THE LAND BETWEEN TWO RIVERS

Also by Tom Sleigh

THE LAND BETWEEN TWO RIVERS

WRITING IN AN AGE OF REFUGEES

TOM SLEIGH

Graywolf Press

This publication is made possible, in part, by the voters of Minnesota through a Minnesota State Arts Board Operating Support grant, thanks to a legislative appropriation from the arts and cultural heritage fund, and a grant from the Wells Fargo Foundation. Significant support has also been provided by Target, the McKnight Foundation, the Lannan Foundation, the Amazon Literary Partnership, and other generous contributions from foundations, corporations, and individuals. To these organizations and individuals we offer our heartfelt thanks.

Published by Graywolf Press
250 Third Avenue North, Suite 600
Minneapolis, Minnesota 55401

www.graywolfpress.org

Published in the United States of America

ISBN 978-1-55597-796-2

2 4 6 8 9 7 5 3 1
First Graywolf Printing, 2018

Library of Congress Control Number: 2017938020

Cover design: Kyle G. Hunter

Cover art: Sadik Gulec / Shutterstock.com

To the memory of Seamus Heaney and Andy Needham,
and for Christopher Merrill

Contents

THE LAND BETWEEN TWO RIVERS

I

The Deeds

1

"When we drove into Qana last year," Joseph told me, scanning the gray concrete houses on either side of the road, "we heard flames roaring, the sound of the jets, people screaming, and the ringing of cell phones." He looked at me and shrugged. "The relatives of people were calling to see if they were OK." Joseph worked for the Red Cross during the 2006 war with Israel and was one of the first to enter the village after an Israeli bombardment killed twenty-eight Lebanese civilians. Soft-spoken, slight, he was solicitous on the surface, but underneath he seemed watchful, even wary. When I hired him as my driver and interpreter to take me south from Beirut, I knew only that he drove a taxi with his father and worked as a draftsman in an engineering firm to pay his way at Lebanese University. But then he offered to take me to Qana. He could show it to me, he said; he could tell me what he'd seen.

To get to Qana, we needed military clearance, and so we'd stopped at the central army compound in Sidon, one of the major cities in southern Lebanon. The Lebanese intelligence officer who handled foreign press was dressed in blue jeans and a checked Oxford, his shirttail hanging out. His wire-rimmed glasses gave him a bemused air, and his thoroughly unmilitary bearing unsettled me. I knew that he knew that I knew he had all the power, and while he seemed to enjoy this, he also seemed to appreciate the absurdity of his own position. Why should he be the one to control who went to the south of Lebanon?

"This is not my decision," he said. "You need to get permission from the military authority in Beirut."

"But," I explained, "when we came yesterday to the base, I was told that we were to talk to you, and that you could grant us permission."

"Who are you writing your story for?"

I tried to explain that *VQR* was a general-interest magazine and that I wanted to tell the Lebanese side of the story of the 2006 war against the Israelis. He could barely keep from rolling his eyes: How many times had someone like me come in and said the same thing? And which side of the war would that be—the Druze, the Shia, the Sunni, the Christians?

I wasn't exactly a seasoned reporter—as a matter of fact, I'd spent most of my writing life as a poet. This was my first so-called assignment, and the role of foreign correspondent felt a little outsized. As the officer stared me down, I realized his checked Oxford was, in fact, a cowboy shirt, complete with snaps and pocket flaps. And when I noticed his cowboy boots shining under the rickety metal table, on which a comic book and various official-looking papers were spread in casual disarray, I began to feel a little desperate, realizing that whatever I'd expected to find in Lebanon would be of an order of complexity beyond any of the books I'd read, or the people I'd talked to, in preparation for the trip. I started to babble about how close to Washington, DC, my magazine was and how it was read by important DC politicians. I could picture my editor grinning, exhorting: *Shovel faster, boy-o, shovel faster.* At last the officer smiled—quite genially, in fact—and lifted his hand the way a casting director might to spare himself one moment more of a bad actor. He asked Joseph where we wanted to go.

Joseph, his face tense during the entire exchange, wanting to help but knowing how capricious the military authorities could be, said simply, "Qana." The officer wrote a few words in Arabic on a scrap of paper and said, "This will get you where you're going. Show it at all the checkpoints." He then shrugged good-naturedly: "Beirut has many good nightclubs and shops. I hope you will visit them." I assured him I would. Then he looked at me and said, "Everyone says that we Lebanese are good at two things. Fighting. And shopping." I nodded and smiled, he nodded and smiled, and Joseph and I went back to the car.

On our way south we inched along in the dust cloud kicked up by dump trucks, convoys of United Nations Interim Forces in Lebanon (UNIFIL), and Lebanese Army transport vehicles. All the coastal bridges had been bombed to rebar and rubble and were now being jackhammered apart by work crews. As the sun beat on the sea in the distance and the rocks riled the waves into scuffed-up patches of foam, I remembered that Qana was the place where Jesus worked his first miracle. At a wedding feast, Jesus turns water into wine and inadvertently humiliates the bridegroom for serving up plonk, at least compared to Jesus's miraculous vintage. That I was on my way to this scene of biblical faux pas and realpolitik slaughter in a cab I'd rented for the day—the logo TRUST TAXI emblazoned across the rear window—was just the sort of irony that made Lebanon Lebanon.

Checkpoint after checkpoint, we flashed our flimsy scrap of paper and my passport at the soldiers lounging in their flimsy wooden booths, or just as often leaning on stacks of tires painted red and white. Between checkpoints, I studied the map, locating Qana, then searching out each of the twelve official Palestinian refugee camps in Lebanon—though by now there was nothing camp-like about them. These were established neighborhoods built alongside Lebanese neighborhoods, in the capital city of Beirut and throughout the country, and they were home to somewhere between 250,000 and 400,000 refugees, depending on whose statistics you believe. Three generations had grown up in these makeshift cinderblock-and-rebar quarters since the Arab–Israeli War of 1948 and 1949, when over 700,000 Palestinians had fled or been driven from their homes by the Israeli forces. In the subsequent armed conflicts between Israel and Lebanon, Israel had labeled them "terrorist strongholds," while Palestinians saw them as centers of resistance against Israeli aggression.

I hadn't expected violence when I came to Lebanon. I'd originally been scheduled to leave the United States in December 2006. But when a prominent Christian politician, Pierre Gemayel, was shot dead by three gunmen, and the country seemed on the verge of civil war, the trip was postponed to May 2007. By that time, everything was supposed to have calmed down. But the violence that had been building for months erupted the moment I stepped off the plane—and only got worse, in a series of car bombings, shootings, and a full-fledged siege by the Lebanese Army on a Palestinian refugee camp where Islamic fighters, led by Fatah al-Islam, had holed up.

To Joseph, now twenty-two, none of this seemed unusual. He was a child of war. During the first five years of his life, Beirut was a chaos of sectarian zones, a dizzying swap meet of shifting alliances, arms deals, and gangland struggles. He lived through the Israeli and the Syrian occupations, which ended, respectively, in 2000 and 2005. And that's not counting the everyday threat of political assassinations carried out by car bombings, an occurrence so frequent that you'll see television ads for car-bomb detectors. "ProSec: For a World of Security." A man dressed in a fashionable leather jacket holds a device emitting an electronic beam that senses plastic explosive under his Mercedes's fender. A useful gadget, really, in a country where five anti-Syrian ministers of parliament have been assassinated in the last two years. What a thousand kilograms of Semtex will do to a motorcade—enveloping in the blast not only the target vehicle but anything moving within fifty yards—obsesses Lebanese news channels.

I confess that as we drove I was feeling a little paranoid, eyeing cars and their drivers. On TV, two nights running, I'd watched cars exploding into flames—just as they do in movies—and later I visited the scorched remains. There were no "security zones," just a casual-looking ribbon of yellow caution tape declaiming in Arabic and English, STAY BACK. I could stand close enough to see how the blast heat had annealed the body paint to a glassy blue-black sheen. Doors and windows blown away, upholstery fire-gutted. One skeletal chassis resembled the fossil remains of some docile, plant-eating dinosaur. The locals who walked by barely gave it a second glance. When Joseph spoke of this kind of destruction, he was dead-pan, unimpressed by its drama for an outsider like me. "Welcome to Lebanon," he said. *Welcome to Lebanon*: how often I heard it re-peated, followed by a half-humorous, half-stoical shrug, when I asked about the car bombings. Cabdrivers, hotel clerks, soldiers, politicians, professors, Palestinian refugees: *Welcome to Lebanon*.

2

"This is the first time for me to be in Qana since last year," said Joseph. "It's strange to see it so quiet." Where bombs had fallen now resembled construction sites, rubble piled high on the side of the road, though clearly much of it had been removed. "There was an-other massacre here," he told me, "during the 1996 war with Israel. They bombed a UN compound where the farmers came to keep safe. There is a memorial. People from all over Lebanon come here to see it." One hundred six people died when Israeli howitzer shells col-lapsed the roof. The 2006 massacre was the result of two bombs—one almost certainly precision-guided and made in the United States—that exploded into a three-story building with a subterra-nean garage where members of the extended Hashim and Shalhub families had gone for cover. Twenty-eight of them were killed.

The Israel Defense Forces insisted they had evidence that the build-ing was housing Hezbollah fighters and weapons, including missile launchers. But according to Peter Bouckaert of Human Rights Watch, these claims were disputed by a top Israeli military correspondent who wrote in *Haaretz*, "It now appears that the military had no in-formation on rockets launched from the site of the building, or the presence of Hezbollah men at the time."

"Our team," Joseph told me, "was called by the military on July thirtieth, at one fifty a.m., and we left Beirut as soon as they called. We got to Qana at four a.m., but the Hezbollah soldiers ordered us not to enter the village. They were waiting for the Israelis to tell them that it was safe to go in, that the bombing was finished. The

Hezbollah soldiers said they would shoot us if we tried to enter without their permission. We could see nothing but smoke and rubble. We wanted to enter the town, but they held us back for two and a half hours."

Joseph told me it was common practice for the Israelis to issue general warnings about impending bombardments. But at Qana, he said, the villagers had been too afraid to leave when all the roads out were being so heavily bombed. When I asked him how he felt about Israel, he began to talk about the United States—something that happened again and again, from Lebanon's former prime minister, Salim Hoss, to taxi drivers and hotel workers. "Before 9/11, all of us wanted to go to America to work or study, but that has changed. America is seen as not friendly to us. And also because of Bush and his support of Israel." He glanced sidelong, as if worried he might offend me. "In our eyes, there is no difference between what Israel wants and what Washington wants. They are the same voice speaking."

As we drove past makeshift scaffolding around half-rebuilt cinder-block houses, Joseph was careful to distinguish between the actions of the Israeli and US governments and ordinary citizens. And he had equally complex feelings about Hezbollah, which most Lebanese of whatever sect regard not as terrorists but as both a resistance movement against Israel and a mainstream political party. But nothing is ever simple in Lebanon. Joseph was ambivalent about their religious and social agenda—feelings only deepened by his Christianity, which in Beirut is almost a form of tribal identification. Since the Lebanese Civil War (1975–1990) pitted every sect against every other sect, with the major division falling between Christian and Muslim, survival depended on religious solidarity and the willingness to band together with other sects in sometimes surprisingly short-term alliances. Even the current legal system is divided. Lebanon recognizes eighteen different religious sects, called confessions, and each confession has its legally binding religious courts that handle social issues like marriage, divorce, intermarriage between faiths, and inheritance. So eighteen different law codes operate simultaneously. For example, according to Muslim codes, a Muslim woman can't marry a Christian, but a Christian woman can marry a Muslim—though according to Muslim law, she cannot inherit.

Joseph, despite navigating these divisions, was a fairly secular Christian who loved the Rolling Stones and didn't seem much interested in politics as they broke down along sectarian lines. "During the Civil War, things were not good between Muslims and Christians," he explained. "My father is a fireman—after a battle, the firemen picked up the bodies and put out the fires—and so he saw the worst part of the war. People stayed with their own people. But for my generation, it is different. As a boy, I played with Muslim children. To me, religion is much less important." Still, he said, "If you are a Christian, you tend to live among Christians, marry a Christian. I have many Muslim friends, but your main connections are to other Christians." Each sect is similarly divided over its view of America. "Because America is seen to be anti-Muslim, Muslims hate Americans. But we Christians tend to love Americans, because America supports us. Both points of view are wrong. All the leaders are wrong," Joseph said, as we drove under a banner of Hezbollah's leader, Hassan Nasrallah, a chubby, bespectacled cleric with a bushy black beard. Beneath his smiling face ran the Arabic caption: THEY FOUGHT THEY RESISTED THEY WON. "We Lebanese are good at blaming the other side. There is enough blame for all sides. We must look at ourselves, but we are bad mirrors. All we see are the things done to us by the other side."

Joseph let down his reserve for the first time. "I live war. I've lived only eight years my whole life in peace. But I lose my nerve when I hear this thing from this mother." He spoke softly, but fiercely: "I saved children out of one home, two were suffocating under rubble and bricks, two had broken bones, they were two and seven years old, and their parents, their faces, they were stone—I cried as I worked, their mother did not cry, she said, 'This is for Hassan Nasrallah.' If I wasn't in uniform, I would have killed her. I would die for my children. She said it was a sacrifice for Hassan Nasrallah. I would not sacrifice my children for anything. Yes, to see the reactions of the parents killed us. We all have martyrs, but I do not call a boy or a girl of seven or eight years a martyr. How many sins did he make?"

He parked the car near a mosque pocked by shrapnel. "We saw bodies of children. There was rubble and dust. We were four ambulances in all. Our first job was to look for the living. Then we took care of the most serious cases. I could hear lots of screaming, but it was sometimes hard to see where it was coming from. We found five children. I did CPR on one until we could get him to the ambulance. One had broken bones, and the other was wounded in the thigh. We put them in the ambulance, and then the driver took them to a hospital thirty kilometers from Qana. Three of the people we pulled out of the wreckage died on the way to the hospital."

We walked by a house that had collapsed into itself, just the doorframe standing and a fragment of the back wall of what had once been someone's living room. Joseph and I stepped through the doorway, and he pointed to a pile of mangled rebar and concrete. "This door was blocked by rubble, but the door was still on its hinges. We could hear two women screaming inside, but they wouldn't open the door. They didn't believe us when we said we were Red Cross. So we had to break down the door. We were all completely covered in dust and it was hard for them to see our uniforms. We could still hear the jets circling overhead, and they were scared that we were Israelis. They had a flashlight and lit our faces so that at first we were blinded. But they hugged us when they saw we were Red Cross."

We walked past a bombed vacant lot where an old man in a Mercedes was assessing his property. A tall, dapper fellow, he offered us a cigarette, and told us how the Israeli bombs demolished his five stores and the villa that he'd built here for his retirement. "The Israeli drones must have spotted weapons here. Hezbollah was hiding rifles and grenades between my houses. So that's why they bombed me. I am lucky to have family in Detroit. They all sent me money to rebuild. But since I have a green card to work in the US, Hezbollah would not give me any money, even though it is their fault this happened." He then insisted that UNIFIL—the UN peacekeeping force—had told the Israelis about the weapons cache in the corner of his lot, and I could sense him trying to control the anger and frustration in his voice. "They are supposed to help us but they help the Israelis."

Joseph gave me a skeptical glance, but many Muslims in southern Lebanon make this same charge against the UN forces. Whatever the merits of such accusations, the UN has been powerless to stop the fighting. During the five years prior to the war, the Hezbollah militia and the Israel Defense Forces shrugged off UNIFIL and played cat and mouse with each other's fighters. According to the rules of the game, each side was supposed to restrict raids and combat operations to military combatants. Civilians were more or less off-limits. But it turns out that between the time of the 1982 Israeli invasion and the 2000 pullout, the five hundred Lebanese and Palestinian civilians killed "by accident" totaled more than the combined dead from the Hezbollah militia, the Israel Defense Forces, and the South Lebanese Army, Israel's proxy army. And this number was thirty times the number of Israeli civilian deaths. This kind of grim accounting breeds an internecine calculus of how many people you have to kill to get the other side to stop killing, and continually weighs blood shed against how much blood remains to be shed in order for the scales to balance.

3

In a little village just beyond Qana we met an old man scornful of both Hezbollah and the Lebanese government. "Six died at that house up the way and ten were wounded," he told me as Joseph translated. "And none of the buildings that were bombed belonged to Hezbollah. But we, we have nothing left. In our fields we found two Israeli missiles ninety centimeters long. And as you can see, our house is destroyed."

The old man's disdain for Israel began long before last year's war. From 1978 to 2000, the Israel Defense Forces had occupied a so-called security zone in southern Lebanon to protect their northern border population. The zone expanded by 1985 to comprise about ten percent of Lebanon's territory. This sparked Palestinian and Hezbollah militia resistance. When things quieted down, the Israelis told themselves that their policy was working and had to continue. And when things heated up again—car and suicide bombings, Katyusha rockets, guerrilla-style ambushes—the Israelis insisted on the absolute necessity of the zone. On the opposing side, the notion that Israel would withdraw once resistance stopped seemed ludicrous to Hezbollah and to neighboring Syria, which was embroiled in its own conflict with Israel over the Golan Heights, a casualty of the 1967 Arab–Israeli War. Such is the nature of wartime logic: all signs of goodwill are interpreted as weakness, and any sign of weakness is to be exploited. And, of course, the weakest of the weak, those most easily exploited, were the unaffiliated civilians.

The old farmer and his wife now lived in two rooms—the only ones still standing—of what had been a seven-room house spacious enough for sons and daughters, children and grandchildren. Down the middle of his yard he'd cleared a path through the rubble, which led to the remains of the bathroom, where only the mirror and a hanging lightbulb remained. "My wife and I stay here, but everyone else is gone to Tyre or to Beirut. We have sixty-three children and grandchildren, and when the bombs dropped we thought it was our last day on earth—the sea, the air, the ground, from every place there were explosions. One minute, and everything was destroyed."

From the wreckage of his garden, the old man plucked three pink roses and a white flower that Lebanese Christians associate with the Virgin Mary. He gave them to me. Across the street was a dump truck painted with the Islamic symbol of the eyes of Fatima, the daughter of the Prophet. Fatima and Mary seemed weirdly at odds at that moment. As we left, he told us that his orange groves would go unharvested this year; his fields were seeded with Israeli cluster bombs, making it far too deadly a business to try to pick oranges.

While we walked to the car, Joseph took me to where the most recent massacre in Qana had occurred. "When we arrived, we began to collect the dying people. I'm used to it, it's ordinary to me, I grew up with dead people, people eighty or ninety years old who died not from old age but from war. They had no names, nothing to remember them by, they were just bodies to be picked up. Nobody could tell what body part belonged to what body. And all the time you were deciding what piece of flesh to put in which body bag."

On most days, we would have seen buses of people who'd come to pay homage at the site, but there were none that day, probably because of the heightened security. And so the village was extraordinarily quiet for the middle of the afternoon. Off in the distance you could smell the oranges rotting, and see the hills' outcrops. I thought of Armani clothes strewn across a showroom by a bomb blast in a Beirut shopping district (it was just as the intelligence officer in Sidon had said—fighting and shopping); I recalled the seismic pattern of the blast wave that knocked out windows on one side of a building but left the other side's windows intact when the wave caromed among concrete walls. Such sights were beginning to seem commonplace. But I wasn't prepared for what Joseph told me next.

"I couldn't see anything, there was so much smoke and dust. But right here, yes, it was right here"—Joseph pointed to a scraped-bare, chalk-white patch of ground near the edge of where the three-story building must have been—"I saw what I thought was a child's hand. We had no tools, really, to move the rubble, and so I began to move rocks with my hands to dig the child out. And as I dug, I uncovered her head and had dug her out to just under her armpits. People were screaming, and I could hear a cell phone ringing. And I thought that if I could just lift her up under her armpits, then I could pull her free. And so I reached under her armpits and pulled, but she was not there. I mean the bottom half of her was not there. She had been blown in half."

We stared at the spot he was describing and suddenly, at the same moment, saw the gleaming, flesh-colored, plastic thigh and leg of a baby doll. I nudged it with my shoe, wanting to pick it up as a kind of gruesome souvenir, but restrained myself. It seemed a co-incidence so bludgeoning that it made you disgusted with reality and the atrocious nature of a war that could unleash such banalities of heartbreak and despair. Joseph shook his head—as if there were something absurd and unsubtle and ludicrously contrived about that leg lying there in the heat of afternoon—then holding out his arms before the bomb site, he said, "All this—how embarrassing."

Beginning our drive back to Beirut, we passed under a poster of Hassan Nasrallah that declared, in Arabic, DEFEAT HAS GONE WITH YOUR PATIENCE. Of course, the poster meant to praise the patience of the Lebanese people in their victory against the Israelis, but the real meaning lay in the ambiguities of the syntax. "What have they won?" Joseph asked softly. He stared into the dust cloud billowing from the military convoy in front of us. "Here, they declare a holiday for the liberation of the south. But why not a day for Qana's dead? We do not care for the dead."

He looked at me, then looked away, and I told him that we could talk about something else—but he cut me off midsentence. "I hope this is the story you are after. I hope you are satisfied, Mr. Tom, with what you have seen. But what did they win? They lost children, houses, they lost the trust of the people. I left the Red Cross because of the war. Do you remember *Top Gun*? Tom Cruise? He says the first rule of engagement is that you do not kill civilians."

4

In September 1982, between eight hundred and two thousand Palestinians (depending on whose estimates you credit—Israeli intelligence or the Palestinian Red Crescent, the Muslim version of the Red Cross) were slaughtered in Shatila and in the southern Beirut neighborhood of Sabra. The Christian Maronite militia, outraged by the assassination of their leader, Bashir Gemayel—his head was blown off by a two-hundred-pound bomb—bayoneted men, women, and children, trampled babies to death, and slaughtered whole families in retaliation against the PLO, which had just been driven out of Beirut by Israel a short time before the massacre. Gemayel's militia carried out the killings, but Ariel Sharon's invading army looked on and refused to intervene, occasionally launching flares over the area so that the two nights of hard work could be carried out more efficiently. And once the killing was over, they lent Gemayel's men bulldozers to help in the digging of mass graves. Hundreds of thousands of Israelis protested, but the Israeli government never condemned the incident.

But as Hicham Kayed, a Palestinian filmmaker, led me through Shatila's poorly lit, narrow, winding streets, raw sewage spilling out from pipes here and there, I was more focused on keeping up with him and trying not to collide with anyone than on thinking about the massacre. As I stumbled and slipped on the hard-beaten dirt-and-gravel street, I kept glancing into the small, rudimentary storefronts—an open doorway leading to shelves piled with canned goods or clothes or used automobile parts and tires, and a surprising number of electronics shops selling all kinds of ancient gadgets and computer components. We were going to meet Hicham's fixer, a man who knew Shatila intimately and secured permission for Hicham's shoots.

At the fixer's apartment block we climbed narrow, unlit stairs to the rooftop from where we could see over the entire neighborhood, rooftop courtyards like the one we looked out from looming over the expanse of cinderblock buildings. The sun was just starting to set, the moon had risen, and there was a heavy fog creeping in from the Mediterranean. Down below, you could make out thick vines of electric cable dangling just above the heads of passersby. The swooping lengths of bundled wires were fastened to the sides of the buildings by what looked like U-bolts, and the jungle of branching wires, to my outsider's eyes at least, gave the neighborhood a provisional feel. It was as if the Palestinians had an unspoken understanding that their exile in Lebanon would end, and everyone would exercise "the right of return"—go back to their homes in Palestine and resume their lives before the Nakba, the Arabic word for "catastrophe." This is what Palestinians call the flight from their homes during the 1948–49 war between the Arab states and the newly founded state of Israel—a war that the Israelis, by contrast, call the War of Independence. Between *catastrophe* and *independence*, there is a vast and fiercely contentious literature about the founding of Israel, war atrocities committed on both sides, and whether the Palestinians fled or were driven out by the Israelis. But up on the roof, the Sabra and Shatila massacre and the Nakba seemed historical events only.

We sat on an assortment of old wooden and plastic chairs while chickens roamed free from their coop, pecking for grain, their little eyes focused monomaniacally on finding that next kernel of feed corn, heads jerking up and down as they wandered among our chairs, taking no notice of us. Hicham pointed to the chickens and joked, "Look at them, they all look like they are running for office."

He had talked earlier that day about the way every political party in Lebanon was mired in a version of its own corruption. They were all hypocrites spouting democratic slogans, he thought, and all they cared about was maintaining power. "At least Hassan Nasrallah and Hezbollah say what they stand for. Maybe I don't like what they stand for, but at least you know who they are." When I asked him if there were any younger politicians who gave him hope, he looked at me incredulously, smiled, and shrugged. "No. Absolutely not." Amused by the gormlessness of my question, he asked, "Why would there be? The Lebanese president must be a Maronite Christian, the prime minister a Sunni Muslim, and the speaker of Parliament a Shiite. Each of them wants to be the boss, and not just for their term of office—but forever. So whoever is in power tries to change the law to keep himself in power. This is why they are afraid to give Palestinians citizenship—a civil right that Palestinians should not have to ask for. The Christians want to give Christian Palestinians citizenship because they think that will give Christians more power. But not Muslim Palestinians—the Christians are afraid they will support Hezbollah. So to us to be a citizen means almost nothing. And many Lebanese still resent the way the PLO carried on a war against Israel from our soil. But what we are asking for is this—our civil rights. So no group or party in Lebanon wants to give you your right as a right but as a business move."

Some Muslims are more sympathetic than the Christians to the Palestinians' situation, but the religious solidarity doesn't go as far as you would expect. The PLO (Palestine Liberation Organization), with its often arrogant, gun-toting, thuggish behavior toward the local Shia population, alienated many southern Lebanese. Many blamed the PLO and the Palestinians in general for Israel's continued military presence. Plus, the various sects, especially the Christians, worry how the Palestinians might change the way power is divvied up in Lebanon. And so the Palestinians are denied Lebanese citizenship and are subjected to legalized discrimination.

"Because I am not a Lebanese citizen and have not asked to be one," Hicham said, "the law makes it difficult, if not impossible, for me to inherit my father's house. I might be able to live in it, but I cannot sell it or rent it. There is even a chance that it might go to a Lebanese religious organization," a possibility that gave him great amusement. "And for years there were seventy professions that Palestinians were barred from entering. Those restrictions have been loosened, but you still have to be a member of a professional syndicate, and only citizens can join them. And since we are denied our civil rights, and are not citizens, we cannot join, and so we cannot work." Professions such as architect, engineer, doctor, pharmacist, lawyer, and journalist were proscribed. Hicham waved his hand as if gesturing to the whole camp: "And you see how everything is old and in need of repair and how crowded everything is. We cannot build beyond the borders of the camp so we have to build up. And for years we were forbidden from bringing in building materials, and the army makes sure of that by the checkpoints they man outside the camps. The government claims that if we are allowed to bring in materials and repair our homes, then Israel will think we no longer wish to return to Palestine. So the government is really taking care of us by not letting us live in decent housing." He gave me an arch look. "The government is looking out for us by supporting our right of return by forcing us to live in overcrowded, substandard conditions." He grinned and shook his head.

All the while the fixer's wife, a young, pregnant, black-haired

woman in a head scarf, brought coffee and fruit that she peeled
and cut into quarters and handed to each of us on plastic plates,
encouraging us to eat, eat. Her little boy ran in circles, pretending
to be one of the airplanes that you could see in the distance. A min-
aret's loudspeaker announced a funeral service for the next day, the
crackling voice high-pitched and resonating in the calm evening air.
The moon had risen and Hicham's fixer passed out water pipes to us,
what they call a "hubble bubble" for the bubbling sound the water
makes when you inhale. We took a toke, drawing the cool smoke
into our lungs. When Hicham finished exhaling, he said, "We are
like your American Indians. This is our reservation. We have control over our internal affairs in the camp, but what is there to control
when you cannot own property, you cannot work outside the camp
except illegally in the worst jobs no Lebanese wants, you cannot go
to school unless there is a place left over by the Lebanese, and you
cannot have any say in Lebanese politics?" And then he shrugged at
the absurdity of his own situation. "Yes, of all possible governments,
this one is the worst."

5

We smoked in silence for a while. Staring out over Shatila, I couldn't
help but think of what it must have been like to live through such
a massacre, and of the Palestinians' determination to endure by re-
building the camp after its destruction. Only a few days before, I'd
visited Quneitra, a Syrian town in the Golan Heights—a town that
had been "razed to the ground." The very term—*razed*—had always seemed like literary artifice from histories of the war between
Carthage and Rome. But in Quneitra, the word was inescapable.

Before pulling out of Quneitra at the end of the 1973 Yom Kippur
War, the Israeli army evicted the thirty-seven thousand Syrian Arabs
living there, then stripped buildings of fixtures, windows, doors,
anything that could be carted off, right down to the hinges and
knobs. Once the town was completely picked clean, bulldozers and
tractors moved in and knocked down most of the buildings. It was

odd, disturbingly odd, to hear birdsong in the clear, quiet air, and to see a herd of cows, heads bowed to graze among the ruins overgrown with flowers and weeds, roses run wild in what used to be somebody's garden. Now, Quneitra served the dual purpose of a Syrian memorial and propaganda site.

When, later that day, I'd ducked into a carpenter's shop in a Palestinian camp near Quneitra, I met an old man who invited me back to his home. His house was modest but comfortable: cushions and an industrial-style brown carpet covered the concrete floor, a ceiling fan whirled close to a modest chandelier, family pictures and crockery were stacked in a wooden hutch, and plastic roses sat snug in a wall sconce. This was luxury compared to the bare, unadorned Palestinian homes I'd seen in Lebanon. The signs of domestic order—including an old computer and a TV—were hard won. "All you see in our camp we have built by ourselves," he told me. "We do not have paved streets, no sewer system, no drinking water. People build their own sewage system, and it flows to an open outfall pipe at the end of the village. The international community keeps promising to improve things, but it's just a lot of noise: nothing changes. Still, our lives here are much better than in Lebanon. At least in Syria a Palestinian can work in any job, and we have most of the same rights as Syrian citizens. We are issued identity cards that are temporary, but they are valid until our return to Palestine."

As he spoke the room filled with his neighbors, who listened intently. Most of them were too young to have experienced the Nakba or even remember a time when the right of return still seemed more than a vague possibility. He paused to sip his tea, then continued in a low, strong voice, staring straight ahead. "In 1948, the Israeli army invaded my village. Right before my eyes they killed my mother, and four of my brothers. My father was hit by a bullet and died. We left the house while shots were still being fired. I was three years old, and I remember it with complete clarity. The house was blown up, and we were forced to go to Lebanon, then Syria. When we got here, we had nothing but tents, we had no shoes, no clothes against the cold. My first school was a tent, and my teacher wept for us. To live in such conditions, in a tent, was like living in a spiderweb in the heart of a well. I was raised here until preparatory school, then I went to Damascus to high school, and then to Saudi Arabia."

He paused again to sip his tea, then said in a quiet voice, "It was like a lake of blood and the deeds are stained with blood." I assumed he was speaking in metaphors, until he asked, "Would you like to see the deeds?" He called his nephew on the cell phone. A few minutes later a heavyset young man of about twenty arrived on a motorbike to show me the deeds to the family's property in what is now Israel. I could see that the paper was discolored with blood, the legalese obscured by three long, brown, faded stains. "The deeds were found by accident when my uncle and cousin came over to our house—after the soldiers dynamited it—to see if there was anything they could do to help us. I saw my home blown up. But the worst thing I saw, the worst thing I ever saw, was my brother, still a baby, suckling at my dead mother's breast."

This was no rehearsed performance trotted out for my benefit. The effort to say this, to remember it, had cost him, and it had also cost us to listen. The old man's words seemed to have nothing in common with the doublespeak of Lebanon's ruling elite or Syria's police state under Bashar al-Assad. Everywhere in Damascus propaganda photos of the president stared down at you, declaiming in Arabic and English: I BELIEVE IN SYRIA and I BELIEVE IN JUSTICE. Bashar's father, the previous dictator, had once, after putting down a rebellion by the Sunni Muslim Brotherhood, bulldozed whole neighborhoods in the Syrian city of Hama and killed an estimated twenty thousand Sunnis. Over Quneitra there was a banner that declared, apparently without irony, PEACE IS OUR TARGET: THE PEACE WHICH RETRIEVES OUR OCCUPIED SYRIAN GOLAN.

But I found the old man had accusations and agendas as well. I kept thinking of a quote from Robert Frost. "Politics is an extravagance," he wrote, "an extravagance about grievances. And poetry is an extravagance about grief." I confess that it was easier to accept the old man's grief than his grievance. His voice hardened and grew louder, almost fierce: "The Israelis," he said, "should return to the place where they came from. The Arab Jews, we love them, they are our brothers. But we wish that the colonial European Jews would go home to Europe." He paused for a moment and said, "The blood of my brother is on these deeds. This proves that this land is for us, and not for them. Our only hope is that America will wake up. The Jewish lobby manipulates American opinion, even though they know nothing about Palestinians. Daily, the Israelis commit crimes that Europe and America do nothing about. The Nazis' crimes are documented, and their crimes are as bad as the Nazis'. The war criminals should be prosecuted, but the Americans help them. And as Arabs and Palestinians, we do not know how to talk with America and Europe. We must learn to do that better so that people in America will see the truth. I saw on Al Jazeera a film that told the story of Israeli crimes. But the Israelis know how to get their story told. My last word is this: we will resist the Jews by word, by sword, until the last drop of blood."

6

Later that same evening, having left Quneitra, I spoke with a high-ranking member of the Syrian government. He wore a dark blue suit, a black-and-silver silk tie, and displayed the smooth manner of a professional diplomat—the courtly, subtle smile that indulges an opponent in his errors, the calm, reflective voice that seems somehow edged by steel. He had received his doctorate from a European university, and as we talked, he confessed a penchant for Graham Greene—for Greene's obsession with betrayal, his weighing of treacheries and brutalities committed for good causes and enlightened reasons, his portrayal of characters who are inevitably corrupted by their own goodness. In fact, he had written his thesis on Greene. We sat in the minister's office, a well-appointed, utterly nondescript room in one of the ministries in Damascus, and I was immediately drawn to his intelligence, his nuanced explanation of Syria's support for the Palestinian people in their struggle with the Israel Defense Forces. That, and his deep appreciation for the opportunity to meet a writer described to him as "an important American poet." In other words, it was farcical; it was like fog talking to fog, his words designed to get his message across and appeal to my vanity, my words intended to appeal to his civility.

Meanwhile, I kept wondering how much personal responsibility, if any, he bore for the imprisonment of Syrian activists who received brutally hard sentences, twelve years in the case of prominent human rights activist Dr. Kamal al-Labwani. Who was this functionary, really? Who was I talking to him? It was clear to me, however, when I left his office, that I had made a good impression, and he, in fact, had made a good impression on me. I liked him. He offered to do anything he could to make my trip more enjoyable, and I have no doubt that he would have. Like him, I was shoving feeling out of sight, avoiding either grief or grievance in order to maintain a sense of cordial decorum. I was as guilty as anyone of speaking the language of policy.

On my way out of the ministry building, I remembered a kitschy painting at the Quneitra propaganda center: Bashar al-Assad and his father, dressed in white robes and mounted on white Arabian steeds, their hands brandishing sabers at an enemy in flight, no doubt the Israelis being driven from the field by heroic *père et fils*. Somebody had painted the thing, and somebody had placed it right next to the door with the obvious intention of glorifying the Assads (though in my mind it underlined the Assads' wounded pride at having lost the Golan). I got a weird sense of multiple exposures, the old man's straight talk overlain by my minister's spokesmanese overlain by the painting's anti-Israeli mythmaking.

But Assad wasn't the only one putting out propaganda. As I traveled back and forth between Lebanon and Syria, every government source I talked to—and without exception, these ordinary men and women were courteous, hospitable, even likable—directed me to websites showing powder-burned children and heroic rescue workers pulling them from rubble. Another click of the mouse would link me to almost hysterical charges and countercharges about the authenticity of such photos. It's as if each side's partisans—and certainly our own media are no exception—fear that the emotional immediacy of grief will verify the justice of one side's grievance, or its own sense of grievance will be weakened by having to feel the other side's grief.

But given the hard conditions in the Lebanese Palestinian camps I visited, there's something a little luxurious about decoupling politics and grievance from poetry and grief—hence the old man's desire that the Palestinians find a way to get their side of the story told in the West, not as propaganda, but as a collective truth. Mahmoud Darwish, who was nothing if not ambivalent about his status as the Palestinian national poet, a man who went through the official Nakba, as well as the personal Nakba that every refugee undergoes, has a poem called "Murdered and Unknown":

Murdered, and unknown. No forgetfulness
has remembered to forget them, no remembrance
has scattered them to gather them in again.
They lie hidden in winter's brown weeds in the ditch
beside the two lane highway that runs back and forth
between two long stories about heroism and suffering.
"I am the victim." "No. I alone am
the victim."

The voices seem to compete for the honor of victimhood, as if Darwish were satirizing as much as memorializing the collective wound. Or as a Hezbollah official said to me about the Israelis, quoting an Arabic proverb, "He hit me and then he cried." Of course, it didn't seem to occur to this official that this same logic might also apply to Hezbollah.

Once you refuse to see someone else's grief and focus strictly on your own grievance, it becomes far easier to reduce your rival victim to a villain—someone you need to protect yourself against and, if necessary, harm before that person can harm you. But in Qana, where Joseph told me he wanted to kill the woman who said her child was a sacrifice to Hassan Nasrallah, he resisted the impulse. True, his grievance sprang from his own grief at what he saw, and certainly his urge to kill her was tied up with his sense of grievance, possibly with his Christian upbringing, his lifelong experiences of war, and his understandable anger at what he thought was her unfeeling response. But some powerful inkling of the woman's grief, her need to see her child's suffering and death as a sacrifice for the community rather than just another random event of war, must have kept him from harming her, must have let him get on with what he'd come to do: save lives, not take them.

Darwish's poem hints at something darker. Most of the people I met—the old Palestinian man, Joseph, the people I talked to in Qana—were just trying to lead their lives. Some of their relatives indeed had been murdered, and were, for all the world cared, virtually unknown. No one would much notice if the survivors thought of themselves as victims or not.

7

It was pitch-black as Hicham drove us back to downtown Beirut, the night strangely edgy, the streets almost deserted except for soldiers in camouflage who manned tanks and armored vehicles at checkpoints throughout the city. The UN had just approved the formation of a special tribunal to look into—what else?—the assassination in 2005 of Rafik Hariri, a Sunni and the former prime minister of Lebanon— and one of the richest men in the world—who was killed by a car bomb of three hundred kilograms of C-4, the explosive equivalent to a thousand kilograms of TNT. Twenty-one other people, "murdered and unknown," died with him in the blast. Because Hariri had had a conflict with Bashar al-Assad, it was widely assumed that the Syrians were behind the assassination. But then a story was also circulating that he'd been killed by a Palestinian suicide bomber, a follower of Osama bin Laden. And there were other stories, all equally plausible, all equally unsupported by hard evidence.

Hicham tensed up when we drove through a neighborhood in which hundreds of flickering candles, celebrating the approval of the Hariri tribunal, lined the streets. While making a left turn, we were stopped by a group of Sunni men. They wanted to know if we lived in this neighborhood, and if we didn't, what were we doing here? Hicham explained that he lived on the next block, and so they let us pass. I had never seen Beirut so deserted, and it seemed that the bombs, and the anticipation of violence at the announcement of the tribunal, had worked a kind of fatal magic on the populace. Everyone was hunkered indoors, eyes glued to TV screens for news of the next bomb, the next killing, the next atrocity in a never-ending series of atrocities.

After Hicham parked the car and we said a hasty good night, I caught a cab back to my hotel. I paced nervously in my room, waiting for some sign of violence to break out, for the pro-Syrians to attack the Hariri supporters, and vice versa. And then I heard it: the rattle and crack of gunfire down in the street just below my window. I ran to the light switch and turned off my lights, but my curiosity got the best of me, and like a fool I opened my balcony doors, stepped out, and looked down into the street. Two small boys were running away from a string of lit firecrackers.

The moon was high now, and I could see on the horizon a silver light that must have been reflected back into the sky by the invisible sea. Below, in the dark, a little farther down the street, a Lebanese soldier, palm leaves woven in his helmet mesh for camouflage, lolled behind his tank's gun turret, talking amiably to another soldier. His friend was making an obscene gesture known the world over, and the one up on the tank burst out laughing. I gripped the balcony with both hands and tried to catch my breath, all the while half expecting to be shot and knowing that I wouldn't be. I caught a heavy whiff of jacaranda mingling with the sulfurous odor of gunpowder drifting up to my window. I was shaking with fear, and felt utterly ridiculous, a real drama queen. *Welcome to Lebanon,* I said to myself, *welcome to Lebanon.*

"A Violent Prone, Poor People Zone"

Dawn came twice to Nairobi that morning, once when the sun rose at six, then two hours later when the sun and moon aligned in an annular eclipse, the sun flickering like a halo round the blacked-out moon. Starting in West Africa and sweeping across the continent, the eclipse sputtered out over the Indian Ocean, just off the coast of Somalia. In that country, refugees were streaming across the border into Kenya and its neighbors, or had left their homes for camps inside Somalia. Their exodus led to the vast refugee camp complex centered around Dadaab town in Kenya's North Eastern Province. At 450,000 people and growing at the rate of more than a thousand people per day, in 2011 the camp had swollen into Kenya's third-largest city, and the biggest refugee camp in the world. But many thousands of Somalis choose not to go to the camp and head straight to Nairobi to the neighborhood of Eastleigh, which Kenyans have nicknamed "Little Mogadishu." That's where I was headed as I walked to the corner to catch a *matatu*, a dirt-cheap minivan so crowded I had to hang out the doors. Eastleigh, Dadaab—over the past two years, they've been cardinal points on the compass of what K'naan, a Somali rapper, calls "a violent prone, poor people zone."

But that's only one part of the story. As Andy Needham, an Irish Aid press officer working with the UN, put it, "Journalists come to the camps because the story's right in front of them. It makes for good photographs like, you can take one look and see the problem for yourself. But refugees in the city—and let's be clear here, there are thousands of them, most of them undocumented, hard to trace, hard to reach out to—that's a story that goes almost untold." And I could see what Andy meant: in Nairobi, there were no camps, no food distribution centers, and so the refugees disappeared into the city—for if you went to Nairobi rather than Dadaab, you had to make it on your own. There wasn't a lot of obvious drama that would appeal to Western media, no suffering chic to spice up your story.

But in following "the story" from 2009 to 2011 in both Nairobi and the camps, I came to understand a basic paradox that was true of both urban refugees and those in the camps: no matter how hard the refugees' lives were—starving children, bodies racked by fevers, head-scarved Al-Shabaab members (the Islamic militia that controls much of southern Somalia) cutting off hands for petty offenses, burying women up to the neck and stoning them to death for adultery, passing out AK-47s to children as the top prizes in a Koran recitation contest—the refugees knew full well that there was always another step down. Like Edgar in Shakespeare's *King Lear*, who disguises himself as a mad beggar to survive the violence of civil war, they also knew that "the worst is not / So long as we can say 'This is the worst.'" And yet that brutally perverse truth was also the source of much resilience in the face of suffering: yes, a starving child was terrible, but also terribly ordinary. One refugee woman whose house had been blown to pieces by a mortar told me, "I would starve for my children." But she knew full well that if she died, the chances increased that they would die.

This calculus between the awful and the ordinary is always at work in Nairobi, so that one of the most dangerous things about the city is how deceptively functional it can seem. But Nairobi was so crime ridden—carjackings, muggings, kidnappings, murder—that the locals dubbed it "Nairobbery." As the matatu jerked and revved over potholes, that calculus was engineering a traffic jam and a riot, both of which I'd get trapped in later that afternoon: for if you got caught in the traffic jam, you got caught in the riot—a riot in part sparked off by tensions between Somalis and Kenyans, their not-so-willing hosts.

Beneath the assumption by many Kenyans that Somali pirate money finances everything Somalis do, there runs a darker undercurrent: Somalis used to be slavers, they look down on Africans, they think of Kenyans as kaffirs. Somalis are lazy, they're dirty, they bring crime and war. And weren't Somalis responsible for al-Shabaab, which was kidnapping and killing NGO workers and reporters, threatening Kenya with jihad, and refusing to let in food aid despite the famine that's killing their own people? Hadn't they made Eastleigh into an al-Shabaab outpost? Even now, to protect the borderlands, the Kenyan army had been forced to push deep into Somali territory to hunt them down. Yes, Somalis needed to be stopped before their anarchy and chaos and piratical ruthlessness hijacked the Kenyan ship of state.

James Brown was blasting over the bus's speakers, exhorting us to "tighten up!" British and American soul and pop were ubiquitous in Nairobi—Motown, Michael Jackson, even a disco-era Bee Gees hit like "Stayin' Alive." But despite some Kenyans' views on Somalis, they had allowed close to half a million Somali refugees into the country—a display of exceptional generosity, given the poverty of many Kenyans, and the Fall of Rome mentality of the Big Men, the ministers of President Mwai Kibaki's government, who adhere to the motto "Now it is our time to eat." One day Kimani, a burly ironical driver at my hotel who worked long, hard hours, pointed out to me in the careening traffic a government-purchased Mercedes—chauffeur driven, of course—that carried an MP, what he called "one of the Wabenzi."

"You see," Kimani smiled, "*Wananchi* in Swahili means 'the people.' So the Wabenzi are the people of the Mercedes-Benz."

The matatu let me off in front of one of the cinderblock, open-air malls that looked to have sprung up overnight. No pyramids of Giza, they were wholly functional structures that at five stories tall looked top-heavy and precarious. But they stocked as many goods as Pharaoh and his grave-robbers could wish. Partly financed by remittances from the Somali diaspora, in the past five years Eastleigh had grown into a huge commercial center in Nairobi—and one of the most prodigious money machines in all of Africa. I walked stall to stall, ogling the vast flow of stuff. In the mall basement, in the jaws of forklifts, huge imported bales of household items and clothes from China, India, Pakistan, Hong Kong, and the Arab Gulf states were being opened by their various owners and carried upstairs to individual stalls.

I pointed to a black-lacquered elephant, a kind of stool, and, enunciating as if I had pebbles in my mouth, asked, "Where?"

The clerk, a young woman in a conservative white hijab, drawled back, "That thang? Hey Mama, where's that from? India, right?"

It turned out she'd been born in Memphis. "Near Graceland."

"You like Elvis?" I asked. She shrugged, as if to say, *Too old.*

At another stall selling plastic-wrapped dress shirts, the clerk literally lay on top of the merchandise piled any old way to the ceiling. He reclined on the heap, fingers laced behind his head, elbows akimbo, the picture of kingly prosperity and ease. But what you saw in the street, along with the new hotel that had a working elevator and marble-tiled bathrooms, was a man in ragged khakis, squatting on his hams on top of a garbage mound piled high as my neck and extending half a city block, sifting through his fingers a few grains of rice left over in a burlap bag. At least there were rice grains to be gathered. Not even he was at the bottom, for as I was learning, the bottom was a long way down.

"Do you have an appointment for an interview?"

"No, I don't have an appointment."

"So you haven't registered to get your UNHCR mandate?"

"No, I haven't registered."

"Then you have to come back in two weeks' time for an interview."

"But how will we live for two weeks? We have no money, my son is sick, he needs help now."

Or you would hear variants so gruesome that it was difficult to believe you were hearing what you were hearing:

"We had to flee from Congo, my neighbors' daughters were raped, the men who did it came back in the morning and threw the girls' heads in our yard. We need food, we need money."

"I'm sorry that happened, I wish I could help you. But you'll have to come back in two weeks."

And though it sounds heartless, what more could one say? I sat in on many hours of such UNHCR (United Nations High Commissioner for Refugees) intake interviews, and Alan, who conducted them, was unfailingly polite, professional, sympathetic. Between us and the refugees, and their desire for a UNHCR mandate—a document that would make their refugee status legal in Kenya and give access to medical care and free primary school for their children—was a sheet of Plexiglas and a computer. The huge workings of the bureaucracy that Alan functioned inside of were invisible. He was the human face they appealed to, and Alan was the one who had to tell them over and over again, I'm sorry but . . .

As one refugee put it (who claimed he had learned the system only to be denied refugee status), "We come to UNHCR as if she were our mother. We ask her for bread but she gives us a stone." But it turned out to be more complicated: he was a Rwandese Hutu who may have helped in the genocide committed against Tutsis. How could Alan presume that this man hadn't cut down his neighbors with a machete, and was thus in violation of refugee status? UNHCR was not a mother. Nor was the man a child.

Unlike the Rwandese Hutu, most of the Somali women I talked to had only the vaguest notions about their rights to asylum. Issues of protection came up again and again: clan warfare didn't end at the Kenyan border, not if you lived in Eastleigh. In a 2007 study by Professor Cawo Abdi about the plight of Somali women since the civil wars broke out in the 1990s, rape has become so prevalent that women have taken to wearing pants, the tighter the better, under their robes. And if a woman admits to rape, she runs the risk of being ostracized, divorced, or even married off to the rapist. No wonder most women keep that knowledge to themselves.

In my many interviews with Somalis, two starkly contrasting pictures of their world began to unfold: a pre–civil war Somalia in which religion and culture were separate, and the Hobbesian present, in which life was indeed "nasty, brutish, and short." In response to such constant insecurity and fear, Islamist conservatives had managed to erase the boundary between culture and religion, and had induced a kind of cultural amnesia in many Somalis about their pre–civil war mores. This was directly expressed in the stricter and stricter prohibitions women were being subjected to, most visibly in the way they dressed.

This cultural amnesia didn't extend to everybody, of course. Idil Bulgas, my Somali interpreter who lived in Eastleigh, had embraced both Somali culture and Islam, while insisting on the difference between the two. She liked to dress in brightly colored sequined shawls and head scarves to set off the long gauzy tunic of her *guntiino* tie-dyed in midnight blacks and blues, a style worlds away from the austere, head-to-foot black chadors. She was completely at ease with Westerners like me, while scrupulously observing the hadith about not shaking hands with men. And yet there were aspects of Somali culture that she was less than enamored of, particularly in regard to women's reproductive rights.

On the same day the riot occurred, she invited me to the apartment she shared with six other family members. But on the way, we stopped at the maternity clinic where she occasionally worked, a low cinderblock building with a muddy yard surrounded by a cinderblock wall. Inside was almost like outside: the walls were unpainted concrete, the floor a poured concrete slab, the corridor almost bare except for some worn benches and chairs. The maternity ward held twenty beds in all, each with a green mosquito net bundled in rope above the bed, the mattresses broken-backed and stained, the springs groaning ancient coils.

Sister Sankali, the head nurse, who wore only a simple bandeau around her head and a faded flower-patterned blouse and skirt, told me, "We perform sixty deliveries a month. It is always hard to do follow-up. The men, you see, the men do not come the day that their wives deliver. Only the women's relatives are here to help." I asked where the men were. "It's not part of the culture that a man should be present. So they are at home drinking tea," she said, a little razor nick that made Idil smile.

"Somalis value large families," said Idil. "Some men have several wives, whether they can afford to keep them or not, and the women have almost no rights. So when I first started working for my aid agency, they sent me to religious schools to talk about HIV and family planning. In one class I was telling the women about means of contraception when a man claiming to be a sheikh stood up and said that I was talking against the Koran and Islam, and that none of these methods can be used. Then he accused me of being a spy. And so I told him that forcing women to start feeding a baby Nido infant formula so that she can again become pregnant is against Islam. And I reminded him that the Koran says that women must wait for two years between births."

"And was he willing to wait two years?" I asked.

She laughed. "What do you think?"

Sister Sankali nodded. "Just a few months ago we had a woman come into the clinic who needed a cesarean section. But the men in her family did not want that."

When I asked her why, she said, "Women are meant to bear children. If you deliver a baby that way, then that means you will probably have to deliver a baby that way again. So her husband kept refusing until it was too late. Then, to save her life, we not only had to take out the baby but her uterus. That means, of course, that she can no longer have children. So her husband divorced her and she went back to her family in disgrace."

Sister Sankali frowned and shook her head. "And we had an even worse case, the one that haunts me most. We told a Somali woman early on that her baby would be too big for us to deliver it here. We told her to go to a regular hospital because she might need special surgery. But when her baby came due, she came here. We told her that if she wanted to save her and her baby's life, that she needed to go immediately to the hospital. And so she took a matatu to the hospital, but when she finally got there, she didn't have enough money, and so she came back. And by then it was too late to do anything. And so she died."

Sister Sankali's voice grew soft.

"Her husband came by the next day and asked where his wife was. He didn't even know that she was dead."

Later, at her apartment, Idil told me how she did not fit in "at all well" with the way Somali men believe their women should behave. "For one thing," she said, "I dress to please myself"—in stark contrast to the other women in her apartment building who had adopted the fundamentalists' faux tradition of the chador.

Before the civil war, Somali women wore a full-length, lightweight garment leaving the arms, shoulders, and part of the back bare—a practical way to dress, given that nomadic life requires constant mobility in tending sheep and goats, putting up and taking down huts, cooking, and caring for children. Following urbanization, women also adopted a very sheer dress worn with a bra and a slip. They wore light scarves over their hair, again leaving the face, neck, and shoulders uncovered. But what was striking was how unusual this style of dress had become.

With the rise of conservative Islam, women had adopted—or been forced to adopt—the chador, a long black cloak covering the body head to toe. Rape as a weapon of clan warfare, and the shame rape brought on not only the woman but the clan, had also played a role. And so in less than twenty years, a new world for women was born—a world that for fundamentalist imams was scrubbed clean of colonial histories, Western cultural influences, and even Somalia's own cultural history.

And so Idil's distinctive sense of style had drawn attention. "I'm now receiving anonymous phone calls. A man's voice tells me, 'We know you are a good girl, but you need to stop dressing the way you do.' So now I am afraid to go out at night on my own because I do not want my brothers to be responsible for defending my honor if I am treated disrespectfully or even raped."

Life had not always been like this: Idil was born in Mogadishu in 1984, when her father had worked for Siad Barre, the last recognized head of the Somali government. "We had a five-bedroom house, a sitting room, two bathrooms, and my dad had two cars—a Land Cruiser and a Toyota Corolla." Now she and her sister, a nurse, were the sole support of their extended family of seven: they were all crammed into a two-bedroom apartment in a cinderblock building next to a mud compound full of broken-down buses. The bathroom was a hole in the floor, the kitchen nothing but some pots and pans and a charcoal brazier—no running water, electricity wires swooping in through the windows. They had to haul their own water upstairs and boiled at least twenty liters a day for drinking water. And yet they had decorated the sitting room (which doubled as their bedroom) with brown marbleized tile, painted the walls a faded yellow, and strung from the cracked ceiling wedding decorations shaped like stars and glittering paper balls. Light-green curtains patterned with green roses hung in the windows.

"I grew up a tomboy," she said. "I was Daddy's girl. He gave me the same education as my brothers and he told them that they needed to do household chores the same as my sister and mother. I got into fights; I was not afraid of boys. Other fathers did not go out to dinner with their wives; they left the women at home and went off with the other men. But my father and mother always went everywhere together. They would promise us that if we finished our suppers they would bring us a treat home when they came back from the restaurant. And if we were good, they would take us to the beach on Fridays, the boys the same as the girls. So it was natural for me to do the kind of work I am doing, helping women know their reproductive rights."

She pointed to a Bollywood poster of her favorite movie star. "I used to like him, but now I prefer American film stars like Tom

Hanks." And I could see why she would like Hanks, his bland, un-threatening smile. "When I marry," she said, "I will have to marry a Muslim."

"And will he have to be a Somali?" I asked.

"No, not at all. But if he is not a Muslim already, I cannot marry him unless he accepts that there is no God but God and that Muhammad is his Prophet."

"That sounds hard on the fellow, don't you think? I mean, what if he's someone who's more of a good man than most people who are Christians or Muslims. Wouldn't that make a difference?"

She smiled and said, "Well, if he loved me, he would have to convert. Islam is something that I feel that he must feel too."

The antithesis of Tom Hanks, the Bollywood movie star was stripped to the waist, his gym-chiseled pecs and biceps and abs sharply defined bands of muscle. He had slicked-back, black hair and ravishing white teeth. I glanced over at Idil's battered desktop computer, which had just received a message, and saw that her email username was "chasing liberty."

I changed the subject. "How are you getting along financially?"

"The money we bring in is not enough. We pay rent and electricity. We have to pay certain things and not others, and then pay the others when we can." She shrugged. "My uncle is a good man, but he spends all his time chewing *khat*. My brothers have not worked for two years; they look for jobs, but there are no jobs, except with NGOs like mine. To work for a Kenyan business, you need a Kenyan work permit, and they are almost impossible for a Somali to get—unless you have fifty thousand shillings for a bribe. It is only my sister and me." She looked at me fixedly. "Everyone I work with thinks I grew up in the West, I guess because of the way I dress and the way I think. I want to leave here. The only hope for someone like me is to get out of Kenya, out of Africa." She lifted her hands in a gesture of dismissal. "But I cannot leave. I must stay here and help."

On the way back to my hotel, I managed to get caught in a traffic jam and riot. Muslim demonstrators and police and local Kenyan shopkeepers battled it out in front of me, throwing rocks, their faces clenched with rage and fear, the shouts muffled by the rolled-up windows of the taxi I was lucky enough to be riding in, tear gas hanging over the city in a greenish pall. A man across the street, scrabbling in some brown, shriveled shrubs for a stone, began kicking at the dirt out of frustration. While the Wabenzi tooled around in their government-purchased Mercedes-Benzes, he couldn't even find a rock to throw.

Although I felt panicked, I tried not to show it to my driver and friend, Joseph (his name just happened to be the same as that of my taxi driver in Beirut), a tall, roguish fellow who had been driving me day after day through Nairobi's inch-by-inch-hoot-the-horn-every-second traffic with a skill and nonchalance that was pure artistry. He casually opened the glove compartment, took out two handkerchiefs, wet them with his water bottle, and gave me one. We sat there, handkerchiefs pressed over our noses and mouths, coughing, tearing up, while he mocked me in a sly, good-humored way about my journalistic pretensions. "Ahhh, Mr. Tom, you journalists like all this."

Windows rolled up, doors locked, I sat there hyped up on the drama of rocks smashing in shopwindows and windshields, the tear gas smelling like overripe lilies and battery acid. The riot was sparked off by the detention of an Islamic cleric from Jamaica, Abdullah al-Faisal, who had once preached that Americans, Jews, and Hindus should all be killed. The Muslim community had rallied behind him, not because they liked his politics—in fact, Muslim leaders condemned them—but because he'd been arrested without regard for his civil rights.

In a newspaper photo the next day, one wounded policeman held what looked like a white handkerchief to the gunshot wound up near his throat, the blood discoloring his green sweater, his maroon beret weirdly vibrant against the dazed look on his face. A demonstrator masked in a balaclava waved an al-Shabaab flag, another held a discharged tear gas canister that the security forces had hurled into

the courtyard of the mosque. This was the first time in the history of
Kenya, a Muslim worshipper told me next day, that the sacred pre-
cincts of a mosque had been violated in this way—a new low for the
security forces, even for Kenya.

And if they were trying to contain a riot, what exactly was the
point of hurling tear gas into the mosque? Hadn't it literally forced
the demonstrators out into the street where the battle went on for
hours? And rather than containing the violence, the police had simply
retreated when the demonstrators picked up the tear gas canisters
and hurled them back. Abandoning any attempt at control, the cops
huddled in a doorway and let the demonstrators and mob throw
rocks at each other. One young demonstrator dressed in a white
robe sopping with blood was carried off by two men while a police
chopper circled overhead. Joseph and I crouched low in our seats to
wait it out, our eyes watering, the two of us sporadically coughing
while rioters surged back and forth. Then he leaned forward to turn
on the radio and cranked it up full volume as Beyoncé began to sing
"Naughty Girl."

Up in Dadaab near the refugee camps, as my eyes flickered open in
my tent a little before first light, the first thing I saw through the
gauze of my mosquito net was the high perimeter fence surrounding the UNHCR compound. In the cool before dawn, I had a few
moments to let my thoughts wander, and I found they sometimes
wandered back to that man on the dump I'd seen in Eastleigh. For
a moment, I'd considered asking him how he'd ended up there. But
since no one, especially not a *mazungu*, talks to men on garbage heaps,
I kept on going. Maybe he had enemies in Dadaab, someone in a
rival clan's militia who'd shot his father or brother dead right in front
of him, and so he was scared and had fled the camp for Nairobi. Or
maybe he was the one carrying the gun, caught up in the tit-for-tat
killings of clan revenge.

But whether he'd been in a militia or been the victim of one, my garbage heap man probably had no papers—for if he had his UNHCR mandate, he wouldn't be squatting on the dump; he'd be here in Dadaab, where at least he'd have a ration card and wouldn't have to perch on a garbage heap, pincering rice grains between his fingernails. His fingers had moved with almost mechanical precision, and his face wore the abstracted look of someone gardening.

But men on dumps are everywhere. You can't think about them too much, the problems they pose are too disturbing, but then too common to be disturbing for long. People—even people threatened by drought and starvation—have to get on with their lives. And the previous morning in the crowds at Hagadera market, how normal it all seemed in the vitality of buying and selling. I asked a tall, loose-limbed fellow herding a few goats through the dust how much a goat would cost—twelve hundred Kenyan shilllings, about twelve dollars. He gave me a broad easy smile, his beard dyed bright yellowish red by henna, and reached out to shake my hand, telling me his name was Abdi Hussein.

Speaking through my interpreter, Abdi told me, "No one wants to buy goats, because if you cannot feed them, if they die of hunger and thirst, why would you waste the money? A year ago, a goat cost twice as much."

When I asked him how many wives he had, he said that he had two wives and seven children.

"And the henna in your beard, why do you do that?"

"Ah, my friend, for Beauty!"

I told him that he was indeed beautiful, but that I'd cut off my beard because it had way too much gray.

Abdi said, "And you, how many wives and children do you have?"

Doing my best Henny Youngman imitation, I told him, "One wife, one child—and that's more than enough!"

Everybody laughed uproariously. But despite this seeming normalcy (and the international appeal of old Henny), bandits, kidnappers, and rape were also part of the daily round. Just the week before a UNHCR Land Rover had been carjacked in Hagadera, the driver kidnapped, and still no word of his whereabouts. The week after I left Kenya, the online news told how two female aid workers had been kidnapped just outside Dadaab, their driver shot in the neck.

Out over the desert's red sandy hardpan studded with thorn and acacia trees, the ground was heating up. Soon the air trapped inside my tent would grow claustrophobically hot, the desert pulsing like a migraine. Meanwhile, out beyond the UN fences in the camps, the refugees were also readying themselves for the day—but a day of waiting, particularly for the new arrivals. As many as a thousand a day had been arriving for several months, an advancing tide of refugees moving through country where mainly lions and hyenas and nomads have their territory. On foot, in trucks, in minivans, over red sand roads that turn to thigh-deep sinkholes in rain but in the current drought hide rocks and craters that can snap axles and blow out tires, the women wearing *jilbaab*s, the men's faces plastered with red dust, the refugees clutch their cell phones (cell phones are so cheap, even refugees use them), waiting for the call from their kin already in the camps.

Scavenging marabou storks perch in the thorn trees, their pink heads bald because, as I read in a bird book, "a feathered head would become rapidly clotted with blood when the bird's head was inside a large corpse." In the heat-haze scarfing the rocky desert, the marabou's eight-foot wingspan shadowed the refugees' progress toward Dadaab, as they carried bundles under their arms or pushed broken-down carts, often women alone shepherding children. One grandmother, accompanied by seven children, told me how al-Shabaab bandits had attacked their bus. "They made us get down and then they beat the bus driver and robbed him of our fares and took everything they could carry. And then they beat the men, shouting at them that God is as great in Somalia as in Kenya, that they were running from God, running from their country."

At the field office for the camp named Ifo, the refugees would huddle hour after hour under a UN canopy to hide from the sun as they lined up for reception and registration—needles jabbed in arms against polio and tetanus, vitamins B and C eye-dropped into the mouths of children, interviews in cubicles, biometric scans of face and fingerprints, fingerprints inked the old-fashioned way into a dossier, more questions and answers, questions and answers, any security issues, any known enemies—and then they'd be given flour, cooking oil, salt, sugar, soap, a kitchen set, jerry cans, woven grass sleeping mats, baby-blue tarps, and a chance at a second life on a plot of ground the size of some people's living rooms. They'd be housed in tents much like the one I was staying in, only there'd be as many as seven people living in it. They'd be living in a camp in Section X, Block X, Plot X.

From my first visit back in 2009, to my visit now eighteen months later in 2011, the population had exploded from 280,000 to 450,000—and this in a camp that was originally built to hold 90,000. Two generations had grown up in the camps since they'd been established in 1991–92, when Siad Barre lost control, and the country devolved into a permanent state of clan warfare. Given such a world, one consequence of camp life is that nobody ever dies. As one UN rep told me, "Nobody reports a death—I mean, think about it from their point of view: they're not getting enough food as it is, and if you admit that someone's died, that means you've one less mouth to feed, and your rations are reduced—and only an idiot allows that to happen." And so the dead are taken out into the desert bush and buried in shallow graves. During the rains, the bodies often wash up to be devoured by hyenas that eat everything, even the bones—their scat chalk-white from the calcium.

I was told by many refugees that UNHCR rations, distributed every fifteen days, often lasted only ten days, and that meat and milk, regarded as important staples in the Somali diet, weren't provided by UNHCR. Which is where my tentmate, Yoko Kuroiwa, and his NGO, the International Lifeline Fund (ILF), came in. Yoko had the notion that if they had paying jobs, the refugees could provide these things for themselves.

By now the sun was clearing the horizon, and the makeshift concrete slab of the tennis court behind the tent swam up through the dawn twilight. I could hear Yoko, still asleep, breathing softly—in contrast to the strangled groans of agony or joy he gave each evening on the court whenever he made or missed a point. "I am the black sheep of my family," Yoko had told me. "Everyone thinks I'm crazy for not living in Japan. They think I want to be famous, a movie star. Like Angelina!" (Yes, Angelina Jolie had visited Dadaab in 2009—and I heard one aid worker jokingly accuse another of "pulling an Angelina.") While the glint in Yoko's eye could be self-sardonic and exacting of others, when he laughed his completely unbuttoned laugh, he had the gift of putting everyone at ease. I loved watching his wild, savage forehand smashing down through the air: nothing could stop him from pursuing a point; he put his whole heart into every shot.

Our tent had become unbearably hot, so Yoko and I made our way to breakfast and then the motor pool. "Dogfish 1 to Base, we have Yoko from Lifeline and one journalist from New York." Handing back the shortwave transmitter to our UN driver—given the number of kidnapped aid workers, no one wanted to be unaccounted for—Yoko told me, "I've always been a bit odd . . . I went to high school in Iowa, to college in the Netherlands, and I worked in Thailand for six months with some Burmese refugee kids. After that I worked as a journalist back in Japan"—Yoko shrugged, as if to say, *Who hasn't worked as one?*—"but then I got a fellowship from the Japanese Ministry of Foreign Affairs to work in a program called 'Peacebuilding.' And that's how I ended up in Dadaab the first time in 2009. I left for a while, and now I'm back as the environmental program officer for International Lifeline Fund." When I asked how big an organization it was, Yoko said, "It's small, the smallest one in Dadaab. I'm it." So in this alphabet soup of mega-aid agencies—WFP (World Food Program), CARE, MSF (Médecins Sans Frontières, Doctors without Borders), ADEO (African Development and Emergency Organization), LWF (Lutheran World Federation), all under the umbrella of UNHCR—Yoko's ILF was as informal as it got.

It wasn't an easy task Yoko had set himself: giving refugees steady work, not just aid. But with the exception of jobs in the camps themselves, tending to their goats and chickens, and selling things in the market, refugees went unemployed. Their educational opportunities were almost nil once they finished secondary school in the camps, nor could they leave the camp and find work elsewhere; that required a Kenyan work permit that could only be obtained by paying an immense bribe. As Anne Campbell, the UNHCR head of Dadaab in 2009, told me, "The youth have almost nothing to do here, and have had nineteen years to do it in."

Near the outskirts of the camp at Hagadera, we were dropped off in front of an iron gate surrounded by bush and made our way through a nursery to a concrete building partially sheathed in scrap CalTex oil drums. There refugees were busy making small, brick cooking stoves. By kneading together red and black soil with animal dung—"the dung helps hold the heat"—and making bricks from this concoction that were then fired in a kiln, the refugees had produced over twenty-five thousand stoves. Since UNHCR didn't give out firewood, the refugees either had to buy it in the market or gather it from the bush. It was the women's job to gather wood—and the farther out into the bush they went, the greater the chance that they'd be raped. With the huge influx of refugees, Yoko told me, and the ongoing deforestation, and more and more women being raped, the stoves could make a real difference, because they were more efficient and required less wood than open cooking fires. It was a simple idea, but it had a substantial ripple effect. And the stoves were well designed for heating up the women's griddles in order to fry flatbread or to set pots boiling to make porridge.

We set out walking in the hot sun to the outskirts of Hagadera. There, we went household to household, each compound consisting of a sleeping hut, seven or eight sleeping mats to a hut, a separate lean-to for a kitchen, and maybe a couple of pens for a goat or some chickens. The insides of the huts were often decorated with colorful scraps of cast-off UN packing materials: smiling women in colorful robes surrounded by flowers, a sylvan scene of elephants grazing in the bush. Out of all the kitchens we inspected, only one woman seemed to be using her stove correctly, and it was hard to say if that was merely by chance. But Yoko was patient with this setback. As we walked back to the factory, he said, "We will have to start making daily trips out to make sure the stoves are being used properly.

When we deliver them, we will have to spend more time teaching them how to use them."

When we got back to the factory, I was surprised to discover that Yoko had arranged for a rehearsal of a play about how to use the stoves. He and I sat down to watch, as the factory workers hurried to their places. One woman fanned an open fire until a man playing a worker at the factory happened by and told her about the stoves. Then a refugee, playing a donkey hauling a cart with a stove in it, kicked up his heels and gave a little hee-haw as he and his driver pulled up to the woman. They took the stove off the cart, put it down in front of her, and began to instruct her in its use. Then an older man began to dance, jumping high in the air and clicking his heels together while the whole ensemble joined in a song written by the group for the big finale. Everyone was in high spirits by the show's end, and Yoko instructed everyone to wear costumes, saying proudly to me, "The idea for the donkey was mine!" The tall young man playing the donkey looked a little shy but also proud of his role. He promised to bring a belt tomorrow to wear as a tail and to make ears out of scraps of canvas for a repeat performance the next day at a competition. Everyone was excited by the prospect of winning; at last year's competition during a festival of culture, they'd won first prize.

As we walked back through the middle of Hagadera to meet our Land Rover, Ali, my interpreter, went to visit some friends. I should have insisted he stay with us, because now Yoko and I, two mazungus, would be walking alone in a large bustling town where only last week a CARE driver had been kidnapped. The anxiety was low level but constant. To do what Yoko did required courage: someone could easily put a gun to his head and push him into a van bound for the Somali border.

We crouched under an acacia tree to wait for the rest of the convoy to arrive for the trip back to the UN compound. One of Yoko's interns told me her husband had died during the drought; al-Shabaab had "taxed" away their livestock; her bus had been robbed on the way to Dadaab; a bandit had pushed a woman riding on top of the bus so that her screaming baby wriggled out of her arms, fell to the ground, and died. Such stories showed me how tough these people were. And yet I couldn't help but feel an underlying hopelessness in their situation: *Gunmen came into my house and my brother, my husband, my son . . .* and so they kept coming to Dadaab, they got their ration cards, they entered into a limbo of waiting and dependence.

As for being resettled in a foreign country like the United States, which has taken in many more refugees than other countries, the chances were—and are—slight. Only in 2011 did the refugees who'd arrived in Kenya half a lifetime ago in 1991 become eligible for resettlement. If you made it through the rigorous screening interviews, there was the almost interminable wait for a plane flight to be arranged to the host country. Ali, my interpreter, had been waiting for two years for seats to become available. "The average wait," he told me, "is three years. I've waited so long now that I have to take the physical again. But perhaps in another year or so . . . " He trailed off and looked down at the ground, Hagadera sprawling out around us, the call to prayer echoing from a loudspeaker.

In 2010, out of nearly half a million people, fewer than three thousand actually boarded a plane and flew off to their new homes.

————

WikiTravel.org once called Mogadishu "the most lawless and dangerous city on Earth" and warned that "even with guards, the likelihood of being injured, kidnapped, and/or killed is still very high, including potentially by said hirable guards. . . . Traffic drives on the right." As far as I could tell, traffic went every which way—and yes, I grant you that Mogadishu's walls are bullet-pocked in three sizes: thumb size for AK-47s, fist size for .20 caliber, and both fists for .50 caliber. But just as in Nairobi and Dadaab, people go about their business, the women holding babies in their arms, the older kids running in the streets, laughing and shouting in spite of their sharp ribs and swollen bellies, and the men dressed in trousers or *jillabas*, the older ones with henna-dyed beards.

On our approach to Mogadishu, the UN plane banked away

from the coast, high above the sea, so that we could make our landing over water and avoid antiaircraft fire or a rocket-propelled grenade. There, far beneath us but growing larger as we descended, I saw a TransAVIA transport plane downed in 2007, one wing shot away or crumpled when it crash-landed. It had been towed to one edge of the runway and was now being used as a storage container for khat, the leaves of a shrub that everyone chews in East Africa to get a little lift.

Bill, the UN security officer, gave me my choice of flak jackets: *Baby blue or dark blue? Whichever matches your eyes, darling . . .* I chose baby blue, and as I fastened the Velcro straps, it reminded me a little of a baby's bib—only heavier—like wearing four of those lead aprons the dentist puts over you when you get your teeth X-rayed. I put on my helmet, also baby blue, with its rubber chin strap and adjustable inner plastic housing that I never got quite right so that the helmet kept sliding around on my head. Wear all this on a torrid, humid day—the only kind of day there is in Mogadishu—and your sweat drenches you in less than a minute.

My mind kept running on two tracks: the images of Mogadishu as a place where the average lifespan of a person was reputed to be seventeen minutes from the airport to the city center if you lacked an armed escort, where khat-chewing militias spread death from machine guns mounted on Toyota pickups; and the scenes of women and starving children at a clinic devoted to food aid and medical care.

We went through a gate into a whitewashed courtyard overflowing with women and children, some of them sitting on bleachers, some on the ground, others standing in lines and holding their infants. A nurse dressed in a chador was giving instructions through a megaphone about who should line up where so that their children could be weighed and evaluated for further care. As always, no fathers were present, and the only men at the clinic were the supervisor and two assistants. One of the men wrote down the weights of the children placed by their mothers into a blue plastic tub that, suspended from a hanging scale, would pendulum back and forth as the baby squirmed and gawked—a peculiar, senile famine-gawk that I'd seen before in

Dadaab: the infants would lie passive in their mothers' arms, or sit or stand unsteadily, and stare at you without blinking, the way a bird will sometimes seem to stare at you, cocking its head to one side as if to hold you a little steadier in its gaze. Of course, everyone has seen pictures of starving children with the well-meant purpose of letting others know that these children are in need. But the staginess of many of these photos—light glistening off prominent ribs—makes it seem as if this is an exceptional state of affairs. But famine caused by drought occurred in 1999, 2002, 2005, and 2008—which means that if you were born in 1999, by the time you were nine years old, you'd have lived through four famines—and not just famine but all the diseases you'd be prey to because of hunger.

But starving to death doesn't mean that you're just a passive victim (at least not until the very end) listlessly waiting to die. After one infant boy was picked up by his mother from the tub scale, and she sat down with him on the benches, he began playing with the shiny wrapper of a nutritional biscuit he'd just eaten, throwing it up in the air and patting it when it came down. Before the calories enlivened him, he'd lain so still in his mother's arms that I wondered if he was still breathing. His mother, Gijo Ali, told me the old story: how their house had been blown up when she'd been out in the market, everyone killed except for this child and two others who were back in Al-Adala, one of the IDP (internally displaced persons) camps we'd visit that day.

In a place like Mogadishu, you become so accustomed to these apparent juxtapositions—a child playing with a food wrapper against a Toyota truck turned battlewagon—that they lose any sense of being opposites. I was surprised at how quickly I got used to riding around in an armored vehicle, and how expected the AMISOM (African Union Mission in Somalia) soldiers manning the three machine guns of the Casspir came to seem. They were skinny with bloodshot eyes, young, and not particularly threatening looking, though in the few hours I was with them, who could say? (Three weeks later, after Kenya's invasion of Somalia, when I saw al-Shabaab photos of dead African Union soldiers, one with a *panga* jutting from his chest, I lost some of my sangfroid.) "Oh sure," said Andy Needham, the Irish Aid press officer who'd gotten me into Mog, as the old hands called it, "you're laughin' now about your flak jacket, but you might be cryin' by the end of the day." At which point Andy, Bill, and Jason Florio, my photographer, and I laughed even more. As I stared between the legs of Patrice, who manned the gun in front of me by straddling the aisle, balancing one leg on one battered plastic seat, one leg on the other, all I could really see was the baggy camouflaged butt of his "mate," as Andy might say, manning the fifty.

Famous for its role in terrorizing black South Africans during apartheid, the Casspir went round and round the roundabout at KM4, near where a truck packed with fuel cans would explode two days later, killing the suicide bomber who took seventy lives with him. Hunched in his flak jacket and looking a little annoyed, Bill was on the walkie-talkie now to the vehicle behind us: apparently the driver didn't quite know where he was going, and our convoy got so turned around that we ended up disrupting a busy market, our Casspir blocked in by Toyota pickups, vendors pushing carts, and foot traffic. The smell of raw camel meat hit me in the face, the .20 caliber machine gun belt dangling before my eyes. Later, we all laughed about having had the same fantasy: a grenade lofted through the Casspir's roof where the reinforced steel walls of the compartment would ensure the shrapnel from the explosion did its work.

We finally got our convoy back in line and pulled up to a large, walled-in former villa, where we visited the kids at the Saacid agency (*saacid* means "to help"), a home-grown famine relief organization to aid malnourished youth. These were much older kids, some in their late teens: they swarmed around me excitedly, shouting out, "Mister, mister, where are you from?" And when I told them "New York City," they all nodded, "Oh, New York, New York," one boy shouting out, "The Knicks, the Knicks!" And as I asked them where they came from, and they called out "Mogadishu," "Kismayo," "near Bakara market," we somehow got into a guessing game: I tried to guess how old they were, them nodding when I guessed right, but when they guessed my age as sixty, I kept joking that I was twenty, OK, thirty!

Suddenly we were all laughing and high-fiving and kidding around. As a boy in a football jersey kept shouting, "English? American?" while other kids called out, "Who are you? Where are you from?," and I called back the same, scribbling their names down in my notebook, Mohammed, Sharif, Ahmed, Jamal, Deywa, Amina, I watched a starving goat climb into a huge communal cooking pot and begin licking the sides from the meal the kids just finished.

Back toward the airport, behind a blown-out wall, in what had been a vacant lot, a little city of refugees had sprung up. One older woman buttonholed me, talking loud and fast as she told a story I'd heard so often in Dadaab: *Al-Shabaab killed my husband, my son, they stole our cattle, our goats, so many of us were starving my whole village fled* . . . as she talked, and I took notes, I thought of a story Andy recounted, perhaps the most disturbing illustration that the worst is not as long as we can say, this is the worst. A woman was fleeing with her two children, and as the children grew tired and she had to start carrying them, she knew her strength would fail before she got to the camp—and so she left the heavier one behind because the lighter one would be easier to carry.

On my last day before flying home from Kenya, Jason Florio and I went to Eastleigh to take a look at the khat market. I thought of the TransAVIA plane with half the wing sheared off on the runway in Mogadishu—a testament to appetites that go beyond food and drink. Jason put some leaves in his mouth and began to chew. Soon a crowd had gathered round us, some of the men looking a little glazed, but on the whole friendly. But as I had learned over the course of my visits to Nairobi, Dadaab, and Mogadishu, the worst always goes beyond what we think is the worst. And so at first I resisted an invitation from an energetic young man to enter a storefront that opened up into what looked like a small warehouse, no doubt full of khat. But then I followed Jason inside anyway, worried that I'd put a damper on everyone's apparent goodwill. I felt increasingly fearful when four or five men came in after us, and blocked off the entrance. Suddenly, the young man began to run right at us. My mind began to race, I tensed up, I was about to spin around and push through the crowd back into the open market, when he sprang full tilt into a series of handsprings, his body whirling toward us until, with a final flourish, knees tucking up toward his chest, he landed, as if in slow motion, a full somersault right at our feet.

A few minutes earlier, a boy had shouted, "Take me to New York!" and then folded himself up as if to fit inside a suitcase—a suitcase that somehow I'd have to smuggle on the plane, the boy scrunched up inside with his head to his knees, the bag bouncing along on the conveyor belts until it disappeared into the plane's belly. He was a small, skinny boy, not as skinny as some of the IDP and refugee kids I'd seen, but he just might have fit inside a suitcase. The boy had kept on walking until I'd lost sight of him, but now he was back to see the show, hanging on the neck of an equally skinny pal.

The young acrobat motioned us out into the market where a large crowd began to surround him. Everyone's eyes, a little bloodshot from chewing khat, were glued to his broad-shouldered strut as he shooed us back so he could give himself a nice long approach. Khat sellers lined the market from end to end as he took off sprinting at full speed and turned handspring after handspring, again landing a somersault before finishing up by walking on his hands. And then from out of the crowd came another young man riding a unicycle, and in his hands, flying hand to hand, were balls he juggled as he balanced on the pedals, racing forward, back, forward, always keeping the balls moving in a perfectly controlled arc left to right, then reversing right to left, his friend walking upside down with as much ease as he would right side up.

The Land between Two Rivers

What I have to say about my trip meanders the way the Tigris and Euphrates meander, and like those rivers in flood, is sometimes murky in intention, balked in its conclusions, and flows where it has to flow. In Iraq, in which the customs and conventions were often operating invisibly, or easily misinterpreted to be the same as mine, I suppose I gave up on telling a straightforward story. Instead, one night in a helicopter, what I felt in the air, so different from what was happening on the ground, made me realize the truth of Jean Genet's assertion that when you take an oath to tell the truth, you're not telling that truth either to the judge or to the courtroom. Perhaps the point of the oath is to try to surround yourself with a lightness and solitude from which you can speak the truth, adding whatever light and shade you can so as to make "the how" implicate "the why." After all, the judge and the members of the court weren't riding in the helicopter, so a realistic description won't mean anything to anyone unless you add that light and shade that only you, as the witness, could perceive.

But even then, in the helicopter roar, the truth may be hard to hear, even in your own ears.

The container housing unit, known as a CHU, is a white prefab box that contains a sink, toilet, bed, one small window, a heater/AC unit, and not much else: maybe a TV set, a towel rack, and a particle board dresser. When you first enter it, it's about as hospitable as a cell in a substation jail. But after you get used to the white walls, white floor, white ceiling, the fluorescent light fixtures, also white, though glazed to cut the glare, the CHU is a triumph of army functionality.

For the first week of my stay in Iraq, I lived in two CHUs, first at the Baghdad Diplomatic Service Center (BDSC, pronounced "Bedsy") at the Baghdad Airport, then beside the airport in the southern oil port of Basrah, where a former British base is now home to the US Consulate. Both BDSC and Basrah utilize hundreds of CHUs for living quarters and CHU-housed services, such as the barbershop advertising two different "looks": the battering ram of the shaved head, favored by most of the security contractors; and the ram's-wool curls and long sideburns of Liberace, a look that many of the younger Iraqi men seemed to favor. There was a CHU-housed PX where you could buy booze and other food and drug sundries somewhat randomly arranged on metal shelving. And on one shelf in the back, there were souvenir T-shirts and hoodies. Because Iraq in December was about twenty degrees colder than my Southern California fantasy of it, I bought a hoodie for fifteen dollars, a whitish-gray color with the US seal on it. The insignia over my heart was of a cross-eyed American eagle with the stunned look of a cartoon character who'd been hit over the head with a hammer, though of course the spark-like stars wheeling above the eagle are meant to represent the original thirteen states.

BDSC also had its own enormous gym in an air-hangar-sized Quonset hut where my friend Chris Merrill, who heads the International Writing Program at the University of Iowa, and I worked out on the elliptical machines the afternoon we flew in from Jordan. Chris flies all over the globe with US poets and fiction writers to conduct writing workshops in places as various as Juba in South Sudan, and refugee camps in Kenya, where we'd first worked together. Now, we'd be traveling to universities all over the country to talk with Iraqi writers, professors, and students. We'd been asked to talk about literature and creative writing workshops, which many of the professors seemed interested in learning how to teach, and in turn we were curious about the situation of contemporary Iraqi literature. Pumping the machine's handles, I told Chris that I was a little nervous about how violent the country had grown in the past few months. Chris nodded and told me about the orientation his State Department host had given him to Juba. "The guy told me there were a lot of poisonous snakes, like black mambas, and that I should try to keep from getting bit, because there's no anti-venom serum in the whole country. He called them 'cigarette snakes'— you have just enough time to smoke a cigarette before you die." We laughed, and for the rest of the trip, whenever I began to be anxious, I thought *cigarette snake* and settled down.

The next morning we flew south to Basrah in a Dash 8, an eager little commuter plane with a fifty-seat capacity. The loadmaster—which is Embassy Air–speak for the steward—wore wraparounds and a reflective orange-and-yellow caution vest. "File across the airstrip single file," he told us, "avoid the propellers, and climb the stairs into the Dash one pair of feet on the stairs at a time." The only addition to the safety announcement was the loadmaster warning us that the plane might shoot off decoy flares, and that the explosion we would hear was the sound of the flares deploying. If a heat-seeking, infrared guided missile was fired at the Dash, automatic sensors would release the flares, either in clusters or one by one, in the hope that the flare's heat signature, many times hotter than the engine's, would decoy the IR missile away from us and after the flare. On an earlier flight to Baghdad, Chris had experienced the release of these flares. "The explosion," he said, "was really loud, loud enough to hurt your ears, and absolutely terrifying."

The plane began to taxi down the runway, and Chris and I fell silent as the rattle and roar of the Dash ascending filled the cabin. The plane leveled off at cruising altitude, and through the pitted glass, I saw the Tigris winding through Baghdad, the city hazy in the morning light. As we flew south, the Euphrates and Tigris, which almost meet in Baghdad, again diverged into widely meandering beds before coming together outside of Basrah in a river called the Shatt al-Arab that empties into the Persian Gulf. Field on field of green wheat and barley surrounded small isolated farmsteads nestled inside groves of date palms. Underneath us, I watched the shadow of the Dash ripple across the vast green plain between the Tigris and the Euphrates. The name Mesopotamia means "the land between two rivers," and here and there, you could see long, straight irrigation canals and artificial reservoirs divided by dikes, watering the fields. I was astonished to actually be seeing what I had known since grade school as "the cradle of civilization." I remember reading about cuneiform writing, and thinking that it looked like the marks a flock of crows' feet would leave in our muddy garden if it froze solid overnight.

As we began to see the outskirts of Basrah, I thought of the great Ziggurat at Ur, and how, twenty-five years ago—and a year or so before the first Gulf War broke out—I'd come across a cuneiform tablet in the Louvre, translated into French, about the destruction of Ur. I copied it out on the back of an envelope, took it home, where it sat on my desk for months while I read the odes of Horace. And then one day, I found it on my desk, and thought that if I could treat it like a Horatian ode, I might be able to do something with it in English. So via a French translation of an ancient Akkadian original, and utilizing a meter that I'd come across in Horace, I translated a poem into English that I called "Lamentation on Ur." I hadn't meant the poem to have overt political overtones—I thought of it as a general comment on the destruction and fragility of civilized life:

Lamentation on Ur
—from a Sumerian spell, 2000 B.C.

Like molten bronze and iron shed blood
      pools. Our country's dead
melt into the earth
      as grease melts in the sun, men whose
helmets now lie scattered, men annihilated

by the double-bladed axe. Heavy, beyond
    help, they lie still as a gazelle
exhausted in a trap,
    muzzle in the dust. In home
after home, empty doorways frame the absence

of mothers and fathers who vanished
    in the flames remorselessly
spreading claiming even
    frightened children who lay quiet
in their mother's arms, now borne into

oblivion, like swimmers swept out to sea
    by the surging current.
May the great barred gate
    of blackest night again swing shut
on silent hinges. Destroyed in its turn,

may this disaster too be torn out of mind.

But then the Gulf War came along, and suddenly the poem was taken up as an antiwar poem: so current events had transformed what I thought of as a general statement into a topical political statement.

Now, after two US–Iraq wars, and a decade of trade sanctions between them, I found myself looking down on the brown-and-green alluvial plain of southern Iraq, which had figured in my mind for over forty years as a kind of shadow world that had haunted me as not only civilization's cradle but also the crucible that gave shape to the bogeyman of the "Islamo-fascist." US policy in the Middle East was like a moral migraine that kept flaring up in the imagination of the American body politic. From the first Gulf War in 1990, which I'd demonstrated against and watched the police stand by while my fellow demonstrators were beaten up by skinheads; to the second Gulf War in 2003, which I also demonstrated against, though this time I was appalled by a group of younger male demonstrators who were itching for a confrontation with the police and stormed a police barricade while the cops radioed for backup that luckily never arrived, or all of us would very likely have had our heads bashed in; to the subsequent disastrous occupation that ended in 2011; to 2014, in which sectarian violence had escalated back to the levels of 2008, and al-Qaeda had made a huge comeback in Anbar province: in the past quarter century, it's no exaggeration to say that two generations of Americans grew up either ignoring, deploring, or approving of our involvement in Iraq. But whatever one's position toward the wars, I'd arrived at my opinions with virtually no idea of what our bombardments had done during either war, and with almost no sense of day-to-day Iraqi cultural life, except for the image of the head-chopping, suicide-bombing al-Qaeda fighter who wanted a reversion back to a seventh-century caliphate. (My trip took place a few weeks before the final split between al-Qaeda and ISIL in February 2014. Al-Qaeda and ISIL, however, are not so much formal organizations as ideologies that have given rise to several different groups of Islamic fighters.)

I remember teaching a class of undergraduates at Dartmouth College in which a young Iraqi woman, who had lived through the bombardments of Desert Storm, sat among us. The students had no idea she was from Iraq, nor did I, until she wrote a paper about surviving the bombing. I asked her before class if I could use her paper as part of the discussion, and whether she would mind talking about the bombardment that she had lived through. She agreed. Slight and wearing a beige head scarf, with perfectly plucked, absolutely symmetrical eyebrows, she was a very soft-spoken young woman whose command of English was perfect, though more formal than the English most of the students spoke.

We were reading *The Iliad* and talking about the anatomical particularity with which Homer describes the wounding and death of the individual heroes. I asked them to think about the only war they knew at that time, the first Gulf War, and to discuss their sense of whether or not, given the images of backs and lungs and livers and bellies pierced through by spear heads, it was possible to justify the slaughter of war, including the civilians killed as "collateral damage." Almost the entire class, women as well as men, said that it was possible to justify the slaughter, based on American interests abroad, on overcoming dictators for democracy, and on the hope that a better life could come out of battle. I then asked them what they would say to someone who had actually lived through the bombardments intended to achieve these worthy goals—and said that this someone was here, sitting among them, as one of their fellow classmates. How would they explain to their classmate the necessity of the bombs? Silence fell on the room. Everyone looked deeply uncomfortable: I realized I'd betrayed them, as well as the young Iraqi woman, who sat very still in her seat, though I hadn't meant to. I'd assumed there would be at least some opposition to the "just war" thesis, and I was disconcerted when I realized that not one of them had moral qualms, or at least qualms they were willing to express. And then one boy said, "I guess if I were that person, I'd think that most of what I just said was pretty stupid." And when I asked the young woman to talk about her experience, she said something like: "We sat in our house with the lights off. The bombs went on for a long time, and when they stopped, all of us were so tired, we went to sleep." She plucked her head scarf a little further over her hair, fell silent—and then the class ended.

⁂

I proved myself to be inept at putting on my bulletproof vest, attaching this to that in all the wrong places, before figuring out how to Velcro the waist panels tightly around my stomach so that they were under the vest, not over it, and adjusting and readjusting the shoulder straps to make sure they were tight. I didn't look very military: in fact, I looked like I was wearing a bib, a sort of Rambo Jr. By contrast, in his Irish conspirator's raincoat, his shirt buttoned all the way to the top button, his black trousers and worn-at-heel, split-toed shoes, Chris projected, despite the flak jacket, a timeless, jazz musician hipness.

Now that I was strapped into my vest, it felt fairly lightweight, around eight pounds—thick enough, according to the specs, to give reasonable protection against handguns. But when you consider that a bullet fired from a military-style weapon is the equivalent of a five-pound sledgehammer smashing into you at forty-five miles per hour, serious bruising and broken ribs are pretty much guaranteed. I put on my helmet and snapped the chin strap fast, but I had to keep pushing the helmet back from sliding down over my eyes. Rather than protected, I looked—and felt—like an overgrown infant.

We were going to the University of Basrah from the consulate compound near the Basrah Airport. In front of our armored vehicle—a Chevy Suburban SUV reinforced with steel plating—a beefy but terminally polite security contractor dressed in khakis, a brown knit shirt, a gray windbreaker, lightweight hikers, and sporting a buzz cut, gave us a briefing. "Once you're inside the vehicle, please stay away from the doors. We'll let you in and out. If we take fire, or if I give you the signal to get down, I'd appreciate it if you could get on the bottom of the vehicle. I'll climb in back with you and cover you. Once we get to our destination, you can leave your armor and helmets in the vehicle. Then we'll open the doors, and we'll proceed single file to our destination. Everything clear?" His low-key manner and his faintly smiling friendliness were fairly typical of the manner of most of the security contractors. For such large men, they had the gift of disappearing into the background—they didn't talk much to the people they were guarding: in the twelve or so missions Chris and I were on, never once were there more than a few words of conversation between us, and the driver, and his partner riding shotgun. A good thing, I suppose, since that meant they were concentrating on the cars around them, and whether they might be a threat. Many of these men had served with elite units in the military, like the Navy SEALs, and I met one contractor who had been in Iraq since he came there as a soldier in 2003. The big draw was the money: while the ordinary sergeant was making around $2,500 a month, security contractors were making between $15,000 and $22,500 per month.

We passed through the consulate checkpoint, manned on the

consulate side by security contractors and on the Basrah side by the
Iraqi army. One Iraqi soldier was dressed in fatigues and wore a purple
beret, his automatic weapon pointing at us as he nodded a greeting
to our driver. We sped out on the highway, and Chris and I got our
first real look at Basrah.

My only coordinates for Basrah were the Douglas Fairbanks silent
movie in 1920 and the Alexander Korda spectacle of 1940, both titled
The Thief of Bagdad. Basrah is the city to which in the Korda film the
deposed prince and his companion, the thief, flee from the treach-
erous, power-hungry Grand Vizier. Minarets and spires, flying carpets and horses, a huge genie, a giant spider guarding the magic jewel
of an All-Seeing Eye that shows you the entire world, a happy ending in which the prince marries the Sultan of Basrah's daughter, the
Grand Vizier gets punished, and everyone lives happily ever after—I
was going to write that the Basrah of the movies and the Basrah I was
seeing from the SUV had nothing in common, but the All-Seeing
Eye was like a more sophisticated version of drone surveillance, the
Grand Vizier was either Saddam or George W. Bush, depending on
your point of view, the giant spider could be military hardware, and
the genie—well, the genie imprisoned in his lamp, but furious to get
out, could refer to a whole range of psychic, societal, and spiritual
pressures threatening to tear the country apart. And if you were looking for Technicolor spectacle, natural gas, burning off from the refin-
ery stacks, flared and rippled all across the horizon. At night the city,
ringed by oil fields, can look like it's on fire.

The outskirts were a hodgepodge of two- or three-story cinderblock apartments, often left unpainted or undressed in either brick or
stucco. Unpaved streets, no central sewer system, large puddles of
wastewater floating soggy flotillas of trash. But I also got a sense of
thriving commercial activity from the shopwindows, their large bright
signs painted with the graceful calligraphic swoops of Arabic script.

Just behind the contractor riding shotgun, I sat on a jump seat
that faced the rear of the vehicle. Chris and Dale Lawton, our public affairs officer from the Basrah consulate, sat in the back seat facing me. While they could see the SUV in our convoy ahead of us,

I saw the SUV bringing up the rear. I heard a loud hum, like a fan blade, coming from behind the seat where Chris and Dale were sitting. Dale, who had set up our meeting at the university, leaned forward and said, "We'll have to talk a little louder because of the jammer." When I looked puzzled, Dale explained, "That noise is the sound of the radiowave jammer. If someone wants to detonate an IED by using a cellphone, the jammer will block the radiowave that would set it off."

The jammer's constant whir was nerve-racking and I found myself tensing up every time we traveled to one of our meetings. Not that there was much I could do against an improvised explosive device or a well-placed shot from a rocket-propelled grenade. A direct hit would most likely take us out. And many IEDs were powerful enough to blow a vehicle like ours ten feet into the air.

We turned off the highway and drove down a suburban street with three-story apartment buildings on either side, as well as private homes behind head-high walls. This part of the city looked much better off—cars parked along the street looked in good repair. Our convoy paused at a steel gate. The Iraqi guards threw back the black-painted steel stanchions, and we passed into the entrance of the University of Basrah. One of the Iraqi security guards, a muscle-bound man wearing a tight polo shirt under his black jacket, and a gold chain around his neck so that he looked a lot like Sylvester Stallone, waited on the steps while our guards established a five-point perimeter around our SUV, two in the rear, two in front, and one at the center of the hood, facing outward toward the surprised-looking students milling about outside in a small courtyard.

The SUV doors were opened by one of the security contractors. The students couldn't help but gawk as we walked through the halls and into a large seminar room where we shook hands with the male professors but were careful not to shake hands with the women unless they initiated it. For a nonbeliever and a male to touch a woman who is a stranger could be seen as a violation of the hadiths.

Because our trip coincided with Ashura, the day on which Shia Muslims all over the world commemorate the death of the Prophet's grandson, Imam Hussein, pictures of him were everywhere: silk-screens fluttered from streetlights and were plastered on walls. In many shops hung little framed portraits. He was depicted as having a lush black beard and shoulder-length hair. His rugged good looks exude the glamour of a Bollywood movie star. Most significantly, he was strung up on banners along the pilgrimage route to the Iraqi city of Karbala, the place where Hussein died in battle in 680 CE. The battle was fought over who would be the leader of the Muslim world. The divisions among the original followers of Islam would open up, after Hussein's death, into the doctrinal, political, and economic differences that fourteen hundred years later separate Sunni from Shia.

Since the American troop withdrawal in 2011, Ashura had sparked off even more sectarian murder than usual: car bombs, suicide bombers, exploding roadside IEDs, Sunni gunmen executing Shia, and vice versa. The pilgrim trail, with its comfort station tents providing food and drink, and sometimes a place to sleep, made easy targets for Sunni radicals who, inspired by Osama Bin Laden, thought of themselves as the Iraqi al-Qaeda.

Before I came to Iraq, the media image I had of al-Qaeda was of Osama bin Laden waging jihad like some kind of evil superhero. But here, al-Qaeda was far more ambiguous. It was a mainly Sunni movement, fueled in part by anger about having been pushed out of power by the Shia once Saddam fell. But it also included foreign fighters from all over the Middle East, and even the United States. They were all waging jihad in order to establish a worldwide caliphate. At least, that was the lofty-sounding ideal. But the opposing militias, such as the Mahdi Army, organized at the behest of the Shia imam, Muqtada al-Sadr, were equally extreme. As Saddam Al-Jabouri, a college student in a city near Basrah, said in an oral history I'd read on the plane to Iraq:

> The biggest issue was females on campus. People involved with
> the Mahdi Army tended to believe that having females in school
> was against Islam. . . . There were beatings and kidnappings

targeting women just because they wanted to go to school. . . . Sometimes these enforcers would check people's cell phones for pictures. If you were a guy and you had a picture of a woman on your phone, for example, they might rough you up or take your phone. This kind of crap . . . someone from these enforcers would . . . haul you off to one of the party offices, where you would be questioned and lectured about religion and society from these goons. It was not just beatings and lectures they doled out, however. Some people who defied these zealots wound up dead. Look, it was the same religious bullshit that al-Qaeda in Iraq and its followers imposed on Sunni areas. The exact same thing, only one group did it in the name of Shi'ites and the other in the name of Sunnis.

(Mark Kukis, *Voices from Iraq: A People's History, 2003–2009*, 84)

The boys in the room were dressed in jeans and button-down shirts, most of them sporting the Liberace look, their long sideburns razored sharp while the top was allowed to flourish, though no one had anything as extravagant as an actual pompadour. The girls all wore head scarves, and to my great surprise, especially after what I'd read in the oral history, there were as many, if not more, girls in all the classes we would visit. It looked as if times had changed, though whether or not there were jobs waiting for these young women, I don't know. But in our travels we met as many female professors as male. Of course, if the conservatives among the Shia and Sunnis had their way, the universities would quickly be purged of women.

We tried to tailor our meetings to the participants. If we were speaking mainly to professors, we asked them about the cultural situation. If there was a mix of students and professors, we spent most of the session talking about creative writing.

But one consistent fact about all our meetings: there was always lots of laughter, often sparked off when Chris and I, in an effort to understand the sometimes thick accents, had asked the professors and students to speak loudly and slowly. One or the other of us, enunciating loudly and slowly ourselves, would say, "Our ears are old ears, and we don't hear as well as when we were younger because we spent too much time listening to loud rock music."

From that moment forward, the room relaxed. Education in Iraq is extremely formal, and a professor expects, and receives, a certain deferential treatment. But the workshops worked best when the professors joined the students in trying the exercises: one particular department head read his poem with such theatrical brilliance, in which he'd developed the metaphor of love as a kind of net, and done it with such a sophisticated and playful sense of humor, that the whole room was transfixed and burst into loud and sustained applause. But mainly what we heard from the professors was heartbreakingly articulated by the head of the department at Basrah. He spoke a flawless, pure English, with just the faintest English accent. "For years and years I have longed to visit the places in England and America that my study of literature has made real for me. But now, at my age, I do not think that this will ever happen." Looking grave, he clasped his hands, and stared down at the table, while the other professors quietly nodded their heads.

When I asked him to say more, he shrugged. "First we lived through ten years of war with Iran. This was followed by another ten years of war and occupation by the United States. And now the violence today . . . More than anything, we need contact with the outside world: our cultural isolation under Saddam was extreme. We need exposure to new ways of thinking, new ways of doing things."

When Chris asked about censorship, one of the women writers replied, "There is no official censorship, but everyone is aware that there are red lines that are dangerous to cross. Religion and sex, those are still difficult subjects, and even more difficult to talk about from a woman's point of view."

But despite all that, the picture we got of literary life in Iraq—and particularly in Basrah from the head of the Writers' Union—was one of tremendous vitality. In his rumpled sports coat, his tie askew under his unbuttoned collar, he spoke quickly and decisively about Iraq's literary movements for the past twenty years and finished up by saying, "In Basrah alone, we have three major literary festivals, many new literary magazines, both print and online, and more and more published books. What we need most of all is to have our literature read beyond the borders of Iraq. The years of Saddam put an end to open artistic expression in our country. When I was a young man, I was put into prison with my colleagues here"—he nodded to three other members of the union—"for a year. We were accused of 'subversive activities.' But now there is a huge amount of activity among younger writers, and I'm very hopeful for the future. After all, I started out in prison, and now I'm head of the Writers' Union!" Throwing his arms in the air, he laughed uproariously, as did everybody at the table.

Such hopefulness was infectious, and the students had their share of high spirits. As an example of this younger generation's confidence, one female student challenged a professor's love of Shakespeare by saying that when she read *The Merchant of Venice*, it hadn't seemed in the least believable. Chris and I made some well-meant remarks about naturalism not always being the most effective way to make a statement, when we were politely interrupted by the professor, a burly fellow dressed in a black leather jacket, looking very hip indeed in comparison to the suits and tweed of the older professors. He had gotten his degree in Shakespearean performance at Leeds University, and said that his specialty was to talk about the differences between Shakespeare's plays onstage and on the screen. And in a history lesson that the young woman, as well as Chris and I, quickly realized was generational insider knowledge, he told the young woman, "Look, what you read wasn't really Shakespeare, but a Ba'athist translation in which Shylock was reduced to a completely anti-Semitic stereotype. It wasn't translated into verse, it wasn't even a play—it was written as if it were a story. What you read was Saddam propaganda, not Shakespeare." In other words, Shylock was depicted as a proto-Israeli—a figure to be denigrated and despised.

These little insights happened over and over. In another workshop, a student had written about her grandfather's garden in which there were, as I heard the phrase in her somewhat thick accent, "six trees and two white dogs." I began to talk about how much I liked the repetition of the detail about the trees and dogs—but Chris and Dale interrupted me sotto voce, almost hissing, when I persisted in my folly, "Doves, not dogs!" I was a little surprised by their insistence, but thinking my ears had betrayed me, I said, "Yes, doves, of course! Doves, not dogs!" Afterward, on our way to the SUV, Dale said, "Sorry to have interrupted like that, but dogs are considered unclean by most Muslims. Dogs would have a completely different meaning for them than they would for us. They'd find it disgusting to even think of letting their dogs sleep with them, or come in the house, for that matter." And in all the traveling we'd do in Iraq, I'd see only one dog, on the muddy outskirts of Basrah, and that was obviously a stray.

But our education in dogs didn't stop there. To my surprise, another student wrote about a dog named Rocky that he liked to play with as a child until one hot summer day, his father put Rocky on the roof of their house. And poor Rocky, since this was the first time it had ever happened, and because there wasn't any shade, or so Chris and I assumed, poor Rocky jumped off the roof into the garden, and looked to have died from his fall because of the blood trickling out of his mouth. But he got up after a few moments, and began to play again in the garden. When Chris and I talked about the story, we focused on the dog as a kind of subtle metaphor for the troubled relationship between the boy and his father. But as soon as we said that, a student raised a hand, and said that far from being a metaphor, it was simply what was done with dogs in Iraq in the summertime. They were put on the roof under a little shade, and with some water, and no one thought anything of it. About this cultural difference Chris remarked that what was customary for an Iraqi was, for writers, their material. And so we learned about such subtleties as how dogs were treated—surely a detail that Flaubert or Proust, both sticklers for such things, would have loved.

But no matter how off the mark Chris and I sometimes were in our comments, the students' concentration, and self-delight in the process, went far beyond anything I could have imagined. It was as if Wordsworth or Dickens or Hardy—who came up again and again as a focus of study—had climbed down off their pedestals and were rubbing shoulders with the students. As places to write about, the Lake District, London, or Wessex had nothing on Baghdad, Basrah, or Erbil. And as the ones guiding them, our enthusiasm for what they wrote, and our way of pointing out how some detail—dogs? doves?—could create certain interesting emotional effects, added to the feeling that someone was really listening to them. Writing workshops were like a magnifying glass held up to their daily lives, providing us more grain and texture than I ever could have thought possible.

When we flew back to Baghdad from Basrah a few days later, the last hop of our trip from the Baghdad Airport to the embassy compound was by helicopter. The skinny, curly-headed gate agent told us to line up and proceed single file out onto the tarmac where a light-lift, open-sided helicopter waited for us. The blades whirling overhead made a loud roar as one of the security contractors motioned me to the far side of the helicopter. I stashed my suitcase and computer behind a low steel bench that the contractor, stabbing his finger at it, pointed to as my seat. I looked for the seat harness, but saw only a seatbelt with a little buckle hook. I took the hook, began to fit it into the metal slot, but for some reason, I couldn't get the hook to slide past the slot. I felt ridiculous, and then absurd, when the contractor, in one swift, impatient movement, fit the hook in the slot, and tightened the belt for me. I smiled and shrugged, but the contractor had already turned away and taken his seat next to me on the bench. The chopper's sides were open to the night air, and I instinctively shoved myself back on the bench as far as I could get—not very far, it turned out, certainly not far enough to quell my unease about hurtling through the air with no door in front of me.

The contractor gave me thumbs-up, and I at least knew enough to give thumbs-up back, and then the chopper blades accelerated and got louder. He slid the lenses of his night-vision goggles past the lip of his helmet and down over his eyes to keep watch for snipers on the ground, and then we slowly ascended, the nose of the chopper dipping slightly as the tail lifted, and we soared straight up until the pilot adjusted the pitch of the rotors and we shot ahead, eventually climbing to about a hundred feet over the city.

Everything was dark down below for the first hundred yards, and then we were crossing over Baghdad, the lights of the cars on the road flickering softly, houselights shining in the windows. The pilot occasionally flicked a switch on the instrument panel, and then, as we rose higher and the night air got very cold, the contractor slid the Lexan-glass doors closed on the passenger part of the tiny cabin. The chopper shimmied back and forth in the light wind, soft buffets, almost the way a child might pet a cat on the head. Just above the pilot's helmet, silhouetted against the curved glass of the windshield, shimmered another little galaxy. Switches glowing in the darkness, an overhead instrument panel lit up the pilot's hand as he leisurely lifted his arm from time to time to switch one off or on.

For a moment, I felt immensely happy: I had the reverie of myself as a child, looking up at Day-Glo stars stuck to the ceiling over my bed—a memory I knew to be false, since I'm way too old for such things to have existed when I was a kid, nor were my parents the type to indulge me with Day-Glo stars. I knew, even as I took pleasure in it, that my fantasy was out of sync with the reality on the ground, not to mention the contractor hunching forward, his gun in his lap, intently scanning the darkness below. At least the contractor had his orders and his night-vision goggles. What I had to go on was the drone of helicopter noise, its surgical detachment from the neighborhood alleys and streets, and the way my own hypervigilant senses magnified and crystallized the light and dark flow of the city beneath me. One of Saddam's former palaces, encircled by a moat that testified to the dead dictator's love of water, glowed dimly below us, looking like an Arabian nights fantasy in bad taste, and reputed to have a torture chamber in the basement. Aloft in the chopper and looking down, I found and continue to find it hard to know what tone to take when the truth is both atrocious and banal.

And if you were on the ground looking up? In the oral history, I'd come across this account of a pregnant woman, Rana Abdul Mahdi, who lives in Sadr City:

> I saw a helicopter floating very high in the air away from me, and I watched as it fired a rocket toward me and my little sister, Zahra. She was eight. I felt heat all over my body, and then I was on the ground as the street filled with smoke. There were bodies all around me, and I saw my sister with all her insides spilling out her front. She was reaching for me, motioning with her hand for me to come and help. . . . I saw my left foot was gone. It was sitting there in the street a little ways from me.
>
> (Kukis, *Voices from Iraq*, 180)

In one of our Baghdad workshops, a slight young woman named Mariam, wearing a black-and-white headscarf, with a round face and large black eyes and just a hint of mascara on the lashes, stood up to read her poem. The way we generally conducted workshops, Chris would talk about writing as an artistic and academic discipline, and I would set up the assignment: a very simple one based on Joe Brainard's poem "I Remember." I asked the students to shut their eyes, accompanied by much embarrassed giggling, but as the exercise went on, the room grew quiet until there wasn't a sound, nobody was moving, everybody was deep inside his or her own reveries. I asked them to think back to their childhood homes, to remember their bedroom, to tell us what the room looked like, what the day was like, to perhaps think about a favorite toy or game. I asked them to remember what the weather was like, what their parents were doing. And then I would ask them to imagine that Chris and I were from another planet, from Mars, say—which in a way, we were—and that what was familiar to them might be completely unknown to us. I told them to go wherever the memories took them, that gritting your teeth and trying too hard wouldn't help, that you were letting the sights and sounds lead you where they would, and all you needed to do was to get out of the way and go where they took you. As new memories occurred to them, I asked them to repeat *I remember* for each new memory, *I remember, I remember* . . . and then I asked them to change *I remember* to *I don't want to remember.*

As soon as I said this, we could always sense a major shift in their inner weather—you could see it in how they would hunker down, or the lines around their eyes would clench a little tighter, or furrows would suddenly come into their foreheads. This physical change happened every time we did the exercise. It was as if the war, and the postwar killing, rose up irresistibly in the students' minds. We had cautioned them that painful memories, as well as pleasant ones, were part of a writer's material. But what was most impressive about the students was how they didn't shy from the hard facts. Did writing in English afford them a little distance, a sort of protective shield? Or maybe it was the novelty, or the release that came, in writing about their own lives? In any case, many wrote about the pervasive violence, sometimes directly, but more often as an undercurrent: violence, after all, was one of the defining characteristics of their generation. For such difficult material, they wrote with a poise and depth of understanding that almost never happens among US students. Most of them were in their twenties and had never known a time when their countrymen weren't at war, either with the United States or with each other. I can't imagine them ever telling us in casual conversation some of the things they wrote.

Mariam stood very straight in front of her classmates and read to us with a quiet, unself-conscious dignity. Her pronunciation was excellent, so I have a good memory of what she wrote. She said that she was woken in her bedroom near dawn by her older brother, who had bent down to kiss her gently on the cheek, and to ask her if she wanted anything special in the market. And when she looked up at him, to tell him no, he said to her, very gently, that this would be the last time she'd be seeing him. But she was so sleepy, she didn't quite take in what he meant, and a moment later he was gone. Later that morning, she wrote, she was in the kitchen having breakfast with her mother. And then their neighbor came in and gave them the news. She wrote that as she heard the news, she felt herself get smaller and disappear: she had no hands, no face, no body to feel with. There was no kitchen, no mother, no her. The neighbor, she wrote, told them about the "car accident." She wrote how she remembers her brother's words coming back to her, how gentle he was when he kissed her on the cheek, how he would always bring her special things from the market. And then she sat down, seeming completely self-possessed, except for the sadness that had come into her voice and hung now in the room. No one said anything for a while, as what she hadn't said—didn't need to say, since everyone in her generation already understood—resonated for a few moments. Chris and I looked at each other, but were slower in grasping what it was she'd left out. And then it dawned on us too: her brother had been a suicide bomber and blown himself up in the car.

For all the violence going on in Iraq, in my little white box of a CHU it was eerily calm. And no wonder: the entire complex of CHUs was covered by a huge steel roof and surrounded by twenty-foot-high, reinforced concrete blast walls—"to keep bombs and missiles from falling right on your head," was how the fellow who gave me the key to my CHU put it. This kept the whole compound perpetually in shadow, but it added to the feeling of isolation and quiet.

There's a poem by Tomas Tranströmer in which he's in a motel room so anonymous that faces of his old patients begin to push through the walls. The CHU was something like that, a refuge from the violence, a deprivation chamber I was grateful to retreat to, but also a little theater of the mind in which what happened during the day came back to haunt me in the ammonia smell of disinfectant mixed with drying mud that exuded from my CHU. Mariam's face came back many times, and the face of her brother, though I could never quite make out his face because it was always too close to hers. I could see the shape of his head as he bent down to her ear, but his body was lost in shadow. His gentleness and the violence of his final act resisted my attempts to explain or understand. Of course, I was imposing on his entire past the moment when he'd pressed Send, making that moment more significant than a thousand other moments which, as he lived them, would have had their own weight and value. A back-page newspaper photo of smoke pouring up, a vague ghost face pushing forward into the white walls of my CHU—except for the glimpse Mariam had given me, that was all I could see.

Meanwhile, inside my CHU, I led a radically simplified life: no decorations, purely functional furniture, and not much of it—and a mask against sarin and other forms of nerve gas, packed neatly in a small cardboard box with a convenient black plastic handle. The warning label read **DO NOT REMOVE**.

But after a while, staring up at the white ceiling, letting my thoughts drift, I'd remember the daily body count—the bodies, which had seemed so abstract back in the US, began to take on solidity and form. From the very first night in my CHU, I'd established a routine (maybe more of an obsession) of going online to check on that day's violence. During the night and day it took me to reach Iraq, twelve liquor stores, run mainly by Yazidi Kurds, had been shot up in drive-bys from SUVs: nine customers and owners had been killed. Although no official group stepped forward, conservative Shia, whose version of Islam decrees death for drinking alcohol, were probably the gunmen. Then on Sunday, forty-six more people were killed, this time by Sunnis terrorizing mainly Shia neighborhoods: the places they hit were crowded shopping areas, markets, and auto repair shops. If the bombs had gone off in corresponding New York City borough neighborhoods, they would have been the Fulton Mall in Brooklyn, Hunts Point Market in Queens, and the lower reaches of Fourth Avenue's garages in Gowanus.

I arrived in Baghdad three weeks before Christmas. The December death toll numbered 226 civilians. By the time I flew home to New York a few days before Christmas, that number had risen to 693. And by New Year's Eve, while I was humming along to the patter song of "A Modern Major-General" at the Gilbert and Sullivan Society's production of *The Pirates of Penzance*, and sipping a glass of champagne in my seat, the New Year would ring in 1,126 killed in December, 9,852 for the year (Iraqibodycount.com).

Death and more death. Throughout my travels in Iraq, as a kind of bedtime ritual just before I went to sleep, not a day went by that I didn't read about ordinary Iraqis being blown up, shot down, or kidnapped, tortured, and dumped by the roadside.

Some prefer to call the T-walls that surrounded the CHUs Bremer walls, after Paul Bremer, the head of the Coalition Provisional Authority during the first two years of the US occupation. If Bremer goes down in history at all, he would probably prefer to be known as the namesake of these walls, rather than the inspirer of the insurgency, which is how he's viewed by many Iraqis today. He is the man who implemented the decision to fire the entire Iraqi Army in one day, putting four hundred thousand men out of work at the stroke of a pen. Not content with that—and in an attempt to get rid of the ruling political class, Saddam Hussein's Ba'ath Party—Bremer also fired every middle-level-management civil servant in the country, between thirty-five thousand and eighty-five thousand people. One can understand his desire to enforce a standard of justice on Saddam's apparatchiks, but most Iraqis think the purge went too far and should only have affected the top political class. But whether out of a sense of justice, cultural ignorance, or lack of political savvy, all of middle management got the ax.

The dismissal of the technocrats and bureaucrats who knew how to run the banks and oil refineries, the hospitals and power stations, and who oftentimes had joined the Ba'ath Party in order to keep their jobs, left an administrative vacuum that still exists today. Add the dismissed soldiers to the ministry clerks and you've got close to half a million people suddenly without work. You'd think it would have occurred to Bremer that these hordes of unemployed men, with wives and kids to feed, might be ripe for resistance to American rule.

But Bremer, following the Bush administration's policy that you could invade Iraq, overthrow Saddam, and turn the country immediately back to the Iraqis to run as a democracy, seems to have dismissed the thought. He and the Bush administration seem not to have considered the difficulty of building functional, democratic institutions in two or three years. Nor did they fully appreciate the historic tensions between Sunni and Shia, or fully comprehend the division between the Iraq of the conservative imams and the more laid-back civil society. That said, most Iraqis would say they are glad Saddam is gone. But they also think, though their politeness toward guests might prevent them from saying so, that the US's ignorance of Iraqi society and history has had disastrous consequences.

Not that some of these consequences weren't foreseen. In fact, Donald Rumsfeld, in a secret memo written in 2002, a year before the war, seems to have had more than an inkling of them—only to ignore them. Weirdly enough, I downloaded this memo, declassified in 2011, from the former secretary of defense's own website. One of Rumsfeld's undersecretaries of state, Douglas Feith, gave the memo the inadvertently hilarious nickname "The Parade of Horribles." The term derives from the nineteenth-century custom of New England mummer's parades, in which one's fellow townsfolk dress up like monsters and grotesques, and lurch down Main Street on the Fourth of July. The memo presents twenty-nine Horribles—including number thirteen, in which no weapons of mass destruction are discovered. (Rumsfeld himself placed three check marks after this Horrible.) Other Horribles include sectarian battles between Sunni, Shia, and Kurds (one check mark); US postwar involvement lasting eight to ten years, not two to four (one check mark); the cost of the war becoming ruinously high (no check mark, though the cost of the failed reconstruction is in the neighborhood of $206 billion—$60 billion from the US, $146 billion from Iraq (according to the 2013 *Learning from Iraq: A Final Report from the Special Inspector General for Iraq Reconstruction*); and world opinion turning against the US because Iraq would "best us in public relations and persuade the world that the war is against Muslims" (five check marks). The insurgency, the currently escalating civil war between Sunni and Shia, and the country's fragmentation in Anbar province because of the rise of the Islamic State—the Parade of Horribles set in motion in 2003 just keeps getting longer and longer.

The chronicle of the spectacular failure of the reconstruction is documented in the Special US Inspector General's Report on Iraq Reconstruction. Titled *Hard Lessons*, the 2009 report—an internal government document commissioned by Congress in October 2004—is a little masterpiece of understated but savage irony that at times seems like a deliberate parody of policy-wonk-speak to achieve its less-than-flattering conclusions about Donald Rumsfeld, Paul Bremer, and Dick Cheney. In excruciating, and sometimes excruciatingly funny, detail, it shows how their mistaken conviction that the Iraqis would welcome the United States with open arms lies at the heart of the most catastrophically disorganized and wasteful reconstruction effort in the entire history of humankind. (And that's no exaggeration: the Marshall Plan, a relative success story, cost in today's dollars around $103 billion—roughly half of the combined cost to the United States and Iraq. Ultimately, the Watson Institute of Brown University estimates that the total cost of the war, $2 trillion, could rise to more than $6 trillion, if you count interest over the next forty years.)

In one particularly surreal chapter head, "Flying Billions to Baghdad," we learn that 640 bundles of cash, each bundle containing a thousand $100 bills, were strapped to one pallet, which weighed about fifteen hundred pounds. In the first year alone, over "$12 billion—or 237.3 tons of cash—" was flown to Baghdad, where the pallets were unloaded. Then shrink-wrapped bricks of cash, nicknamed "footballs," were loaded into "trucks and Chevy Suburbans," and personally delivered "to their respective ministries to pay salaries and other costs." And who would be the wiser if a football got tossed out of bounds now and then? Or if a van stopped off at a friend's house on the way? Or if $1.2–$1.6 billion found its way to a Lebanese bunker—a fact revealed by Stuart Bowen, the inspector general who tracked the money down.

Another chapter heading in a draft version of the report is a quote from Charles Dickens: "We spent as much money as we could, and got as little for it as people could make up their minds to give us." There was so little thought given to the reconstruction that one of the Department of Defense generals, Steven Hawkins, who was assigned to come up with a plan for reconstruction fifty-six days (yes, fifty-six days) before the invasion, said he had so little support from his own military commanders at Central Command (CENTCOM controls American military operations in the Middle East) that he went to an officers' club trade show and swiped paper and office supplies from the display tables so that he could give his staff something to write on.

Perhaps the most damning comment on the reconstruction is how many younger Iraqis view it. As the specter of Saddam Hussein fades, most would say that there wasn't much to choose from between Saddam's thuggery and the US occupation. In fact, for some Iraqis, Saddam was at least a homegrown thug, while the United States was a mere parvenu. In the oral history, I noted this bit of testimony by Azhar Abdul-Karim Abdul-Wahab, a lecturer in the political science department at the University of Baghdad:

> You cannot discuss Iraqi history without mentioning Saddam, whom I viewed as a kind of occupier. I tried to put it in those terms to my students. Saddam stole freedoms from Iraq. He stole money from Iraq. He brought wars on Iraq. All the bad things an occupier might do Saddam actually did. I told them this. For the most part their reply to me was the same. At least he was an Iraqi, they would say. At least he was an Iraqi.
>
> (Kukis, *Voices from Iraq*, 55)

All of our convoys followed the same pattern of tight security, except for our visit to the University of Sulaimani in Iraqi Kurdistan. With the exception of Kirkuk, where the violence is as bad as any place farther south, travel in Kurdistan feels relatively safe. While there were the usual three vehicles in convoy, they were manned by Kurds, not international contractors. Just before the road switch-backed up the central massif to Suly, as the Kurds call it, we stopped at a roadside restaurant where we ate thick yogurt with oven-baked bread—a luxury and freedom of movement unthinkable in Basrah or Baghdad. Alongside us ran a snow-fed river that on his previous visit Chris had swum in to cool down after a run. The water ran swiftly beside the road, the ply of the central current ridging up into waves and whirlpools in the hazy sun—so unlike the slow gray meander of the Tigris through Baghdad, or the huge, silty marshes outside Basrah.

The Kurdish language, suppressed for many years, now holds sway over Arabic. The Kurds are intensely nationalistic, and Kurdish identity trumps sectarian loyalties. After the fall of Saddam, who made numerous attempts at genocide against the Kurds, security has been one of their prime concerns. Unlike the US occupiers, they learned early that major reconstruction efforts are doomed to fail if security can't be guaranteed to companies interested in investing in the Kurds' huge oil fields. As long as Kurdistan can keep from being torn apart by the war in Syria, or co-opted by either the Turks to the north or the Iranians to the east, not to mention their warring countrymen to the south, they stand the best chance of any part of Iraq to offer their citizens a decent life.

This sense of hopefulness is palpable among the students. In one workshop, several of them had just returned from Venice Beach, California, and were agog over Beyoncé and Lady Gaga. In fact, many of the students had traveled abroad, and didn't seem nearly as culturally isolated. Despite the fact that these students lived in Kirkuk, one of the few cities in Kurdistan still deeply embroiled in sectarian killing (the presence of ISIL has made the situation even more difficult), their responses to the writing exercises were far more upbeat and not nearly so fatalistic.

One of the teachers, a young woman without a head scarf who was Christian, told us how she had become friends with Harold Pinter.

"He would call me," she said, "over Skype, and ask question after question about our daily lives. We became good friends." Pinter had championed Kurdish human rights for years, especially when they rebelled against Saddam during the first Gulf War. After encouraging the Kurds to rise up against Saddam, the United States refused to support them when Saddam cracked down with helicopter gunships strafing columns of refugees escaping by foot, or riding on donkeys, trucks, and tractors. But after Saddam fell in 2003, the Kurds aggressively pursued their own self-governance, putting a high priority on security.

In fact, the Erbil consulate compound looked like just another suburban neighborhood. Even though it was cold, on a windless day you could lounge in the sun on the roof and look out over the entire city: white stucco houses, yards full of orange trees, the oranges shining among the leaves, and far off, the Zagros Mountains jutting up on the horizon. And even though the security officer was concerned that a twelve-story building, still under construction, overlooked the entire consulate, in Baghdad it would be suicidal to allow such a tall building to share the compound wall. At a small consulate like Erbil's, one man with a rocket-propelled grenade could destroy the compound in less than an hour. Yet the consulate staff went about their business. The Kurdish security guards even gave us clearance to go to an art opening at the British Council. The opening was held to celebrate a book of photographs about Kurdish life. Chris and I stood in line with everyone else helping themselves to the abundance of local cheeses, baklava, and other honeyed pastries.

Before my trip, I confess that I used to wince whenever I used the term *creative writing*. It seems so treacly and diminishing and ludicrously inadequate. And it seemed like such an American approach to the arts, particularly in comparison to how the Iraqi writers talked about it. In a meeting with what American educators might call "gifted and talented" high school students, two of Iraq's best-known writers, one a poet, the other a dramatist, spoke about the art as if it were a form of existential inquiry leading to secular transcendence. By contrast, Chris's and my focus on exercises, on forming good writing habits by trying to write every day, and our insistence on reading, seemed a little lacking in mystery, if not downright square, in comparison to what Naseer Hassan and Hamed al-Maliki were proposing as primary qualities for being a writer: the Rilkean attributes of vision, inspiration, and the ability to express profound feeling.

When Chris and I traded views on books, or began to reminisce about poets we'd admired and learned from, our conversations almost always took a technical turn. Chris, who'd studied with Joseph Brodsky, once said to me, "You know, Brodsky had the habit of saying provocative things about poetry, things that you wouldn't think someone who came to English as a second language would pick up on. I remember once in class he talked about how British poets often established the metrical norm for a poem in the first line, but that American poets, if they had any kind of norm at all, tended to establish it in the second line."

That Chris and I could be having this somewhat arcane conversation about rhythm in poetry somehow heartened me in the midst of the escalating violence.

And yet Hamed and Naseer had a point. Who cares if the metrical norm is established in the first or second line, if the poem doesn't lift off the page because of the quality of the emotion?

I remember thinking at the time how the Polish poet and dissident Aleksander Wat wrote in his memoir, *My Century*, that his years as an editor, focusing on the minutiae of stylistic effects, had eventually made him lose faith in literature as anything other than a series of calculated rhetorical procedures. Wat had become so accustomed to talking about literature as nothing but verbal effects that he "felt in charge only when I had taken hold of the actual end of the thread and could see an entire work unravel into its components. And I gradually became cynical about what I considered the spurious integrity and unity of a given work" (Aleksander Wat, *My Century*, 210). He had come to think about literature in a way that resembled our American faith in workshops. Again, a stark contrast between our kit-bag-of-techniques approach, and our Iraqi counterparts' faith in the primacy of the imagination.

I admit that Wat's weariness with literature has beset me from time to time, a kind of poetry gloom that overtakes me when certain values in poetry that I love are forgotten in the world of workshops, "scenes," and hyperbolic blurbs. Complexity of feeling, a style that embodies emotion, as opposed to riding on top of it with lots of verbal pyrotechnics and rhetorical display, a sense of the deep past resonating behind a line, and the feeling that the poet, as Seamus Heaney once said, aspires to make poetry an independent category of human consciousness, partaking of, but not beholden to, politics, religion, psychology, or sociology—well, it's an ideal that I myself find hard to live up to, and from time to time, it's difficult not to lose patience, not only with oneself but with all the forces in the culture that want to instrumentalize our relations to art.

Or if that sounds too hifalutin, call it the Facebookery of art, the Gradgrindization of art, as Charles Dickens might put it. But the meetings Chris and I had with Iraqi students and professors and writers, and the poems and stories they wrote, began to restore the balance for me between the thread that unravels and how my Iraqi counterparts spoke about literature.

This balance was something Wat also rediscovered in the silence of the Lubyanka Prison, the worst of the many prisons and camps he was condemned to during the Stalinist purges. And while Wat's historical situation was radically different from mine, not to mention Hamed's and Naseer's, in Iraq I understood a little about how Wat regained his love of literature:

When we go back to the twenty, fifty, or hundred greatest works of world literature that we read as young people, we cannot, nor do we wish to, be freed from the charms of that initial reading. Still, we were prematurely exposed. What could we have known of their roots in human life? Under conditions like those in Lubyanka—cut off from the world, aware of the vast roaring

world outside, the deathly hush inside, where time slows terribly
while we continue to grow terribly old biologically—under those
conditions we sought to recover our initial freshness of perception, the way Adam saw when he saw that "it was good." . . . In
Lubyanka, to my joy, I rediscovered the sense of integrity—the
whole that "precedes" the parts and is their soul. I had fully recovered my ability to see things synthetically.

(Wat, *My Century*, 210)

I don't claim that my poetry gloom is either as profound, or
as extreme, as Wat's disaffection. But my trip to Iraq shifted the
frame, not only on how I viewed Iraq, but about literature in general. In a world so fraught with violence, Seamus Heaney's idealism
about the place of poetry was no longer an abstraction but, as Keats
would put it, "proved upon our pulses." And this sense of ground
walked over, as opposed to a flyover on TV, complicated my political feelings—in fact, you could say that for the first time I actually
had feelings, as opposed to convictions. For years, my political views
about the country were off-the-rack lefty, views that cost me nothing and were easy to espouse. But during our trip, I had constant
misgivings about being mistaken for a cultural ambassador, which
was almost inevitable, given the fact that the State Department was
funding much of my trip. But those misgivings forced me not so
much to come to terms with them, as to understand how difficult it
is to live out what Yeats once said the purpose of all art was: to hold
reality and justice in a single thought. Well, my hands weren't clean.
And to wish that they were would mean not going to Iraq because,
for one thing, I didn't have the money to afford the security I would
want to buy: and if you were buying security, your ideological purity
was already compromised because your privilege protected you from
the violence ordinary Iraqis risked every day.

On our way back from one mission in Baghdad, Chris and I
learned that a suicide bomber had gotten inside the Green Zone, or
what, since the US troop withdrawal in 2011, had been rechristened
the International Zone—the IZ, as the locals put it. That meant the

rest of the city qualified as the Red Zone. But the Red Zone, the IZ, no matter—sure enough, a day later, the bomber blew himself up not too far from where we'd just conducted a workshop.

But such incidents, after the workshop with Mariam, now took on a subtly different quality. I had begun to feel such rage about the relentlessness of the killing, the zealotry that could inspire it, the religious mania that seemed to brutalize people into killing other ordinary Iraqis who most likely weren't particularly religious, except as a formal, societal, or familial instinct, and who had no doctrinal grudge against anyone. Their only sin was to be in the wrong place at the wrong time. But since Mariam's story, written and read with such understated feeling, my rage, and the comfort it gave me because of my certainty that it was justified, could never take hold of me without my also seeing the image of her brother, gently, very gently, bending down to kiss his sister, to ask her if she needed anything at the market, and whispering, again with the utmost gentleness, that this would be the last time he would ever see her.

Tales of the Marvelous,
News of the Strange

It snowed the night I got back to New York from Amman, Jordan. The Syrian refugees I'd traveled to meet, their faces and voices, seemed somehow more vivid than the snow, which in any case would melt and turn to ice by morning. On the shelf beside me was the book I'd been reading on the plane home during the past night and day—a collection of medieval Arabic tales, including the story of al-Khansa', the woman warrior who made war against the tribe of the Banu Mazin who had killed her brother, Sakhr. She had sworn that she would only stop killing the Banu Mazin when a thousand Mazini women, who had lost their brothers to the rage of al-Khansa', came before her weeping and mourning. The Mazini women, exhausted by the slaughter, knelt before al-Khansa', all of them crying for the brothers of their hearts. Al-Khansa' felt inspired by their grief and composed these lines:

I won't forget you,
Sakhr, I won't forget
you ever. I'd kill

myself if it weren't
for all these
women weeping for

their brothers
whom I killed.
It's only in

murdering those who
killed you, Sakhr,
that I can find

even this moment
of peace. A thousand
of their brothers

aren't enough
to make up
for your death—

for their brothers
were nothing compared
to you, Sakhr—

but their grief is
all that keeps
me from joining

you down in the dirt
and darkness of
your grave.

The poem like a cool wind passed through her, and she felt pity for
the women and had food brought to them and ate with them, and
this sharing of salt brought peace between her and the Banu Mazin

after seven years of constant war. And she returned their weapons, their gold, their mules and goats and camels and horses, everything in fact that she'd seized in her raids. And then she took off her coat of mail forged and hammered by Da'ud, she unstrapped her Indian sword, and laid down her long lance. And as I finished the story of al-Khansa', I envisioned Jordanian activist and journalist Nahed Hattar's serious face staring back at me—from YouTube, from Al-Jazeera, from a video that shows him lying on his back, head cradled in a man's arms as he bleeds to death on the bottom step of the Palace of Justice.

2

The Christian cabdriver who'd given me a ride to the hotel just minutes before was a large fellow with thick graying hair swooped back over his ears. Though his fine features were beginning to be swallowed up in fleshiness, his face was still handsome. "I lived in Columbus, Ohio, for five years," he explained, "with my older brother. I married an American woman but we fought all the time—and so we got divorced. That's when I came back here and met my second wife: a Romanian woman—they make the best wives of all—mine is beautiful and a good mother—but she's very strong willed. She wants to leave Amman and go to London. I don't understand why these guys with their long, ugly beards are allowed to immigrate to the US, but people like me aren't."

By "guys," Ahmad meant Muslim fundamentalists, and by "people like me," he meant Christians. And as I'd learned on other trips to the Middle East, a phrase like "long, ugly beards" means far more than style and grooming. Beards often signify conservative Muslim values; of course, long beards are also characteristic of certain Christian patriarchs—nothing is ever simple in these matters. In the charged atmosphere of Jordanian politics, to notice if someone is bearded or clean-shaven can become survival information. Would it surprise anyone in Jordan that Nahed Hattar had been gunned down for his left-wing, anti-ISIL views by a man with a long beard?

As we drove past the low-rise apartment and office buildings that line most of Amman's major streets, Ahmad expressed deep frustration about being a Christian in Jordan, his complaints both plangent and, to my outsider's ears, bordering on Islamophobic. But in his own mind he had plenty of cause, given what he characterized as the growing political aggressiveness of the Muslim Brotherhood. "These guys," he said, "they don't like Christians and they want to take us backwards. My brother said he'd sponsor me in the US, but I don't have the money to take my wife and my three daughters. Things haven't worked out for me here: everybody says that there isn't any difference between Christian and Muslims, but I'm telling you, when I was working for an American oil company in Jordan, my boss was a guy from Texas who said, 'Ahmad, I want you to sit next to me at this business banquet.' And when I said, 'Boss, shouldn't you be sitting next to the Turkish boss?,' he said, 'I can't stand that guy. I'm sitting next to you.' It wasn't good business, but my boss preferred me to everybody else in the office. He treated me well and we became good friends. But then he left, and a Turkish guy took over, and hated me. He used to say to me, 'If you come late, Ahmad, I'll do to you what we did to the Armenians.' And it wasn't just once he said it, but every day. I couldn't take it after a while, and I quit. I've got lots of experience in business administration and in managing construction projects. I speak Arabic, English, Italian, Romanian, Greek, and French. But in the last five years, Muslims are only hiring Muslims—it doesn't matter how many languages you speak or what your experience is; they won't say it to your face, but if you're a Christian you're wasting your time—that's how it is, and everybody knows it. You see that row of office buildings?"

In the direction of the Belle Vue Hotel tower, he pointed to a set of glass-fronted, modernist cubes lining the street near the second traffic circle. And despite the shakiness of the economy and widespread unemployment, you could see the Jordanian government's commitment to infrastructure in the wide, well-maintained roads and the steel-and-glass architecture.

"There used to be lots and lots of Christmas lights and decorations on these buildings, but now the business owners don't bother putting them up anymore. The guys with the long beards are against it. They're the ones who killed Nahed Hattar."

"For what?"

"Like the *Charlie Hebdo* guys. Blasphemy."

On his Facebook page Hattar had shared a cartoon, which he himself did not draw, that mocked the religious views of Daesh—a derogatory term for ISIL.

As we pulled into the hotel drive, Ahmed turned to me and said, "And so this guy dies—a Christian just like me. I don't want my daughters to grow up around this kind of thing. The extremists have taken over the schools, and since I want my kids to grow up around other Catholics, I pay to send them to Catholic school. When the education ministry tried to update the textbooks this year by including pictures of women without head scarfs and men without beards, and mentioned Christians, the teachers' union refused to teach from them. Some of the teachers and parents held a demonstration and burned the new books."

I wondered if Ahmed wasn't exaggerating, but in a *New York Times* article that confirmed the book burning, I read how one teacher had fiercely objected to a picture of a clean-shaven man vacuuming his home while on the wall there hangs a crucifix—three slights to tradition in one picture. Verses from the Koran and hadith are routinely inserted before lessons, even in physics and mathematics textbooks. An Associated Press article cites a passage in a sixth-grade textbook which says that if students "don't embrace Islam," they "will face God's torture" and the "pit of hell." Eighth graders are told that "jihad is a must for every Muslim." Dr. Zogan Obeidat, a former ministry of education official who has received death threats for his views, wrote in *Al Ghad* newspaper, "If ISIS ruled Jordan, they wouldn't even need to change our textbooks."

Ahmad shook his head as we sat together in his Hyundai, an immaculately clean, almost elegant little gray car that seemed at that moment a kind of fragile sanctuary. "I would like my kids to grow up in Rome," he said. "I loved living in Italy—everywhere in Rome, there were so many beautiful things to look at: the buildings, the gardens, everything was so beautiful—not like here. Here I feel stupid and old."

"Anyone who can speak as many languages as you do would be counted as brilliant in the United States," I said.

"Thank you," he smiled. He gave a fatalistic little shrug. "I used to feel intelligent, but after driving a cab all day, too many angry people on the road, too much traffic—I don't know, all I can do is sit and watch the TV set and feel exhausted. I need to get out of this country, but I don't know how. My wife has it fixed in her head that the only place she'll go is London. But I tell her we can't afford London: five people in a tiny one-bedroom apartment? No, it would be a disaster. I tell her that we should go to Romania, because at least there we have family, we could get help in finding work—but she shouts at me that she'll never go back to Romania, that the only place she's moving is London. I feel broken by all this."

He stared off through the windshield as if searching for some inner reserves that no longer existed. "What am I going to do?" he asked me.

"I don't know," I said. "But I hope you get to Romania or London. Good luck to you." I paid my fare and included a huge tip—it was all I could think to do. He drove off down Islamic College Street—as if he needed yet another reminder of his status as a Christian. In front of the hotel the statues of two grazing oryx antelopes, an endangered species—one of them bending down to nibble at the concrete, the other with its head up, ears pricked as if listening for danger—seemed like an apt metaphor for the fragility of Jordanian society. Muslims and Christians, native Jordanians of Bedouin heritage and the Palestinians who had come during the Nakba and the Six-Day War, the Iraqi and now the Syrian refugees—it wouldn't take much to plunge the country into chaos. Meanwhile, I could almost hear Ahmed's Romanian wife yelling at him for not taking them to London, while Ahmed sighs wearily and says, "We can't afford it."

3

In another tale, Harun al-Rashid is bored, so he calls on his vizier to distract him. The vizier tells him that there is a man in the prison who has only one eye, one leg, and one hand, but that he is a marvelous storyteller. The Prince of the Faithful replies, "If he amuses me, then I shall reward him as he deserves." And so the prisoner is brought out of the dungeon, washed and perfumed, and dressed in a beautiful and costly robe.

"Prince of the Faithful," says the man, "should I tell you something that I heard, or something that I myself have seen?"

"Something that you have seen, as it is always best to hear what really happened. That way leads most surely to wisdom."

"Then I will tell you how I lost my eye, my leg, and my hand. Know that I was the son of a king. My older brother hated me because my father preferred me above all his other sons, and intended to give me his kingdom when Allah called him. My brother began to tell lies about me to my father: he said that I wanted to kill my father and take over the kingdom.

"And so my father banished me from the palace, and turned me out in the wilderness with only the clothes on my back. I fled to the mountains, afraid my brother might pursue me, but when I finally reached them, I was already dying of thirst and hunger. But as I wandered, looking for something to eat and drink, I came across a stone door built into the mountainside, and in front of it a statue of a bronze warrior with a great ax. I tried to open the door, but when I took hold of the brass ring set into the stone, the warrior swung his ax and chopped off my hand.

"I thought I would die, when out of the air came a beautiful red bird that brought in its beak a magic salve that took away all my pain. I was so desperate that I again approached the door, and again, the warrior attacked me and chopped off my leg. And again the bird gave me the magic salve. I made a crutch out of a fallen tree limb, but this time I cried out to the warrior, 'What do you want in order to open the door for me?' And he cried back, 'I want your eyes, so that I can find my way through the world.'

"And when I looked at him, I saw that he had no eyes. But his hearing was so keen that it was impossible to move even a step without him knowing it. I thought to myself, *By Allah, I will die here unless*

I find food and drink. And so I said, 'Guardian of the Mountain, I need one eye or else I will wander through the world as blind as you are, and my hearing is not as keen as the wolf's, as yours is. Have pity on me, for Allah's sake, and accept the gift of one eye.'

"He agreed and reached out his hand, but I was careful to anoint my eye with the salve, so that when he plucked it out, I felt no pain. He put my eye into one of the empty sockets in his head, and when he saw what he had done to me, he was filled with remorse.

"'Oh son of Allah, forgive me,' he cried out. 'This is the first time that I have seen what my ax has done to its victims. To make up for the suffering I've caused you, I'll throw back the door to the mountain, and inside you will find a vast treasure.' And he took hold of the brass ring and pulled the door open.

"Smoke poured from the interior, I heard laughter and singing, and as I limped into the vast cavern, ahead of me sparkled gold and rubies without number, pearls the size of a man's fists, and a lavish banquet where I ate and drank my fill, feasting for three days and nights, while djinn came and went, fulfilling my every wish. I asked the most powerful djinn to bring me a wife, which he did, and my joy was complete since she was kind, wise, and more beautiful than the rising moon.

"But one day, she woke to tell me that she was sick. And I ordered my djinn to cure her, but he said, 'Master, there is no one who can cure what Allah has decreed.' And so she died. And all my pleasures turned to dust. I left the cavern and wandered city to city, begging as I went, saying to one and all, 'When I saw, I was blind. When I walked, I was lame. When I took what the world gave me, I could not hold what I was given.'

"And so I came to your city, great Prince, and was so hungry, I stole bread, and was arrested by the guard, and put into your prison. Have mercy on me, and God will bless you all the days of your life." And Harun al-Rashid said, "That is a marvel that you have told me, and surely the strangest tale I have ever heard."

And he made this man one of his most trusted courtiers, and he lived happily until He who takes all took him.

4

In the front seat next to our driver is Rania, a young woman from Saudi Arabia who works for the UN in Amman. "When I was a student," she tells me, "the other women students and I had to enter our university through a special entrance meant for women only. We had separate classrooms for women only where we would take off our niqabs and hijabs, and where our professor would be broadcast to us on a screen. We could see him, but he couldn't see us. Our teachers were all men, of course, and were often in the same room with the male students. But the camera focused on our professor at his lectern so the male students and female students never saw each other. We wore headphones and each of us had a microphone. When the time for questions came, we pressed a key on our computer keyboards to let our professor know we had a question."

The use of technology and modern, secular science to impose traditional roles on men and women makes me curious. "Rania, do you still feel at home in Saudi Arabia after living in Jordan?" Yesterday when I went to the University of Jordan, there were lots of women professors and students, and the men and women all sat together in the same classroom.

"When I'm in Riyadh," she says, "I like to see my parents and my brothers and sisters. But because women aren't allowed to drive, it's difficult to have your own life. I want to stay in Amman, at least for now, because the kind of work I do here with Syrian refugees would be impossible there. So I like to visit, but I'm more myself here."

"How do you feel about those restrictions?"

"I don't really think of them that way. You in the West always talk about restrictions, but we think in terms of obligations: when I'm back home, my obligation is to my society and to my work and to my religion—not to myself."

"But you just said that you feel more yourself in Jordan."

"But that's because I'm here in Jordan. Each of us has a role to play, and if we understand our role rightly, then we will know how to fulfill that role in a way that will be right for us. So yes, I'm more myself here, but that's because I'm here, not home in Saudi Arabia. What's right for here wouldn't be right there." She turns halfway around in her seat and gives me an amused smile, her white hijab glimmering in the sun. I want to object that her logic is circular, but I can see that for her it isn't. And so I smile back at her amusement at what she sees as my linear reasoning, and for a moment our differences vanish and we laugh together.

5

I'd gone into the jewelry store next to my hotel to see about buying presents for my wife and daughter. The owner is dressed casually in a close-fitting brown sweater and Calvin Klein jeans, his brown slip-ons polished to a high gloss. The jewelry is tastefully arranged in vitrines of various shapes and sizes, and he has taken care not to overcrowd the separate pieces. "Welcome, my friend—I've been sitting all day like a spider in his web, and you're the only customer I've had all day. Sit down and have some tea."

He emerges from the back room with small glass teacups, the steaming tea so heavily sugared that its sweetness is a kind of bitterness. I place my hand on my heart and nod my thanks before sitting down beside him. Across from us, the counter display shows off antique jewelry of "Traditional Bedouin Design"—at least that's what the beautifully calligraphed placard says that hangs next to a pair of crossed *janbiyas*, daggers with golden hilts and upturned blades.

I ask to see some earrings and a bracelet inlaid with carnelian stones, and we quickly settle on a price. When I praise his English, he shrugs. "I grew up in the US in Seattle. I only came back here after I finished college. I've been back here now for eighteen years. We're Muslims, you see, and we wanted to come back to Jordan to raise our kids."

His name is Mahmoud and unlike Ahmad, my beleaguered taxi driver, he's more optimistic about the future, in favor of the King and the present government. "My heritage is Bedouin, and it's traditional for the Bedouin to support King and Army." And although

Mahmoud doesn't say it, I can tell by his confident manner that he thinks of his heritage as the backbone of Jordanian society—if there is such a thing in a country that is over half Palestinian, and is now trying to cope with a million and a half Syrian refugees. When I mention Nahed Hattar, he says, "Christians and Muslims get along just fine in Jordan. You've seen the Christmas decorations in the hotel lobby, yes?" And despite Ahmad's despair, I had noticed the mural of the Christ child in the manger, and the dough-faced wise men standing around ogling the little Christ, who peers back with a distracted air, as if he were looking off into the future and doesn't much like what he sees.

"Hattar was foolish. But to kill someone for posting a cartoon? That was mad—but exactly what you'd expect from these *takfiris*." Takfiri, which means "apostate," is what Jordanians call ISIL members—perverters of Islam.

"Do you think the fact that Hattar grew up a Christian had something to do with it?"

"Maybe, maybe not—he's what the news channels call a secular Christian, which means that he was raised in a Christian community—but he's not a believer. To say he's secular is a roundabout way of calling him an atheist."

"And isn't he also a Marxist?"

"Yes and no—he believed in Marxism, but he denounced Marxists as armchair revolutionaries."

"What else is he?"

"A supporter of Assad."

"Assad?"

"I know what you're thinking, but there are many Jordanians who support him. To them, Assad is not a murderer, Assad is fighting ISIL, he's being picked on by the US with your drone strikes and air support. They aren't happy about fellow Muslims being bombed. Look, most Jordanians"—he shrugged—"most *Arabs* hated Clinton's and Obama's policies in the Middle East. And because of that, I'd say about half of Jordanians wanted Trump to win."

"But what about Trump's attitude toward Muslims?"

"Trump didn't say he was going to get rid of all Muslims, he said he was going to get rid of these extremists with their long dirty beards." And he added with an arch smile, "There are times when I myself wouldn't mind seeing all these Syrians deported—especially when the West, except for Germany, has done almost nothing to help solve the problem." Mahmoud frowned, then sipped his tea. "Have you seen Hattar's cartoon?" He stood up and typed a few words into his computer's search box.

I bent down to the screen and saw a jihadi inside a tent in what I took to be Paradise. The man's nose was huge and bulbous as an antique bicycle horn, and he was smoking a cigarette in bed, his bare feet sticking out from under the covers, while two naked women at his side await his pleasure. These are his houris, his eternally youthful wives who, according to hadith, don't defecate, urinate, menstruate, or get pregnant. In fact, their flesh is so pure that you can see through them to the very marrow of their bones, which are also transparent, like crystal—not like the women the cartoonist has drawn. Allah, who should never be depicted, wears a golden crown, his long white beard, bushy white eyebrows, and gargantuan face making him look like a fairy-tale giant as he pulls the tent flap aside.

The cartoon is titled "The God of Daesh" and the caption reads:

Allah: "May your evening be joyous, Abu Saleh, do you need anything?"

Jihadist: "Yes, Lord, bring me the glass of wine from over there and tell Jibril [the Angel Gabriel] to bring me some cashews. After that send me an eternal servant to clean the floor and take the empty plates with you."

Jihadist continues: "Don't forget to put a door on the tent so that you knock before you enter next time, your Gloriousness."

I said, "I heard there were hundreds of death threats on Twitter." "Yes. The guy who killed him was one of these Al-Qaeda sympathizers who went to Iraq during the war—when he came back, he was supposedly 'rehabilitated.' He became a part-time imam and started preaching in two mosques. A lot of people think that the government put him up to it: but Jordanians like to read conspiracies into everything." Mahmoud shook his head. "I feel sorry for Hattar. I didn't agree with him on everything, but he was a respectable man, he showed a lot of courage in presenting his views. But he went too far—he knew the mood of these guys and yet he did it anyway. On the other hand, his family did ask the police for protection, and the prime minister refused. That was a mistake, obviously."

"Did you find the cartoon offensive?"

"Well, as a Muslim, I do find it offensive"—he shrugged and shook his head—"a little bit, I guess." Mahmoud pursed his lips. "Well, actually no, it wasn't so much offensive as I just thought it was kind of silly. Like a fourteen-year-old boy trying to gross out his parents. That kind of silly."

Mahmoud again types something into the search box, and suddenly there Hattar is: balding, his large eyes owlish behind black glasses, wearing a striped shirt and jacket; nothing in his appearance suggests that he's been imprisoned by the government sixteen times since 1979, or that his commentary is so controversial it's outlawed in Jordan.

The day bright and calm, his brothers and sons surround him as Hattar approaches the steps leading up to the Palace of Justice. The guards stand around flat-footed as a man dressed in a robe and with a long, tangled beard comes up to Hattar, and at point-blank range shoots him three times, once in the head, twice in the chest. He collapses on his back on the concrete, and a young man kneels down and cradles Hattar as blood soaks through his shirt and suit and pours out across the flagstones and pools around the man's shoes, while a woman behind them screams.

The police guarding the Palace of Justice do nothing but gawk while Hattar's brother chases and tackles his brother's murderer—ironically enough, by grabbing him by his beard.

Mahmoud offers me more tea and shrugs. "The Hattars are a

well-respected family. One of his relatives is the woman who works
in the store when I'm not here." When I'd passed by yesterday on my
way to interview some Syrian refugees, I'd seen her, a young woman
in slacks, her pixie haircut peroxided blond as she balanced on a ladder and fussed over a ceiling display light.

And there was my friend, Ruba Hattar, a cousin of Nahed. A tall,
slender, self-possessed young woman whose quiet intelligence is both
tough-minded and tactful, she works for the US Embassy in the cultural affairs department and had arranged for me to meet with students and professors at various universities. In what I took to be a
quiet sign of mourning, rather than her own Facebook profile picture she had posted a picture of Nahed's hands. One hand curls into a
half-clenched fist, while the one underneath rests at ease on a pack of
Marlboros, some notebooks, a manuscript in progress, and a book—
nicotine, paper, and words, the writer's quintessential tools.

In 1998 King Hussein's security officers tortured Hattar so badly
that he needed surgery to remove a long section of his intestine. When
Hussein died a year later, Hattar pointed out in a column that not
everyone in Jordan was going to mourn the King's passing. And now
Hussein's son, King Abdullah II, who likes to cast himself as a social moderate, had sanctioned Hattar's arrest for "inciting sectarian
strife" and "insulting religion."

For the last nineteen years since his torture, Hattar had needed
to take medication and eat a special diet. But during his month-
long incarceration he was denied these necessities, and so he ended
up in the hospital twice. It was only when his family protested to
the Red Cross and Amnesty International that he was allowed treatment. But as soon as the doctors left, the guards tore out his IVs, refused to remove the needles in his arms, cuffed his hands and feet,
and placed him in a hospital prison cell. As a joke, they wrote a sign
that they placed at the foot of his bed so he would have to see it: *This
man is a dangerous criminal.* But on Ruba's Facebook page, Nahed
Hattar's hands are the soft hands of an intellectual, nearly hairless,
the nails cut neatly to the quick.

Ruba, who is also a poet, had read with me and others the night
before in a coffee shop. Unlike many Jordanian poets who chant

their work in a highly theatrical manner, Ruba reads with a quiet, unforced intensity. Halfway through her poem, I could see her eyes go glassy. Her voice choked up a moment, but then she recovered her composure and read to the end in a firm, understated way. When I asked her for a paraphrase in English, she bowed her head and said, "The poem uses the metaphor of a garden to talk about how Jordan is being torn apart."

6

A poor fisherman goes down to the sea and hurls in his net time and time again, but he catches nothing all day long, leaving him with no fish to sell in the market, let alone to eat. This goes on for three days until he feels as if he'll die of hunger. But on the fourth day, he feels a heavy weight dragging his net down as he hauls it in: and at the bottom of it is an ancient lamp. He takes out the lamp and, thinking to sell it to a junk man in the market, he rubs it with his sleeve. And as he rubs, a plume of smoke arises from the lamp's spout and a fierce-looking djinn materializes, his head so large it blacks out the sun.

"Well, my friend," says the djinn, "I've been at the bottom of the sea now for a thousand years. I'd like to reward you. Ask me for something and I'll grant it to you."

The fisherman cowers in terror and prostrates himself before the djinn, but the djinn takes him by the hand and raises him to his feet. "Your Greatness," says the fisherman, "I'd like a net full of fish."

The djinn laughs and says, "Very good—in a moment you'll have more fish than ten men can carry. But first I'm going to kill you: this is what I promised myself when I was shut in the lamp by a sorcerer a thousand years ago." And so the djinn lifts his sword and cuts off the poor man's head even as his net fills up with every kind of fish that swims in the sea.

7

"We came to Jordan when I was sixteen. My father was ill, but because of the war, he couldn't get treatment." Maysara sipped his Coke as Rania translated. I'd been told not to ask political questions since it could potentially endanger him, and he himself insisted on no photographs. His story felt depressingly familiar—doctors and medical supplies co-opted by the war, his father could stay in Syria and die for lack of treatment, or leave the country for Amman in the vague hope that the Jordanian medical system might save his life.

"The doctors took out one of his kidneys . . . but he died anyway. By this time, the war had gotten much worse, so we decided to stay. We came to one of the camps and stayed there for a month. But we hated it so much that we left as soon as we could find a place to stay in Salt." (Salt is a small city built on the rocky slopes outside Amman.) "There was nothing to do in the camp so I slept a lot. I felt like life was empty. You woke up and you stood around and you went to bed. That was it, day after day. The ones who came before me, they wanted to know why I was so restless, but I couldn't stand it. I guess they got used to it, but me—I couldn't see any future there. And so I ran away to Amman—I had no papers, so it was illegal, but I didn't care. I had to leave." His razor-cut black beard and swept-back black hair, his black vest and blue sweater, his faded blue jeans, made him look a little like James Dean in *Rebel without a Cause*. But there was nothing melancholy about Maysara, nothing pensive or wounded—despite his father's death and being a refugee, he was resolutely optimistic, but in a smart, hardheaded way. He harbored no illusions about returning to Syria because the Syria he'd known had been destroyed.

"My sister is still in Azraq Camp," he said, "going to school, but all the rest of us are here in Salt." He lit a cigarette and sat back in his chair.

"I'd just finished my school back in Syria, and I wanted to go to college, but all the records of my schoolwork were blown up. I'd like to go back to school, but without the records I'd have to start all over again. My family needs me to work. I'm the main support of my mother, my brother, and my three sisters. My brother had a job in construction, and he even went to school here to get a construction certificate. But the job he was working on ended, and he's been without a job for several months now."

"Do you hear anything from your relatives back in Syria?"

"Nothing, not a word. We've heard nothing for three months from any of our relatives."

"Where are they?"

"In Daraa."

"Did you leave Syria because of what happened in Daraa?" Maysara didn't answer, and he seemed to go inward for a moment. He shrugged, and nodded—then looked down at the café table. The jukebox behind us played a loop-and-sample version of *rai*, its high-pitched wail and thump joyous and unhinged, a contrast to the blankness on Maysara's face. The mirrors behind him reflected his hunched shoulders. He was a small, well-knit man, energetic, with a quick smile. Given his tough demeanor, and his athletic swagger—he held a black belt in Tae Kwon Do—it was easy to envision him marching in the streets of Daraa with other kids his age when Assad's Ba'ath Party headquarters were set on fire. In fact, his hometown was a major catalyst in the revolt. When Daraa children were arrested for writing on walls "Down with the regime," and were then tortured by Assad's security police by having their fingernails yanked out, Daraa became a symbol of outrage over the dictator's ruthlessness—outrage that would explode into civil war. And of course Daraa has paid for being the city where the war began. It has been barrel-bombed so heavily that most of the buildings have had their walls knocked down so that you can see into the rooms as if looking into old dollhouses—except that everything is covered in dust and smells of smoke.

I could see that Maysara was growing withdrawn, so I changed the subject. "How are you making it now?"

Maysara said with a slight smile, "Do you like sweets?"

I shrugged. "Of course. Who doesn't like sweets? Last night, I went to Habibi and had *kanafeh*." Habibi is the most famous sweetshop in Jordan, and kanafeh, a sweet cheese pastry cooked over a circular gas grill, is a favorite everywhere in the Middle East.

"I work in a sweetshop making sweets."

"How did you get that job?"

"I started off selling shoes in a shoe store when I was sixteen. In those days, I didn't have a work permit, and the boss paid me about half of what he'd need to pay a Jordanian. So I looked around for another job and found one baking sweets, but when I told my other boss I was quitting, he accused me of stealing from him, and said he'd go to the police if I left him and say I was a thief without a work permit."

"So what did you do?"

"It made me angry that he would say that, and so I decided to risk leaving him. When he reported me, I told the police that he'd threatened me—and when they investigated, they found that he'd made the same threat to three other Syrian refugees who'd worked there before me. A lot of Jordanians accuse us Syrians of taking jobs away from them. But the fact is, there are certain jobs Jordanians won't do, and so people from Syria, Egypt, and Asia do them. And in jobs that Jordanians will do, we can do it better for less." Whether or not this was just Maysara's way of expressing pride in his homeland, I'd read how Syrian ceramic tile layers do excellent work for two dollars per square foot—about half the price of Jordanian contractors. "In fact, at the sweetshop where I'm working now the guy assigned to teach me how to make sweets got jealous of me because I was such a quick learner. And the boss said, 'Maysara, you're the best worker I have.' And another sweetshop offered me more money, so I went to work for them. But after a month the boss came to me and said, 'Maysara, that other guy left and we want you back'—so now I'm back working at the shop I started at."

"What are your sisters doing?"

"The ones in Salt are going to school. But the one in Azraq Camp is engaged to be married to one of our relatives who also lives in Azraq."

"Will she stay in school after she's married?"

"No, she says she wants to leave school."

"And what about you? What would you like to study when you go back to school?"

"I want to be a translator. To make up for the three years that I don't have records for, I can take a test. So I'm thinking of doing that soon."

"What's a typical day like for you?"

"I'm up at six for breakfast, I leave the house for work, I work from eight until six. I work six days a week. Then after work for two hours I go to a gym and practice Tae Kwon Do. I also teach the kids since they don't have any coaches. Then I go back home for dinner at eight or so, I study for an hour from a book called *Travel for Your Brain* that tests you with logic and math problems, I talk with my sisters and mother and brother, and then I do social media until I go to bed at twelve thirty."

"Do you know how to do Tai Chi?"

"Sure, I've seen it."

"That's what I do—you show me some moves, I'll show you some."

Maysara laughs and Rania looks nervous. But we stand up and go outside in front of the café. I show Maysara a few moves of my Tai Chi Yang style long form: Cloud Hands, Carding Horse's Tail, and Needle at the Bottom of the Sea. He shows me some Tae Kwon Do moves, and by the end both of us are laughing at my attempt to do a tiger claw strike before I stumble through a spin kick.

"You're an old guy," he says, "I don't teach old guys."

"Yeah, I don't blame you. But what would you say if I asked you to let me come and work with you in the sweetshop?"

"Like I said, I don't teach old guys—it takes them too long to learn."

He smiles and laughs and shakes his head, but I can see he likes the idea, so I say, "Look, I only want to learn from the best."

He shrugs, nods, and says, "OK. Tomorrow at ten a.m. Come to the shop and we'll work together." We shake hands on it. Then we get back into the van and the UN driver drops him off—the sweetshop has a brilliant ruby-colored sign like an old movie marquee that translates as Jewel Sweets.

"Do you have a cell phone," he asks, "in case something happens?"

"No, I haven't put a chip in my phone yet. But don't worry. I'll be there," I say. "You know, back in the old days before cell phones, this is how people—old people—did things. They made an agreement and they showed up. I'll be there at ten." We bump fists, we put our hands on our hearts and nod good-bye, and he crosses the street to go back to work.

The next morning I arrived early and peered in through the window. The shop, a long, two-story narrow rectangle with a steel stairway to the factory upstairs, was already busy with customers. On the shelves were stacks of inlaid wooden boxes, some shaped like rectangles, others like hexagons with star and triangle patterns on the lids, and lined inside with various kinds of sweets: *bazarek*, round sesame cookies; *ajwa*, bite-sized tea cakes; *ghraeba*, a tiny donut; cashew fingers, little cylinders of semolina with cashews inside; various kinds of baklava, such as *asieh, kolwishkor, mabroumeh*; *aush bulbul*, a little bird's nest of phyllo dough with pistachios nestled inside; and other delicacies, all arranged in mosaic patterns that harmonized with the geometric design of the box. You could see the same kind of design principles at work in the decoration in the Husseini Mosque in downtown Amman: the principle of using decorative motifs to dissolve the boxes' surfaces into infinitely repeating patterns reminded me of architectural elements in the Mosque's courtyard. For all Amman's secular-seeming glass-and-steel architecture, the influence of Islam permeated everything—right down to a deep-fried pastry I would learn to make, Zainab's finger, named after one of the Prophet's daughters.

Maysara took me upstairs to the factory and introduced me to his six Syrian refugee coworkers. One of them was a boy of eleven, a slight kid with big glasses and long, skinny arms who was everybody's "gofer." He was the brother of their boss, Sayid, a burly man in his late twenties who had been working in this shop since he was eighteen. Sayid spoke some English, and he translated for me as we worked. There was a tall, melancholy, mostly silent but very handsome young man who specialized in cakes. He wore a baker's cap at a rakish angle, which is the only excess I could detect in him. He didn't participate in the banter like Maysara and the others, but he smiled from time to time when a joke landed. And there were two boys in their middle teens who hung on the older ones' words and did as they were told with unquestioning alacrity. There was no real hierarchy among them, except for the familial sort of older to younger brother. All of them had been hired by the boss because they were good workers, relations or friends of relations—and because they worked for less than a Jordanian.

When I asked Sayid about work permits, he nodded and said, "Maysara got his work permit through the shop, so no one can threaten to have him deported or force him to return to one of the camps." The US and European Union had bargained with the Jordanian government to hand out up to 250,000 permits—not so much for the sake of the refugees, but to give the refugees a reason to stay in the Middle East, rather than trying to immigrate to the West. In exchange, Jordan got reduced tariffs, access to low-interest loans, and a host of other financial incentives. When I asked one UN official if the Western democracies weren't simply buying off their own consciences, she said, "I think that's a little too cynical. Jordan has been incredibly generous in allowing Syrians into their country, and the government sees this as a once-in-a-lifetime chance to secure much-needed capital for all kinds of infrastructure— infrastructure which will benefit Jordan after the war ends and the Syrians go home."

But given the intractability of the war, the much-ballyhooed number that many refugees are displaced for an average of seventeen years might come true in Maysara's case. He had handed me a rolling pin, a plastic apron, and gloves, and as I rolled out a lump of dough into a uniform circle about a fingernail's width deep, I asked Maysara and the others what their plans were when the war ended.

Maysara said, "I like it here in Jordan for the moment, but I don't want to go back to Syria. I don't feel stable in Jordan, though, and I was thinking about going to the US. But there are problems with race in America, so I'd like to go to Canada instead."

I looked at Sayid, who said, "I have two children and a wife. This is my home now. Once the war ends, I'll go back to visit, but I have no plans to live there again."

Sayid looked at me tentatively and asked what I thought of Donald Trump. When I told them, they looked a little taken aback, since criticizing the King of Jordan is against the law. But I quickly changed the subject and said, "So, Maysara, what's next?"

Maysara took his knife and cut a strip of dough from the round I'd made. Then he showed me how to roll it into a cylinder, and then pinch it between my thumb and forefinger to lengthen it, smoothing and evening it out as I went. He took the knife and measured off lengths of the blade and cut the cylinder into blade-length sections. We stacked these like logs on a steel tray and put them in the refrigerator. Later, they'd be filled with cream and pistachios and browned for a few minutes in the oven.

Then he took thin strings of phyllo dough from the plastic packages and showed me how to make birds' nests. Taking several strings of phyllo, you carefully wind them into a little nest that can hold various fillings: pistachios and cashews, cream and dates. Next, Maysara showed me how to cut off rounds of dough in thumb-sized lengths to be made into *bazarec*, a cookie crusted with sesame seeds.

As we worked, I couldn't help but think of the Syrian refugees I'd met the day before in a bread factory: one of them had been a sales manager at a car dealership, and held a degree in business administration, but now he was in charge of the ovens; another, who had a degree in accounting, was running the huge flour mixers to help support his brother who had actually made it to Hamburg—but the route had been tortuous: Syria to Lebanon to Jordan to Egypt to Jordan to Turkey to Greece to Serbia to Hungary to Austria and, finally, to Germany. He'd traveled in cars, buses, and boats, but he'd also walked hundreds of miles on foot. Another was majoring in mathematics and had finished his second year of calculus when the war interrupted his studies, so now he was monitoring the long conveyor belt used to cool the bread as it plopped down out of the oven onto the belt. All of them were professionals or college students back in Syria, and now they were working factory jobs for substantially less money than a Jordanian. But none of them complained or said a word against their fate. At least they had steady jobs and work permits.

All morning and into the afternoon we worked. When the time for prayer came, everybody washed their hands and knelt on their rugs. We took a late-afternoon break for roast chicken, and then it was time to bake the kanafeh: Maysara and I took two large round trays over to the gas ring, and while Maysara lit the burners, I held the tray. Then he took it from me and placed it on the ring, turning the tray all the while with a pair of metal tongs. After a few minutes, we put another layer of flour on top of the melted cheese, let it cook for a while until the top was brown, then placed another tray on top. We let it cook for a little longer and then we lifted up both trays and flipped them over. The underside was a dark golden brown, and the melted cheese smelled sweet. We took four ladlefuls of sugar water and poured them over the kanafeh and sprinkled ground-up cashews and pistachios on top. The tray was ready to take downstairs to the waiting customers.

When it was time to go, Sayid said, "Tom, you will come back again and we can teach you more. It takes about four years to master the art of making sweets." He patted my arm and they all gathered around me to shake hands as I gave each of them a little hug. I flagged down a taxi as they waved to me from the upstairs window, the sweetshop sign glowing a bright ruby in the sun: Jewel Sweets.

8

In the gallery surrounding the professors' long oval seminar table, one of the students who sat above us, a young woman in a hijab, asks me toward the end of the class, "Sir, you said that writing poetry frees you from your political convictions to explore what you call political emotions: but do you really think that you, as a writer, can truly escape your ideological formation as an American?"

When I try to answer, insisting that I'm not simply a robot of various discourses of discipline, and that writing poetry is, for me, deeply pleasurable because of the strange twists and turns the imagination takes in the process of writing, one of the professors argues that taking pleasure in the process is fine for me, but what about the good of society as a whole? Don't I owe something to my fellow citizens? Another student wants to know why I would want to be freed from my political convictions. Isn't that self-indulgent?

We go back and forth like this, and I have the image of my-self and the students balanced on a sheer cliff face, all of us trying to climb a little higher. Suddenly, I'm aware of how precarious our hand- and footholds are. In the United States, there's a net under-neath you, no matter how torn and unreliable it might seem. But in the Middle East, even in a relatively liberal country like Jordan, what happens if you fall? Do you plunge to your death like Nahed Hattar?

As we talk, we keep discovering minute footholds and finger-width seams that traverse the cliff face. There's a sense of exhilaration in the room, despite the fact that the department head has begun to no-ticeably frown. He's impatient for class to end so that we can go to lunch. Ruba tells me later that the professor wields an almost god-like authority in the classroom, and that most teachers don't en-courage this kind of informal exchange. But the students have been emboldened to ask questions, and so I keep on answering as best I can. It's as if my presence has enabled the students to smash the usual decorums—not because of anything I say or am, but because I come from outside.

The head of the department decides enough is enough: he's hun-gry and it's time to go. He ends our session abruptly, but not before one young man protests, "Next time it would be good to leave more time so that everyone has a chance to ask their question."

At lunch it so happens that I sit at a different table from the de-partment head. The young professor who sits next to me looks a little wary, but then he begins to tell me how he taught the Koran and Greek mythology together. "Several of my students' parents were greatly upset—Greek myths are false, they would say, and the Koran is true. Some couldn't get over the fact that the Koran is not meant to be literature but a sacred text. I kept suggesting that they could have an aesthetic appreciation for the Koran also—but that disturbed some of the parents so much that I began to worry about what would happen if social media turned against me. . . . I had to walk a very fine line—given how things are these days, I'm not sure I'd teach this course again. And I would never teach this kind of course in the university where I worked in Saudi Arabia. That would simply be impossible."

9

Jafar, the vizier of Harun al-Rashid, is out hunting one morning when his dogs begin to chase after a white-footed gazelle. The gazelle leaps away and easily outraces the dogs, but just as it's about to disappear into the desert, it slows down and turns and waits for the dogs to catch up. This happens so many times that the dogs grow too tired to keep in the chase and so one by one they lie down and pant in the shade of a boulder.

The gazelle approaches Jafar, but rather than shooting the animal, Jafar lifts his hand in greeting. The gazelle stands there staring at Jafar, and Jafar thinks he can discern the light of human understanding shining in the gazelle's pupils, and so he says, "By Allah, are you a gazelle, or a creature of the world of the djinn, or a human being trapped in a beast's hide? Speak to me if you can speak the language of men."

When the gazelle opens its mouth as if to reply, rather than human words, Jafar hears the first notes of a song sung by the most beautiful voice he's ever heard. But one of Jafar's party who has been racing to catch up spots the gazelle at a standstill and, nocking an arrow, he shoots the gazelle in the chest. With a look of outrage and disgust at how it has been betrayed, the gazelle's eyes lock on Jafar's eyes; and as it collapses on its knees just before it dies, it says accusingly, "Blood on you, Defender of the Faithful. Blood on you."

10

In the old part of the city, next to the Husseini Mosque, the sidewalks under the shopping arcades are crowded with men and women selling anything they can: their merchandise is displayed on old bedsheets or blankets or simply laid out on the sidewalk. On one blanket, I see sunglasses, a white extension cord, a box of costume jewelry, various pronged chargers, a purple plastic hairbrush with some old hair still caught between the bristles, water-stained magazines, plastic cups, an ornate jar with a domed top, a money belt, a camera, a baby bottle with a madly smiling yellow bear on top, a toilet bowl float, a handheld showerhead, a string of Christmas lights, a child's fanny pack with three Disney princesses looking alluring, an electric toothbrush, a jar of "Hair Treatment Cream," and blue nail polish.

I bow my head to the merchant and put my hand on my heart: "Salaam alaikum."

"Al-salaam . . . British?" he asks. "Canadian?" The merchant introduces himself as Amar, and picks up the domed jar and offers it to me. He's so skinny that his jeans are falling off him, but his gestures have a shy, courtly formality about them.

"New York," I say.

He points to himself and says, "Amman." He sweeps his arm right and left to indicate everything surrounding us in the old part of the city, al-Balad: the hundreds of storefront shops in the souk behind the twin minarets of the old Husseini Mosque, and the arcades branching off of one another into the food and clothing market. He nods and says, "Welcome."

In a storefront next door a headless female dummy's torso is suspended on a rope strung between a streetlamp and the shop roof. Dressed in a harem girl's outfit covered in glittery red sequins, one strap slipped down over the shoulder to reveal a nipple-less breast, she sways back and forth in the light breeze from the little iron hook that's been screwed into her sawed-off neck.

All down the sidewalk is one blanket after another strewn with the same kind of merchandise as Amar's. I'm reminded of the lawyer turned bookseller whom I met after a poetry reading at a cultural center. He'd salvaged much of his stock from a university library that was throwing out thousands of books to make space for new textbooks. Rather than display them on a blanket on the sidewalk, he placed them on the trunk, the hood, and the top of his old Mercedes. Every inch of the interior, except for the driver's seat, was crammed with books. "I was in corporate law," he said in perfect English, "a suit. I got tired of it and I decided to do this: I love books and I love to read. So I decided to make my car into a traveling bookstore. Now I go to rich and poor neighborhoods and sell my books. I try to get the younger kids hooked on books by starting them off with comics. My mission is to spread the love of reading. It used to be that when the police saw me setting up shop on the sidewalk in more expensive neighborhoods, they'd ask me where my license was because the sidewalk and the street belong to the government, and since they belong to the government, technically I'm required to have a license. But because my car is my private property, and I'm displaying my books on my car, now the police can't stop me."

11

In a miniature watercolor, an *ifrit* named Arghan Div carries in his claws a chest of armor. Ifrits are a subgroup of the family of the djinn, and are said to be enormous winged creatures made of fire. Arghan Div's flaming eyes are slightly crossed, his orange skin is spotted all over like a leopard's, and two grotesque white fangs jut from the sides of his mouth. He's up to his chest in jostling waves, and holds the chest high above his head to keep the armor inside from getting wet as he hauls it to a waiting boat. He seems to be doing this at the behest of Hamza, the uncle of the Prophet, who sits on a throne on shore.

Holding a drawn sword up over his shoulder, one of Hamza's soldiers leads a group of chained, nearly naked prisoners to prostrate themselves before him. Why the ifrit is carrying the chest, whether Hamza has made a deal with the ifrit, or if the ifrit, who is often thought of as a malevolent spirit, is doing this on a sudden whim of good nature, the painting doesn't explain. But in the spirit of the miniature, in which war, domination, and the supernatural are inextricably woven together, here's a tale that might be told about the little painting:

"Hamza," says the ifrit, "you know that I am a fire spirit and that I could burn you up with a touch of my finger. If you want to live, you must tell me a story: if I like your story, I'll carry your chest of armor to your fleet of ships and let you go in peace. But if I don't, then I'll burn you and your ships and your army to a cinder."

Hamza smiles at the demon and says, "My friend, if you do that, what will you have accomplished? It's easy for an ifrit to kill a man."

"All the same, tell me a story."

"All right, since you demand it. Once there was a prince who was attacked by pirates just as his ship left land. And so the prince jumps overboard and swims back to shore while the pirates chase after him. A woodcutter is out chopping wood, and when he sees the prince, the young man calls to him, 'Sir, for the love of Allah, can you hide me from the pirates who are trying to kill me? I'll give you enough gold to fill up not only your house, but all the houses of your neighbors.'

"'Prince,' says the woodcutter, 'I would help you even if you had not offered me a single dirham.' And as the pirates chase after them, the woodcutter leads him back to his hovel and hides him in a shed. But the pirates, in their rage to find the prince, cut the woodcutter down and leave him bleeding on his own doorstep. They set fire to the woodcutter's house and are about to throw open the door to the shed, when the prince, utterly terrified now, climbs between two loose boards and runs into the forest, the pirates close behind him.

"But as he runs, he trips over a tree root and plunges down into an underground chamber which closes after him, so that it seems to the pirates the forest has swallowed him up whole. There in the chamber is a beautiful woman who has been captured by an ifrit. The prince and the woman fall in love at first sight and sleep with one another. But when the ifrit comes home, he is overwhelmed with jealousy and transforms the prince into an ape and turns him out into the forest to live with the other apes.

"One day, a princess is out riding with her servants in the forest, and the ape comes before her and says in a human voice, 'Take pity on me, princess. I know I must look like a monster to you, who are so beautiful, but let me join your company and serve you.' And so the princess, who is astonished by how well spoken the ape is, allows him to accompany her back to the palace, where, because of his manners, he becomes a great favorite with her father, the king—"

"Yes, yes," interrupts the ifrit, "I know how this one ends. The princess possesses magical powers, and fights a pitched battle with the ifrit who enchanted the prince into the shape of an ape. The ifrit turns into a lion and the princess turns into a net, the ifrit turns into a knife but the princess turns into a spear, the ifrit turns into a club but the princess turns into a great fire and burns the club to cinders. Then she releases the prince from his enchantment, and he's so handsome she immediately falls in love with him and they are married.

"But I can assure you, Hamza, that's not how it ended. What really happened is this: the young man and the woodcutter are both caught and killed by the pirates. Their blood soaks into the earth, which gives birth to an ifrit who springs up to take on the murdered men's shapes, or the shape of Satan, or the shape of a sandstorm that buries not only the pirates but an entire city."

12

"In my opinion," she said, "a value isn't a value unless you live by it every day. Unless you live by it, it's only a theory."

In a corner of the community center where about a hundred young adult Palestinians were gathered to discuss ethics, I saw chalked on a blackboard $2Al + 6H_2O = 2Al(OH)_3 + 3H_2$—the chemical notation for what happens when you combine aluminum atoms with water to produce hydrogen.

"So if you claim to be a religious person, but you don't live according to the rules, then you can't really say you are religious." She was dressed in a hijab, and as she talked, her face lit up with the intensity of her convictions.

The older woman who was leading the discussion wrote on the chalkboard *theory vs. practice* and said, "Does everyone agree?" There was a general nodding of heads when she said, "So let me ask this: do you think that religion comes before values, or do our ethics shape religious practice?"

"Religion gives us our values," said the young woman. "There are so many ways to act that unless you have religion, you're only guessing between right and wrong."

The leader turned to me and said, "Maybe our visitor would like to say something about this question?"

Perhaps she assumed I was secular since I was American, nor was she wrong. What came to mind, though, wasn't so much an answer as a conundrum.

"When my father was dying, I had the choice: to tell him that he was dying, or to keep it from him. I chose to keep it from him. Now, my father was an honest man and believed in telling the truth. But he wasn't a religious person at all. Does that mean that I betrayed my father's values?"

The young woman began to nod vigorously and said, "Yes, absolutely: it's not an easy thing to do, but if you're a religious person, you must tell the truth."

From the back of the room a heavyset young man said, "But what about his father? He didn't want him to have to suffer not only his illness, but the knowledge that he would soon die from it. At least his father could still hope that he'd get better." And he said to me, "I think you did the right thing. You may have lied, but you lied in the name of a higher value."

But the young woman shook her head and said in an even more heated voice, "I think that we have to choose between our own personal values and the values of religion. Sometimes they are the same, but when they aren't, you have to choose the values that God has given us."

13

She has been a servant in her master's house for many years and one night as she stands at the window looking out into the narrow street, she overhears two beggars talking, both of whom appear blind.

"The master of the house will be going out to a banquet tonight. Yesterday, when we knocked on the door and they gave us money,

I could see that the master is very rich. Tonight, when the master is out, we'll come back and rob his house."

The servant is surprised to discover that they aren't blind, but instead of telling her master about their plot, she decides to trick them. "Masters," she whispers, "I am the housekeeper. And I couldn't help but overhear what you just said. If you will agree to take me away from this house, I will open the door for you myself so that no suspicion will be aroused among the neighbors."

The thieves are surprised and are about to run away, but she says in a soothing voice, as she throws back the window and shows them her face, which is as beautiful as the rising moon, "Have no fear. Yesterday when you were here I felt my heart being conquered by you."

When the thieves see her, they can't resist her, and agree to come back at night at the hour she appoints.

That night they come dressed in black and each is consumed with love for her. They knock on the door, but she only opens it a crack and whispers to them, "One of you at a time must enter. It will be safer." And so the first thief, bigger and crueler than the other one, shoves the smaller thief aside and enters the house. She shows him gold and silver and precious jewels, and the thief begins to put it all in a large bag. Suddenly, she takes him by the arm and says, "I hear a noise. One of the servants may have heard us! You must hide in this oil jar!" The thief is frightened and climbs into the jar, which she seals shut.

Then she goes to the door and says to the other thief, "Come quickly and help us! There's too much gold for us to carry by ourselves." And so the second thief enters the house, but suddenly she cries out, "I hear a noise! Climb into this oil jar and hide! My master must have returned early!" So the thief climbs into the oil jar and she seals it shut also. Then she goes to the kitchen and begins to boil a cauldron of oil. When it's scalding hot, she goes to each jar and whispers, "It's safe now. I'll open the jar and release you." But instead she pours in the boiling oil and seals up the jars again. A moment later when her master comes home, she tells him all that has happened, and her master, who has long loved her for her goodness and her beauty, says to her, "I want you to be my wife: you have acted with such good judgment that my love for you can no longer be contained." And the servant, who has long loved him also, allows her master to embrace her while the thieves howl and howl until they are silent.

14

If you were a Bedouin who lived on the east bank of the Jordan River before the 1967 Six-Day War with Israel, you either worked for the government or joined the Army and police. But when that war was lost, almost a quarter of a million Palestinians fled to Jordan and the PLO began to use Jordan as a place to conduct raids into Israel. Eventually, King Hussein kicked out the PLO because it threatened to become a state within a state, but many Palestinians stayed.

But the fact that they've been in Jordan for fifty years, and are the majority of the population, still hasn't changed things. Most of the Army officers are still Bedouin, and most of the government bureaucrats are too. If you're a soldier, you can shop at special stores with huge discounts, you don't have to pay taxes, you're given subsidies. According to Mudar Zahran, a controversial Palestinian writer granted political asylum in Britain, if you're a Palestinian, you're stuck with a sixteen percent sales tax, and if you buy a car, you can pay up to a two hundred percent tariff on it.

In 1983 Palestinians who lived primarily in Jordan were issued yellow cards, while those who lived primarily in the Israeli-occupied West Bank were given green cards. But when King Hussein severed ties with the West Bank in 1988, the government enacted a new law redefining Jordanian/Palestinian citizenship. According to Anis Kassim, an international law expert in Jordan, green card Palestinians went to bed on July 31, 1988, as Jordanian citizens, but woke up on August 1 as "Palestinian citizens"—but since there is no Palestinian homeland, they became stateless persons. I was told by a UN protection officer that currently sub-subofficials in the ministry of the interior are revoking Palestinian citizenship on grounds nobody quite understands. But the sub-subofficials maintain that it's for the Palestinians' own good. They don't want Israel to get the idea that Jordanian citizenship means the Palestinians have given up their right of return. And if you're a Syrian Palestinian, no matter if you're in danger of being murdered by Assad, you're refused entry to Jordan.

To make it even more complicated, King Abdullah II is married to a Palestinian, Queen Rania. Conservative East Bankers fear her considerable power in politics, while Western liberals approve of her championing the rights of children and women. But poorer Palestinians are disappointed that her prestige has largely failed to improve their lives. Her infamous fortieth birthday party, in which water in a drought-stricken desert was used to keep down dust so her six hundred guests could walk more easily, inspired thirty-six Jordanian tribal leaders to draft a letter of condemnation to the King, complaining of her alleged abuses—this, in a country where criticizing the King (Nahed Hattar learned the hard way) is illegal.

The Bedouin are worried about the Palestinians taking over Jordan and making it their homeland. The Palestinians and the Bedouin are worried about the Syrians taking their jobs. Everyone is worried about Israel. The government and the Army keep the Bedouin loyal by paying their salaries, but the Bedouin are getting nervous and putting more and more pressure on the King to keep giving them a bigger piece of the pie. The more pressure the Palestinians put on the King to stop discrimination, the more the Bedouin push for economic concessions. The oft-quoted Bedouin proverb—"I against my brother, my brother and I against our cousin, my brother and I and our cousin against our neighbors, all of us against the foreigner"—has been turned on its head by King Abdullah II. By keeping his distance from his own government ministers, whom he replaces at will, he tries to make it seem that he is for everyone and against no one. So even though he is ultimately responsible for the imprisonment, if not the murder, of Nahed Hattar, a year earlier you can see him in a photo op, staunchly linking arms with other world leaders as he marches down the Champs-Élysées in support of *Charlie Hebdo*. By a similarly perverse logic, his government's way of being for you if you're a Palestinian is to discriminate against you as a way to encourage you to want to return to a place where there is no place for you to return to.

15

The city is carved out of sandstone. You can only approach it through a mile-long slot canyon. Because of the wars that surround Jordan, no one comes to Petra anymore. The tour guides stand around with nothing to do. No one climbs on the camels to have their picture taken. The stray cats that glide among the tables in the little outdoor café are skin and bones, and barely move from under your feet when you sit down in the faded plastic chairs. The sandstone pillars that brace what has been dubbed the Treasury—really, a tomb with a huge central chamber carved out of the cliff—look three hundred feet tall. This is the focal point of Petra, an ancient Nabataean city abandoned in the seventh century, and for hundreds of years known only to local Bedouin tribesmen. In modern times, the Bedouin lived among the ruins until 1985, when the government decided to develop Petra as a tourist attraction. And so they were "resettled"—that is, forcibly removed to nearby towns. Just a few years ago, as many as three thousand people a day visited Petra. But the city is nothing but a vast sepulchre. The houses of the living were built out of wood and other perishable materials and vanished centuries ago. Tombs line the narrow gorge that winds its way through the canyon. Carved in relief into each of the tomb facades is a set of ascending steps that lead to a landing. And from that landing is another identical set of stairs, only these descend back to the ground. I was told by a guide that the ascending stairs are the pathway that you climb from the world of the dead into the world of the living, and that the descending stairs lead from the world of the living back to the dead.

As I climbed up the cliffs to the top of the canyon, the winter desert weather was clear and cold, and I could see for miles around—toward Israel, and the wars in Iraq and Syria. The abandoned tombs reminded me of a town I had visited in Syria before the war: Quneitra. In the 1967 Six-Day War, Israel seized the town from Hafez al-Assad, the father of Bashar al-Assad, and the entire population was expelled. When the Israelis finally withdrew in 1973, they stripped the town clean, right down to the doorknobs, and loaded everything into trucks to sell to Israeli contractors.

On top of the cliff, I could hear a flute playing a little three-note tune: it turned out to be a Bedouin woman who was selling plastic key chains as well as miniature plastic replicas of the Treasury. As she played, she danced a little hopping dance, circling round and round. It certainly didn't look traditional, as if she were improvising her own dance steps on top of the cliff looking out over the desert, the barren mountains, and the sun diffusing behind a light haze. The notes went up the scale, then down, then got repeated at random over and over. As I listened, I noticed that at the very edge of the cliff, she and her family had built a shed out of scrounged wood and plastic tarps: smoke from a cooking fire wafted up and vanished into the haze as someone behind the tarp made tea.

At one of the readings I participated in, I talked about my visit to Quneitra in 2007, and how Petra seemed like a sister city, though five hundred years distant. Both were abandoned and both persisted despite the violence they'd been subjected to: Israeli machine guns and tanks, and a major earthquake that had caused a deadly drought. And then I read a poem:

Before Rain

Whatever you do, there are rockets falling,
and after the rockets, smoke climbing

up through walls that are exploding.
Trees grow up where there once were people, weeds

take over beds of lettuces and coddled flowers,
uprearing mole hills unpopulate the fields.

The bricked-in hours of the human have all been knocked down.

No one lingers at lipstick counters, no one
stares into a screen to escape the digital mayhem

of heroes hurdling over the heads of monsters.

The old bones on the mountain that stand upright
and shake when winds blow up from the shore,

old bones that shake when the winds roar

now dangle in the void of an unknown dimension.

Forget all this, says Earth to the stars.

Afterward, a young woman came up to me and said that the poem
meant more than I could ever know to the people assembled. As we
talked, the memory of the mile-long avenue of tombs that I'd seen
from the cliff top, their pediments and columns still looking freshly
carved, gave way to the image of Maysara dipping a huge ladle into a
vat of sugar water and spreading the sweet liquid over the hot kanafeh.
I thought of the caves hollowed out of the soft cliff face across from
the Roman theater in downtown Amman, of the wide showcase
highways that cut through the city's heart, and of the ancient King's
Highway, a caravan route that had in modern times been a central artery running north to south the entire length of Jordan, but
was now a potholed road that went mainly through backcountry. I
thought of the refugees dispersed throughout Amman, of cities like
Daraa that had been bombed to rubble. But most of all, I heard the
little tune played on the plastic flute, shrill, aimless, not in the least
bit beautiful, but strangely right in its piercing atonality. It would be
a long time before I could get it out of my head.

To Be Incarnational

1

I was talking with friends after I got back from Mogadishu, where I had been finishing up an article about the lives of Somali refugees in East Africa. I'd just returned from seeing a famine firsthand, and one of them asked me how I felt after seeing so many starving people. It's difficult to answer a question like that coherently. The statistics—more than 250,000 dead, the majority of them children—mean nothing because nobody is moved by a statistic. Plus, it's an experience so at a tangent to most Americans' ordinary lives that I did what I usually do—I avoided the question by saying something about being divided between here and there. The bright sun and red earth and drifting dust and deep-rutted dirt roads left by Land Rovers vs. the computer buzz and hum of surfing the web to find mention of some British tourist shot to death by Somali pirates.

But then my friend pressed me and said he hadn't asked what I thought, but what I felt—and insisted that I answer him. And honestly, I felt enraged—on the surface, a petty, clichéd rage having to do with our cars and comforts. But underneath that, a rage with more substance, less stupidly self-involved. By watching people starving to death, you see why hunger is so degrading: A hungry person will do anything. If you're a mother walking with your two children to a refugee camp, you might have to leave the heavier one to die in the desert or die yourself of exhaustion. Or if you're a man, and a bandit, you might push your fellow countrywoman, a refugee like yourself, at least until you became a bandit, off the top of one of the alarmingly overcrowded buses making its way to the camp, and, while your fellow bandits are stealing goats or chickens, you carefully search through the woman's little bundles for money or jewelry or a cell phone. And if the woman isn't dead, you and your mates might drag her off into the bush and rape her as part of the bargain.

We have all seen hundreds, maybe thousands, of pictures of starving people. What do we learn from such pictures except to deflect them? We superimpose an image of Christ on the cross, or see juxtaposed, on the same page or screen, a starving body next to a female model in a bathing suit thrusting her breasts at us, or a male model flaunting his waxed, perfectly hairless chest. This confounding mixture affected a whole generation of Israeli boys born after World War II, who were said by the Israeli filmmaker Ari Libsker to have had their first sexual awakening by looking at Holocaust pictures of naked Jewish women lining up before the showers to be gassed, or by reading the genre of Holocaust fiction called "stalags," in which sex-crazed female Nazi guards sexually humiliate Allied POWs. Some will think Libsker is crazy, or anti-Semitic, or indulging in bad taste. But in grade school, I too watched in history class a film the Nazis took of naked Jews lining up, the film jerky in that old-movie way, the black and white grainy as the cliché of an old porno film—and I was shocked and aroused by what I knew I shouldn't see, but couldn't look away from.

Or if pictures of the starving have lost their frisson, then maybe all you do is shrug with a kind of worldliness about how wearying it is to note the definition of the ribs, finely carved against the skin, always brown or black. Unless it's Bobby Sands, the Irish hunger striker in the Maze Prison—and then the skin is white, and made even whiter by the glare of the news cameras, the face collaborating with the camera to make itself seem like a mask floating free from the man, a giant mask the size of a billboard that dwarfs the physically shrinking Bobby Sands, like in the old movie *The Incredible Shrinking Man.* To become a symbol of resistance that, in thirty years' time, nobody will recognize, becomes the revolutionary's compensation, since his face belongs to him again, and is anonymous as it was when he was a boy or just born.

So I said to my friend that I didn't know what to do with such feelings and perceptions, that they weren't exactly useful. If people are starving there, they aren't starving here—or if they are, they aren't dying in the hundreds of thousands—and news photos of starving kids felt, to me at least, like a kind of disaster porn, and my rage was just part of that—a defense against a deeper lassitude, even despair. But I wasn't going to give up my car and comforts, and my rage felt, and feels, like a kind of cant: PTSD lite, you could call it.

And the only way I could adequately talk about what I felt was to describe a starving two-year-old boy. His head lolled in his mother's lap, and he seemed listless, on the verge of coma, or the apathetic drowse that precedes it. But his mother had been given, by one of the matrons of the feeding station in downtown Mogadishu, a nutritional biscuit made of vitamin-fortified peanut slurry called Plumpy'Nut. And as she carefully unwrapped it, whether from the smell or some inner alarm built into the species, he roused himself. She gave it to him, his eyes suddenly focused, and he began to eat. After a few bites, as the sugars hit his system, his whole body gathered strength, and he sat up, suddenly alert. He ate the biscuit slowly, and by the time he'd finished, he was taking in his surroundings, particularly the shiny silver foil that the biscuit had come in. He took the foil from his mother and began throwing it up in the air, playing with it, recovering in a few moments, because of the sugars, the instinct to play.

What good was my rage, then? This boy had shown me something about the starving and the dying that I hadn't known until that moment: that up until they lapse from consciousness, they're still part of their world, deeply rooted in their own attachments— they don't shed who they are, and easy pity won't help you see their individual fates and quirks of character. Nobody, until the very end at least, turns into the sharply defined ribs and swollen bellies of the news photos.

2

I remember interviewing a World Food Program official in Mogadishu, not because I wanted to, but because she'd heard there was a journalist on the trip, and had pressured my friend and UN contact, Andy Needham, to get me to talk to her. So we sat in the shade of a cinderblock office at Mogadishu's port, where she rattled off statistics about the superb job WFP was doing. Of course, she meant well and she was doing good work. But all around us were starving people, and I kept thinking, as she talked, about something Saul Bellow had once said about the statistics and the images of misery and suffering broadcast by mass media. He called it "crisis chatter," and pointed out how inescapable it was: "Neither the facts nor the deformations, the insidious platitudes of the media (tormenting because the underlying realities are so large and terrible), can be screened out." And as she talked and talked, I dutifully wrote down facts and figures, knowing all the while that the interview was a waste of time: no one would be interested in such disembodied abstractions. And in a lull of the blizzarding numbers and percentages about metric tons of wheat and capacity building and infrastructure gain, I found myself asking her questions about how she felt about her work—at which point she looked annoyed, clammed up—and so the interview, mercifully for both of us, I suppose—ended.

So why did I insist on turning the conversation back toward the personal? I suppose I was looking for a link between her passion for the work she was doing and her feeling for the people for whom she was doing it. And in that space between her life and theirs, I felt there was a void that statistics couldn't fill: I wanted the people to be there in the flesh, just as I wanted her to flesh out her passion.

When I think about the art I most care about, it's an art in which bodily reality isn't slighted; in which every aspect of a person's world achieves solidity and clarity for its own sake, and not because it serves a cause or program; and in which artistic devotion to the surfaces of the world insists that the artist keep on looking.

3

For me, the paramount example of an artist whose gaze never wavers is David Jones, the great English/Welsh/Cockney painter and poet. In the journalism and the poetry I've tried to write, his poems are bedrock. So if I seem to be changing the subject abruptly, it's only to come at it another way.

Jones, the author of *In Parenthesis*, a poem in part about World War I, once said that he wanted poetry to be "incarnational." He means that literally—dressing the spirit in flesh. So the Word not only becomes the words that bring the war into focus but also makes them so physically immediate that abstractions evaporate. The terrible physicality of the war registers in our senses before lodging in the understanding. But when it finally does lodge there, the outrage and irony and despair are so finely etched that any form of overt moralizing seems superfluous, if not a spiritual vulgarity. He never attempts, like his fellow Great War poet Wilfred Owen, to come at war from an overt position of moral outrage. All of that emerges from the material, his mixture of Cockney, Welsh, and foot-soldier slang, disjunct army jargon, weapons terminology, Welsh myth and legend, bringing the war itself up close—but the war as a collective phenomenon, no high-ground attitudinizing, no personal anguish outside the ordinary fears of ordinary soldiers.

As a somewhat bumbling, incompetent infantryman, a self-described "knocker-over of piles, a parade's despair," Jones ranges himself against the Brass and the Staff. His is the only war poem I know of in which class consciousness is a basis for solidarity with the enemy. This, too, is not an overt position, but a natural extension of fellow feeling toward young men like himself, caught up in the murderous logic of trench warfare. The Christmas Truce—a spontaneous uprising among the enlisted men, and often against their officers' wishes, in which both sides freely fraternized in No Man's Land, playing football and exchanging gifts and singing carols—partially exemplifies what I mean. Although there are no Christmas truces in Jones's poem, the end of the poem's dedicatory page reads: AND TO THE ENEMY FRONT-FIGHTERS WHO SHARED OUR PAINS AGAINST WHOM WE FOUND OURSELVES BY MISADVENTURE.

By contrast, Wilfred Owen represents the enlightened officer class, the kind father and older brother to "his men." Lest anyone mistake the risks of junior field officers like Owen, their average life expectancy was about six weeks once they'd reached the front. But Owen's war and Jones's war occur over a class divide as wide as the distance between the bells of Magdalen Tower in Oxford and those of St. Mary-le-Bow in Cheapside, where a true Cockney is born within hearing distance of the bell.

By focusing so intensely on the sights and sounds of the war, on the look and feel and texture of its kit, its weaponry, its ambience of trench domesticity, like boiling water for tea, the day-to-day sense of no-man's-land as a place of "sudden violences and . . . long still-nesses, the sharp contours and unformed voids" begin to take on a "mysterious existence" that becomes, in Jones's words, "a place of en-chantment." But enchantment in the sense that Malory in *Le Morte d'Arthur* uses it, such that the landscape becomes one of doomed fatality and dread. Some malign power has placed it under a spell so that the shattered greenery speaks, as in Malory, "with a grimly voice."

In describing the interior of a thicket fringed by "scarred sap-lings," Private Ball, the poet's alter ego, registers how blasted-to-bits foliage and barbwire coalesce into a new version of nature:

> There between the thinning uprights
> at the margin
> straggle tangled oak and flayed sheeny beech-bole, and fragile
> birch whose silver queenery is draggled and ungraced
> and June shoots lopt
> and fresh stalks bled

> runs the Jerry trench.
> And cork-screw stapled trip-wire
> to snare among the briars
> and iron warp with bramble weft
> with meadow-sweet and lady-smock
> for a fair camouflage.

This new, hybrid nature of briars and "cork-screw stapled trip-wire" that warp and weft together with lady-smock and meadow-sweet shows how radically different are the poetic conventions that operate in Jones's war, as opposed to Owen's war. In Jones, there are no Keatsian sound effects, no lushness of orchestration as in Owen's "Spring Offensive," in which the soldiers experience the traditional enchantments of pastoral:

> Marvelling they stood, and watched the long grass swirled
> By the May breeze, murmurous with wasp and midge,
> For though the summer oozed into their veins
> Like an injected drug for their bodies' pains,
> Sharp on their souls hung the imminent line of grass,
> Fearfully flashed the sky's mysterious glass.

Even in Owen's syntax, natural imagery and war imagery are kept separate, as if the old categories of pastoral and chivalric combat needed to be quarantined off from Jones's version of the war. So the drama in Owen's poems is the drama of a mind fending off the dehumanization of mechanized slaughter, while searching for some form of consolation and spiritual mystery in chivalric feeling, if not chivalric ritual.

But Jones's soldiers feel mystery in a different key: the mystery of scientific killing revealed through the ordinary soldier's interaction with technology. Nature in Owen's poems is still capable of blazing forth with immanence, at one still with the pantheism of Keats and Wordsworth. But nature in Jones's war is under the same spell that Jones's soldiers are under—a utilitarian day-to-day reckoning with trauma and mass death in which Nature and barbed wire have fused, in which:

> The inorganic earth where your body presses seems itself to pulse deep down with your heart's acceleration . . . but you go on living, lying with your face bedded in neatly folded, red-piped, greatcoat and yet no cold cleaving thing drives in between expectant shoulder-blades, so you get to your feet, and the sun-lit chalk is everywhere absorbing fresh stains.
>   Dark gobbets stiffen skewered to revetment-hurdles.

The earth is nothing but unfeeling rock, and if it pulses, that pulse is only the soldier's heartbeat as it speeds up from the adrenaline rush of fear, from the physical effort of combat. In Keats and Wordsworth, there would have been no qualification about the cause of the earth's palpitations: it would have been assumed that the earth was in cosmic sympathy with human beings, that the pantheistic reciprocity among all things, animate and inanimate, human and divine, was still available as a mode of feeling—in an Owen poem, summer can still ooze into a soldier's veins; but in a Jones poem, "dark gobbets" of bodies, or body parts, are oozing out blood, staining torn uniforms of dead soldiers skewered to barbed wire supports. Summer oozing into veins, even figured as a drug, belongs to a lyric tradition that for Jones is out of bounds, if not inconceivable. Instead, Jones's soldier is expecting at every second to feel shrapnel rip into his back, and his senses are so hypervigilant that he notices in obsessive detail the red piping on his greatcoat, and thinks in the specialist language of an infantryman: revetment-hurdles and the more poetic "dark gobbets" fuse in a fresh linguistic amalgam, a diction both mongrel and yet dedicated to precise observation.

It's as if the humanist assumptions that condition Owen's relation to war, and his vocabulary for it, are not only inoperative but irrelevant to the men in the ranks. Owen's deeply felt understanding of what he famously called "the pity of war," and the poetry that is in the pity, seems at best, at least in Jones's war, to be nothing but heroic posturing in an antiheroic guise. And at worst, the truly great-hearted, empathic identification that Owen makes with his own soldiers seems like a form of unconscious class condescension.

That said, no one can love Owen and his poems more than I do. The dissonance of his slant rhymes has its own kind of daring, while his eroticized depictions of violence powerfully clash with his moral revulsion. Owen's poems, written during the war itself, and well before the publication of Eliot's *The Waste Land* or Pound's *A Draft of XXX Cantos*, used the poetic conventions that were available to him—conventions that he handled with great originality. By contrast, Eliot and Pound offered Jones a wider set of conventions than the ones available to Owen. And *In Parenthesis* represented a retrospective understanding of Jones's war experiences, since it wasn't published until 1937—almost twenty years after Owen's death in 1918.

So why do I appear to be knocking Owen? And with a concept as slippery as class? Didn't a critic as acute as Paul Fussell knock Jones for trying to "rationalize and even to validate" the Battle of the Somme—a battle that was nothing but a "Bloody balls-up," to quote Robert Graves, in which twenty thousand British soldiers died on the first day alone, one-twentieth of England's total fighting force. Fussell accuses Jones of trying to recover "motifs and values of medieval chivalric romance" by linking the heroic Welsh mythic heroes to the enlisted men in the Royal Welsh Fusiliers that Jones served with. Fussell's implication is that Jones is trying to glorify the ordinary soldier's sacrifice.

But isn't a word like *sacrifice* precisely the problem? In a battle that lasted about four months, with over a million casualties, killed and wounded, a word like *sacrifice* loses all meaning. Jones describes his and his fellows' advance at a walk across no-man's-land as "small, drab, bundled pawns severally make effort / moved in tenuous line." In this description, cool and distanced, there are no sacrificial, symbolic lambs, only the sheep of the ordinary enlisted men, British and German, who find themselves in that grimly speaking landscape through "misadventure." And the use of Welsh legend is opposed to the "official blasphemies" hallooed by one Private Watcyn when he

takes with "blameless technique" the First Objective—the blandi-
fied language that glosses over taking an enemy trench as ordered by
the Brass. But it's not Private Watcyn who is to blame, it's the Brass
and their professionalized sanctioning of killing.

What Fussell misses is how the Queen of the Wood "has cut
bright boughs," not only for the officers but also for ordinary soldiers on both sides, with nicknames like Fatty; or as in the case of
a Welsh and a German soldier who have killed each other, "Hansel
and Gronwy share dog-violets for a palm, where they lie in serious
embrace beneath the twisted tripod." The tripod here is a trench
mortar tripod, not the tripod of the Sibyl. And the palm for both
is made of dog-violets: about as far as you can get from a wreath of
laurel. Also, the melding of satire and memorial, of homoerotic sug-
gestion and the well-worn trope of war fostering love among comrades as well as combatants, levels the elegiac hierarchies of Owen,
in which the poet-soldier both mourns and deplores the death of the
ordinary, inarticulate soldier. But Jones expands the range of elegiac
speech to include lower-class slang and utilitarian turns of phrase,
such that the voiceless soldiers that Owen gives voice to have voices
of their own—and voices that speak independently of a poetic persona like Owen's. Regardless of his estrangement from patriotic
pieties, there's no doubt that Owen thought of his poetry as speaking to, and for, his countrymen—that there might be a way to in-
corporate their speech on a level with his own forms no part of his
technique, no matter how well adapted to his own moral and aesthetic purposes.

By contrast, in another part of the same passage about the Queen
of the Wood, a major nicknamed Lillywhite has been killed by a
shell-wrecked tree falling on him. He is granted that most prosaic of
flowers, daisies, by the Queen of the Wood—much to the incredu-
lity, and disgust, of the anonymous narrator: "That swine Lillywhite
has daisies to his chain—you'd hardly credit it." That register of
speech, and the mixed emotions of the narrator, are more or less foreclosed to Owen—unless Owen is appropriating an ordinary soldier's
speech in order to express his own outrage.

Just as Jones's use of Cockney accomplishes on a linguistic level the leveling of the ranks, so his use of the Queen of the Wood transforms heroic Welsh tradition so that she no longer recognizes distinctions among rank or combatant by observing the "official blasphemies." Throughout this passage, in which the Queen of the Wood confers her honors on the dead, the seesawing back and forth between mockery and rage, sorrow and sincere feeling, makes the ritual of myth and legend responsive to the anonymous narrator's fluctuations of feeling, as opposed to a tradition that, in Fussell's blinkered view, regulates such feeling. But tradition operates in far more complex ways than Fussell's account of it, in which myths and legends devoted to kings and princes must always refer to kings and princes, or can't be used in fresh ways, or turned against their own class-bound associations. In a letter to H. S. Ede, Jones notes that in an English hunting song, the "huntsmen meet to hunt the fox, they hunt a fox, and they kill a fox." But in a Welsh hunting song, when the Welshmen see the fox, "the thing hunted turns out to be a 'ship a-sailing' which turns out to be the moon, which turns out to be made of cheese." *Huntsmen kill fox* is Fussell's version of tradition, in this context anyway. But in Jones's version of tradition, nothing is taken for granted, everything can be powerfully transformed to unexpected substances and purposes.

In this same letter, Jones also notes that "the words bind and loose material things." This is radically different from Saussure's idea of sign and signifier as a system of difference. Jones's relation to words is the relation of a conjuror to what he conjures up out of "the vasty deep." But rather than spirits, Jones conjures Fatty, Lillywhite, and Private Watcyn. He conjures gun emplacements and machine guns and duck-boards. By the same token, the solidity of Jones's feelings, the visceral experiences of dread and fear of death, can't be vaporized into notions of sacrifice. Such notions are way too abstract for what the narrator experiences; and the wild tonal shifts between elegy and irony reflect the narrator's inability to reach the level of abstract consideration necessary to feel "patriotism," "*dulce et decorum*," and all the other noble-sounding notions of the officer class. Even using these notions as targets of moral outrage or satire, the way Owen does, would still be to credit them—and Jones is beyond the reach of those abstractions because he's an ordinary soldier concerned with surviving: the "deeper meanings" can be left to the commissioned officers.

So while Owen is deeply ambivalent about the nature of sacrifice, sacrifice is still an operative concept for him. In fact, the ordinary soldier's death is a sacrament for Owen, even when that death is presented with irony. In that sense, sacrifice permeates Owen's poems—the most notable sacrifice, in an irony he would have been sure to appreciate, being he himself. But for a soldier like Jones, all that's above his head—the war, above all, is a fact of the body.

4

I'm not sure how far I want to press this next point. It goes past Jones and Owen, though it's more closely related to Jones's understanding of how to represent not war so much, as what Seamus Heaney once called "the music of what happens." Jones said that he didn't intend *In Parenthesis* to be a 'War Book'—only that it "happens to be concerned with war." That distinction seems essential—when he says, "We find ourselves privates in foot regiments. We search how we may see formal goodness in a life singularly inimical, hateful, to us," he is stating a basic human problem—how to find formal goodness in a hateful life. So he isn't setting up shop as a war poet, or a political poet, or any kind of poet. He isn't motivated by Justice; his poem doesn't require sponsorship by any of the "monumental certainties that go perpetually by, perpetually on time," to quote Randall Jarrell. Which can't be said of a lot of the poetry being written today about politically charged abstractions like war, poverty, racism, and other forms of injustice.

About a decade ago, I became restless with my own use of these abstractions—and began doing journalism to see these things face-to-face, not flickering on a screen. However, I've found that my politics and biases in writing about politically charged subject matter are fairly useless in writing both journalism and poetry. If I'm dealing with such material, I want to discover my subject as I write, and not have it arise from some prefab stance, or some purgatory of opinions that I simply populate with more opinions. Jones's use of clashing vocabularies and tones, melding of Welsh myth with the everyday concerns of the infantryman, his elided categories, like pastoral combined with detailed observation of barbed wire, achieves a music that can express the difference between what you ought to feel and what you really do feel—not iron smashing against iron, but the difference between exploring a political emotion, say, rather than a political conviction. A political conviction weaves no web, traps no chaotically buzzing flies—it's hygienic and easily put aside when the moment of outrage or conversational animus has passed. A political emotion is recalcitrant, contradictory, and involves you with silver wrappers and nutritional biscuits with odd names like Plumpy'Nut. And that involvement with the material world weaves an ever more responsive web of circumstance and contingency.

To be faithful to a political emotion, you have to keep yourself open to lots of different frequencies so that whatever ethical statement you arrive at arrives as part of the texture of whatever form is driving your language forward. And it's this language as it arrives that relieves you of having to stand guard over your own opinions and convictions, and gives you access to reaches of thought and feeling you might not otherwise imagine. Which is risky, unpredictable, and not always easy to reconcile with your day-to-day political, emotional, or intellectual entanglements.

And because of this unpredictability, I feel a little aphasic in front of a word like *sacrifice*. Or more buzzwordy concepts like *race*, *class*, *gender*, even *politics*. The more I think about what I saw in the refugee camps in Kenya and Mogadishu, the flimsier such words seem. I've always had a tenuous grip on these concepts, and the way they gravitate toward a word like *community*—nowadays, the idea of someone speaking for a "community" feels almost repellent to me: is that because journalists unconsciously assume this is their right— their so-called community of readers? And aren't we told that one of the roles political poetry is supposed to fulfill is to speak up against oppression, to speak truth to power—and all the other high-minded slogans? But Jones shies away from taking a position by trying to be responsive to all positions at once. The overt expression of positions, as I said before, at least in my ears, sounds like iron smashing against iron.

This conviction came home to me partly because of my time in Mogadishu. There I was, dressed in my clown-suit legitimacy conferred by my UNHCR helmet, riding in an armored vehicle with AMISOM soldiers manning machine guns in front and in back. Under such conditions, I confess that Owen's desire to tell home truths to a home audience feels a little alien to me. It's as if my time in East Africa has made my own country exotic to me—or if *exotic* is a suspect word, then a place that I can't see without also seeing, even if it's just an intermittent flickering under whatever immediate task daily life presents me, that starving boy, the silver wrapper fluttering through the air. I can't say for sure if this is because of observing, in a very limited way, what starvation does to people; or maybe this double vision is the result of the heightened intensity of putting yourself in harm's way, even if that harm is calculated to pretty good odds that you'll be OK.

Maybe the real question is what home truths can satisfy if you feel unaffiliated with the place that gave you birth—unlike Owen, who, despite describing himself with great accuracy as a "conscientious objector with a very seared conscience," always assumes that his audience, whether or not they will listen, are his fellow countrymen. But as to Mogadishu, no matter if I spent years there, I'd always be an outsider to what, for Somalis, is an intimate history of killing, based on clan reprisals, the colonial interventions of the past century, and in recent months, the hopeful assertion of business instincts over internecine ones.

And yet there's something I can't deny that feels familiar about Mogadishu—the quality of the sunlight over the intensely blue sea, in which the use of the word *azure* finally seems accurate, as opposed to a well-placed poeticism like Lowell's "Azure day / makes my agonized blue window bleaker." In Mogadishu, I had the momentary illusion that this might be home ground, like that beach I went surfing at as a teenager, near San Clemente and Nixon's house, and where I saw, up close for the first time, a decommissioned tank rusting in the sand. This juxtaposition, at least in Jones's terms of putting your body where the mouth of your ideology is, makes a kind of nerve-sense. And no matter how much of a cultural outsider I might be, my body for that moment belonged to the low coastal hills and barbed wire and shell holes pocking the city walls.

I sometimes think it would be consoling to see that tank as consonant with the AMISOM armored vehicle, a form of Army-junk pastoral, and to feel that the lyric compact was still unbroken, so that I could say with Owen "murmurous with wasp and midge." But outside the bounds of Owen's poem, such formulations go dead on me. It's as if the language of Owen, in which his political commitments begin to swamp his political emotions, were foreclosed to me, except as a beautiful, untouchable, infinitely precious historical curiosity.

And so what's left? If you're talking to a man in a refugee camp and he tells you how many members of his family have been shot down in the front room of his own home, and he tells you this in a completely deadpan way, it makes anything you could say about his suffering sound superfluous—and that's exactly how I feel now when I read poems that overtly declare themselves to be speaking for others.

And yet I also feel a respect for the effort—but often growing impatience with the result, even a ripple of disgust, unfair perhaps, if the poem turns out like most poems of this kind do: to be only what they seemed to be on first reading: alibis for thought, a lot of word masquerading, a rhetorical jumping up and down and waving of hands and yelling and shouting to get someone to pay attention. The marks on the page have less permanence, and less vividness of effect, than the henna staining the camel and goat seller's beard.

And so I've become ever more skeptical that poets can speak for communities: they can speak *to* what they think the community is—they can *assume* commonalities—they can, in a limited way, *propose* certain shared values as if they actually existed, as Whitman did—but somehow, some way, they need to signal that they're aware of the limitations of their singular, subjective viewpoint.

And as for a poet addressing posterity, in our current rising sea level, four hundred parts carbon dioxide per million eco-disaster mode, it's impossible for any poet to know, in the moment of writing, if there's even going to be a posterity to write for or to. Not that posterity was anything but a fantasy made popular by Romantic notions of the artist as representative sufferer—a notion that in our era seems as doomed as Owen's status as an officer, machine-gunned just a week before the Armistice. A black joke, you might say, given the heroic depth and sincerity of purpose in his suffering. But his stance now seems like a holdover from another geopolitical and informational era, no matter that his poems are here to stay.

5

Unlike Owen's hieratic and hierarchic understanding of soldiers, and how and why they die, Jones's soldiers in their official capacities have been turned by the Army into human extensions of their rifles, their big guns, their routinized and bureaucratized Army lingo of "Pass up message from officer in rear—Message from in front sir—they've halted sir—to right of road sir—road blocked, sir." The flatness of such language, its purely British Expeditionary Force utilitarian nature, marks one boundary of Jones's language. But on the other hand, the soldiers, with a Cockney genius for entertaining, linguistically inventive grumbling, resist all that. As Jones says:

> I am surprised to find how much Cockney influences have determined the form; but as Latin is to the Church, so is Cockney to the Army, no matter what name the regiment bears. It is difficult to dissociate any word of command, any monosyllable remembered, coming at you on dark duck-board track, from the great Bell of Bow.

This emphasis on Cockney over Latin, and equating the two, shows exactly what I mean by using class, not as a stick or a piety or an attempt to establish "authenticity," but as a formally integrated understanding that needs no comment from the poet—except after the fact, perhaps, in an author's preface. And what's more, the unselfconscious distance and neutrality of Jones's stance toward this language, his refusal to self-dramatize, to lament or attitudinize or conflate his viewpoint with any sort of implied moral understandings, feel radically new: the voices assume their place in the poem, as if some magnetic force beyond the poet's will were driving a pattern into iron filings.

And so the ironies that emerge aren't the well-worn ones contrasting *dulce et decorum* with "gloom's last dregs," or self-dramatizing agonies of witnessing: "Whereat, in terror what that sight might mean, / I reeled and shivered earthward like a feather." Jones's poem doesn't claim special linguistic privileges, doesn't make language into a private code and insist on its exemption from ordinary usage. And yet the comprehensiveness of what Jones calls his cultural "deposits" gives his language the hallucinatory clarity of intermittent flashes of artillery fire and flares lighting up the darkness. By using so many different linguistic registers at once to talk about the matériel of war and its effect on landscape and the human body, Jones creates an archaeology of war more complete than any ever written. It's no exaggeration to say that if all the millions of pages and photographs and drawings and paintings about the war were somehow lost, and all that was left was Jones's poem, the physical experience of the ordinary trench soldier would be wholly intact.

As Jones says, toward the end of Part 2, in an inadvertent *ars poetica*:

John Ball . . . stood fixed and alone in the little yard—his senses highly alert, his body incapable of movement or response. The exact disposition of small things—the precise shapes of trees, the tilt of a bucket, the movement of a straw, the disappearing right boot of Sergeant Snell—all minute noises, separate and distinct, in a stillness charged through with some approaching violence—registered not by the ear nor any single faculty—an on-rushing pervasion, saturating all existence; with exactitude, logarithmic, dial-timed, millesimal—of calculated velocity, some mean chemist's contrivance, a stinking physicist's destroying toy.

This passage, at least until the shift to the incoming shell, describes exactly the quality of attentiveness to detail that saturates *In Parenthesis*. No one has ever registered the minutiae of war, and the processes of perceiving those minutiae, as accurately or as fully as Jones. Like a PTSD nightmare, every detail is registered in the complete stop-time of trauma, but without the emotional overlay of professional trauma-speak. If I say "shell shock," you know the physical cause of the mental suffering—Jones himself suffered recurrent bouts of shell shock throughout his life, bouts that made it impossible for him to work on his extraordinary paintings and drawings for many months at a time. But if I say "post-traumatic stress disorder," you can see how suffering needs to be swept out of sight, reduced to a professionalized abstraction totally divorced from its material/matériel causes. Or if you prefer something tonier to my PTSD comparison, then Proust's notion of the *mémoire involontaire*, the memory of texture that lies beyond the anti-remembrance of dates and the facticity of "this happened, that happened," would also be the quality of unwilled but helplessly focused attentiveness that characterizes the poem. Jones is not a poet who has a design upon the reader. He is a poet in the grip of a design that Cockney accents underwrite, as well as *Le Morte D'Arthur*:

> Good night china—there's some dryish wood under fire-step—in cubby-hole—good night.
> Cushy—cushy enough—cushy, good night.

This exchange occurs between soldiers going up the line to the front to relieve those coming down from the forward trenches. In this passage, "china" is abbreviated, Cockney rhyming slang for "mate," the complete phrase being "china plate." And "cushy" is simply slang for comfortable, as well as being the adjective to describe a much-desired wound in the hand or foot, disqualifying you from combat, but not disabling you for life.

But as we've already seen in the earlier quotation about the wrecked foliage, Jones's other idioms are wildly at variance from the Cockney. In a combination of Latinate borrowings, over-the-top Atticisms, parodic scientific precision, elaborately involved Hopkins-like syntax, and first-rate reportage, Jones uses a whole other register of speech that the poem deploys as skillfully as Cockney—a register that plays with the mock-heroic, but transcends it by its fidelity to the shock experience, and slowing down of time, of sudden trauma:

> He stood alone on the stones, his mess-tin spilled at his feet. Out of the vortex, rifling the air it came—bright, brass-shod, Pandoran; with all-filling screaming the howling crescendo's up-piling snapt. The universal world, breath held, one half second, a bludgeoned stillness. Then the pent violence released a consummation of all burstings out; all sudden up-rendings and rivings-through—all taking-out of vents—all barrier-breaking—all unmaking. Pernitric begetting—the dissolving and splitting of solid things. In which unearthing aftermath, John Ball picked up his mess-tin and hurried within; ashen, huddled, waited in the dismal straw. Behind "E" Battery, fifty yards down the road, a great many mangolds, uprooted, pulped, congealed with chemical earth, spattered and made slippery the rigid boards leading to the emplacement. The sap of vegetables slobbered the spotless breech-block of No. 3 gun.

By hovering at the edge of parody with that antiheroic mess tin, Jones illustrates what Thom Gunn meant by the phrase "a strength so lavish she can limit it." The use of "Pandoran" to contrast with the later "Pernitric," a Greek myth of disaster balanced against a Greek-derived scientific term for an explosive acid, the words fatally linked by alliterative stress, shows just how sophisticated and original and flexibly various is Jones's diction, range of reference, and musical understanding. The final image of the "sap of vegetables" slobbering "the spotless breech-block of No. 3 gun" is, in its humble, eccentric rightness, one of the best pieces of description in all of literature—it's as if Hopkins's harsh, impacted music for inward states of spiritual torment in his late sonnets had been turned inside out in Jones's "slobbered the spotless breech-block," and applied to the physical torments of the war. The eyewitness brilliance of it, while keeping a cool-eyed distance from any overt moralizing, occurs in another linguistic universe from Owen's description of an exploding shell as the "hot blast and fury of hell's upsurge." And the anticlimax, after the explosion of the shell, of John Ball picking up his mess-tin and hurrying inside a barn for cover, reveals a sensibility that refuses to slight one form of experience for another, but insists on getting all of it in, and in whatever style or idiom the moment of perception demands.

6

That flexibility and strangeness and originality of perception are exactly what the conventions of news photos of starving people lack. To actually see someone starving to death, and accurately describe it, and not simply use words or images as a way to deflect your attention, may require a counterintuitive stylistic procedure, a process of defamiliarization. Jones writes, "If you would draw a smith's arm think of the twisted black-thorn bough—get at some remove from your subject." And his source of remove is, paradoxically, to get closer and closer to immediate physical sensations, so close, in fact, that a kind of poetic kinesthesia of the body takes over. It's as if Jones instinctively recognizes that, as R. P. Blackmur once said, "Style is the quality of the act of perception"—which means that style is in part the hardwiring of how you perceive, in all your individual quirks, your personal histories, your borrowings and burgeonings from whatever cultural deposits you draw on and spring from. Registering that peculiarity of perception is what style is—which rescues the notion of style from mere decoration, or spurious individuality, or the affiliation with whatever school of poetry you subscribe to.

If, as Jones does, you take the notion of style seriously as based on bodily experience of the world, then it's obvious that you need to find formal ways to capture unique experiences: ideology is unvarying, while bodily perception is always changing: so the two won't lie easily in the same bed. This is why Jones's range of styles is so wildly at variance, and yet utterly right for the diversity of experiences he's trying to re-create in all their physical and spiritual and intellectual immediacy.

Here is a passage about men climbing out of their trench and advancing toward the enemy that shows what Jones means by getting "at some remove from your subject":

> Mr. Jenkins half inclined his head to them—he walked just barely in advance of his platoon and immediately to the left of Private Ball.
>
> He gives the conventional sign
> and there is the deeply inward effort of spent men who would
> make response for him,
> and take it at the double.
> He sinks on one knee
> and now on the other,
> his upper body tilts in rigid inclination
> this way and back;
> weighted lanyard runs out to full tether,
>   swings like a pendulum
>   and the clock run down.
> Lurched over, jerked iron saucer over tilted brow,
> clampt unkindly over lip and chin
> nor no ventaille to this darkening
>   and masked face lift to grope the air
> and so disconsolate;
> enfeebled fingering at a paltry strap—
> buckle holds,
> holds him blind against the morning.
>   Then stretch still where weeds pattern the chalk predella
> —where it rises to his wire—and Sergeant T. Quilter takes over.

Not until the final two lines does it come clear that most of this passage chronicles a man's death. And this is because the death occurs in slo-mo, as an ongoing process instead of a noted fact. The technical specificity of the lanyard image, the clinical cool of the observation, the way the "iron saucer" of Jenkins's helmet slides over his entire face, the way Jones omits the "he" in "Then stretch still where weeds pattern the chalk predella," as if Jenkins, because he is dead, has been reduced to a thing, rendering the pronoun superfluous—well, you can see how far this is from the usual poeticizing and atrocityspeak. And the freedom with which Jones moves between prose and free verse—the verse breaking the process of the slo-mo fall into smaller perceptual increments, the prose providing context for the process—tracks Jenkins sinking to his knees, collapsing face forward with his helmet over his face, his fingers trying to loosen the strap and failing, so that the last thing he sees is the dark inside his helmet, but without any metaphysical overtones, shows what Jones means by getting at "some remove from your subject." Never have I read a more accurate and heartbreaking description of a man's death—and accomplished without any of the usual stylistic or emotive maneuvering. And when you see how sustained Jones's poem is in carrying off these effects, you see that his work is a vast unmined resource for poets interested in doing more than what Derek Walcott once called "the standard elegiac."

And perhaps that's why Jones means so much to me now: he goes beyond elegy's abstraction to the body's physical reality, and in the process incorporates many different bodies, and the particulars of their speech coming from their lungs—speech recorded in his poem originating from all registers, and all ranks. He mentions how profanity, and its repetition, conditioned "the whole shape of our discourse," and that sometimes the proper juxtaposition of profanity "in a sentence, and when expressed under poignant circumstances, reached real poetry." And in more normal circumstances, "the 'Bugger! Bugger!' of a man detailed, had often about it the 'Fiat! Fiat!' of the Saints."

As I said, Jones is not a war poet. He isn't interested in setting up shop as a professional elegist. He speaks for no community, but lets a community develop through the multiplicity of voices that the poem accumulates. Above all, he is no village explainer, or self-righteous ranter: he has no message to impart, no agenda to advance. Instead, he says that the poem "has to do with some things I saw, felt, & was part of." In the modesty of his claim, I can find my own way into the war. I can see the place in Mametz Wood, which I visited years before I'd read Jones, where he was wounded in the leg—not exactly a cushy wound, but cushy enough to get him away from the front for a few months.

Most of all, I can see not mass slaughter, but this little vignette of vital, and electrifying, substantiation of one man's limited experience. A German soldier throws a stick bomb at Jones, Jones lobs a grenade back, and kills his fellow soldier—and rather than talk about his sense of guilt or pity or rage, or indulge in journalistic or humanist or philosophical or psychological expostulation, he simply notes two things: that he liked the colored label on the handle of the stick bomb as it flew toward him; and after his grenade explodes, he notes how "you scramble forward and pretend not to see, / but ruby drops from young beech-sprigs /—are bright your hands and face." And in that awful brightness, Jones shows how poetic problems are, as such, problems of perception. That the artist is necessarily empirical rather than speculative. That the question for the artist, according to Jones, is always "'Does it?' rather than 'Ought it?'" And that perception can't be faked because it is important to be "anthropomorphic, to deal through and in the things we understand as [women and] men—to be incarnational."

How to Make a
Toilet-Paper-Roll Blowgun

Anna Akhmatova's "Requiem" begins with an anecdote about the poet standing in line before the Kresty Prison. I visited the stone building, which sits on the banks of the Neva in St. Petersburg, as a tourist several years ago—yes, as a tourist: you can pay several rubles and get a tour of the prison and the prisoners: for Kresty is still a working prison. After the guide takes your ticket, you walk into a tall narrow chamber with catwalks above you that lead to cell doors. When I visited, light coming through the clerestory in the onion dome overhead lit the stone walls, and birds trapped up in the dome whirled and fluttered and rustled their wings. Prisoners lounging against the catwalk railings looked down on us: the reverse of Jeremy Bentham's Panopticon, it was the prisoners who kept surreptitious watch over the tourists. But when the prison was first built, it consisted of two five-story buildings in the shapes of crosses—to encourage repentance—but which also allowed the corridors to be watched by guards from a single convergent point.

Vladimir Putin decreed in 2006 that a new Kresty Prison be built on the outskirts of St. Petersburg, while the present Kresty will be sold at auction and redeveloped—inevitably, as it seems—into a

hotel/entertainment complex. But for now, the entertainment con-
sists of the prisoners themselves and the prison's Who's Who list of
famous political and artistic detainees: Akhmatova's son for one, the
historian Lev Gumilyov, sentenced to Siberia for ten years; her first
husband, the poet Nikolay Gumilyov, executed by a firing squad;
Leon Trotsky, brained in Mexico City by an ice-ax wielding NKVD
agent; and almost every other historical name associated with the
1917 Russian Revolution and the Great Purges and show trials of
1937–38.

I stared at the prisoners dressed in black caps and black uniforms,
and they stared right back. I couldn't see any guards, and we certainly
weren't escorted by anyone but our guide. On hands and knees, the
men scrubbed the stone floor with worn-down bristle brushes. I saw
a mouse, apparently fleeing from the slopping, soapy water, scurry
down the corridor and slip into a crevice in the stone. No doubt this
mouse came from the same genetic stock as the ones that must have
scurried during Lev Gumilyov's term of imprisonment when he was
locked up during the Yezhov terror that resulted in the execution of
over a million people. Such is the background of Akhmatova's poem.
But one day soon, perhaps you'll be able to stay in the Trotsky Suite,
drink your champagne, and turn up the air-conditioning.

In Kresty Prison's heyday, women lined up to give packages to the
prisoners, standing in line, as Akhmatova says in "Requiem," "for
three hundred hours, / And where they never unbolted the doors for
me." In the prison museum—yes, there's a museum—I saw icons
painted on Coke cans, historical photographs, contraband such as a
hollowed-out book to hold a knife, and what you might call crafts—a
chess set, for example, made out of masticated bread beautifully
sculpted into the warring armies. And then an example of the object
that I found most moving of all, and still very much in use when I
visited: a blowgun made of the little cardboard cylinders at the center of a toilet-paper roll. Taped and glued together, the gun on display was over six feet long, the tube bent at a soft right angle at about
the fourth foot: the prisoners wrote messages on scraps of paper,
folded them up, inserted them in the gun, and blew them through

the window bars. The right angle was for reaching windows around corners. It must take two men to handle a gun of this size, just to keep it from sagging or breaking apart. Whatever official policy the guards may have had toward these pipe-blown messages went un-enforced: the parking lot was littered with them. I never learned if the men wrote their names and addresses on them so that the messages could be delivered, but something like that must have happened, for out in the parking lot, I saw several women—wives, girlfriends, mothers?—picking through hundreds of folded messages and put-ting a few of them in their purses.

My visit was almost a decade ago, but over the years I've thought in a desultory way about why the image of those blowguns stays so fresh in my mind. Is it because, when I taught in a maximum-security prison, Patuxent Institution, the guards would never have turned a blind eye to such activities? That kind of laxness would never have been tolerated. And on the prisoners' side of the bars, I'd also spent a few days in jail myself, once for hitchhiking in Nebraska, the second time for stealing food in a grocery store. So I had some slight basis for fellow feeling with the prisoners, both as a teacher and an inmate. For a prisoner, the shutting of iron doors behind you, the clanging of metal on metal, felt a little like you'd been erased: all ties beyond the prison walls were cut off, felt far away, rendered weirdly irrelevant—which, of course, made you long for them that much more. The loneliness and desperation, as well as the fear of the other inmates that besets you, are some of the worst feelings I know. And so those toilet-paper-roll blowguns were, for me, an emblem of our overwhelming need for communication—human breath blowing a message to the world. And the fact that they were made of such flimsy materials, materials whose purpose was connected to our most basic bodily functions, made me admire all the more the ingenuity that conceived and constructed them. It was an expression of common humanity, however absurd or desper-ate the feelings behind it, or however brutal the actions of the men who made them. For me, they represented an affirmative gesture, and out of a poverty of means, an instrument that expresses more about our essential natures, its animal and spiritual side, than that other, loftier instrument that the blowgun somewhat resembles: an object designed no less for communication, though of an artistic kind—a pipe or a flute.

Of course the archetypal flute was the one fashioned by Hermes and traded to Apollo in exchange for the caduceus. Apollo, the god of poetry, consummate musician of both the flute and the lyre, never had to take a shit—at least not in any of the myths I've read. Nor does he have to die, nor can any prison hold him. Which is perhaps why the toilet-paper-roll blowgun has such a strong hold on my imagination: I love its handmade nature, its aura of improvisation and bricolage, its embrace of recycled materials, its resolutely low-tech commitments in a world hurtling toward global corporate fascism. It suggests a kind of poetics based on these qualities, an oppositional poetics that isn't simply a replication of the forces it's opposing. Like Robinson Crusoe's flute in Elizabeth Bishop's "Crusoe in England," it stresses the virtues of the homely, the homemade, but without being blind to the larger world. I doubt that Apollo would think much of such an instrument—tape and glue, the industrial processes that make toilet paper—it all seems a little too humanly involved to be of much interest on Mount Olympus. In fact, the flute Marsyas the satyr played in his famous contest with Apollo had belonged to Athena—that is, until she caught sight of her reflection in the water and hated the way the flute made her cheeks puff out. And so she threw it away, which is when Marsyas picked it up—man to the waist, goat below, no wonder puffed-out cheeks didn't bother him. By the same token, animal–human humanity has clear affinities with the toilet-paper-roll blowgun.

This fancy is obviously not what the prisoners see in it, but the fact that a blowgun ended up in a museum that includes photographs of historic figures, as well as that exquisitely sculpted chess set made out of bread, suggests a surplus aura that goes beyond the obvious utilitarian purposes. The museum curator thought it was worth collecting and showing to tourists. And so the blowgun has about it a kind of artifactual antiquity, as if its presence in a museum gives it a shared pedigree with classical statues and great art. At the same time, it represents a counterimpulse to Apollo's sacred music, a kind of punked-out vitality that has its own unique and historically inflected charge. If one of poetry's traditional purposes is to bring humanity to the transcendent, another is to reach out to ordinary human beings and do what E. M. Forster said was the purpose of all art: "Only connect!"

Of course these purposes are complicated by darker crosscurrents. One of them is the way Apollo takes his music making so seriously—so seriously, in fact, that when Marsyas challenges Apollo (now playing an even tonier instrument, the lyre) to a music contest and loses, the real concert turns out to be Marsyas's screams as Apollo skins him alive. These screams turn Forster's dictum inside out: Marsyas's cries do indeed connect, but with ears sublimely indifferent to human suffering. The mythic vision of engaging Apollo in a divine music-making contest devolves into notes that would seem more appropriate for a toilet-paper-roll blowgun.

But it's the dual nature of Akhmatova's vision in "Requiem" that interests me. The poet casts herself as both Apollo and Marsyas, Apollo because of the transcendent poetic privilege she invokes to speak about collective suffering, Marsyas because she herself is the object lesson in what being skinned alive feels like. The implication that she is both torturer and tortured is heretical, and certainly repellent, but, I would argue, the main source of the poem's power. It's as if in the poem she overcomes her helplessness by wresting the initiative from Stalin, and refigures memory as the skinning knife that Apollo so effectively wields. In part III, she writes, "No, it is not I, it is somebody else who is suffering. / I would not have been able to bear what happened." This radical dissociation intensifies in the next section, in which she writes of her pre–Yezhov terror self:

You should have been shown, you mocker,
Minion of all your friends,
Gay little sinner of Tsarskoye Selo,
What would happen in your life—

How three-hundredth in line, with a parcel,
You would stand by the Kresty prison,
Your fiery tears
Burning through the New Year's ice.

And in these lines from part IX, the apex of this split between torturing Apollo and suffering Marsyas reaches a climax, but also a
kind of understanding:

And I've finally realized
That I must give in,
Overhearing myself
Raving as if it were somebody else.

In Epilogue II, she states explicitly this split between Apollo and
Marsyas, but overcomes the split:

I will remember them always and everywhere,
I will never forget them no matter what comes.

And if they gag my exhausted mouth
Through which a hundred million scream,

Then may the people remember me
On the eve of my remembrance day.

And if ever in this country
They decide to erect a monument to me,

I consent to that honor
Under these conditions—that it stand

Neither by the sea, where I was born:
My last tie with the sea is broken,

Nor in the tsar's garden near the cherished pine stump,
Where an inconsolable shade looks for me,

But here, where I stood for three hundred hours,
And where they never unbolted the doors for me.

The magnificence of these lines is made more magnificent by the poet's wish for a monument to be built, not by the sea or in the tsar's garden, both sites of bourgeois or aristocratic privilege, but outside Kresty Prison, in solidarity with the hundred million who scream through her mouth. At the same time, I can't help but feel the ferocity of Akhmatova's egotism—the torturing Apollo who makes music out of Marsyas's screams has had enough—and she is now demanding her due from the transcendental State. In a sense, Akhmatova's desire for a monument reveals underneath the Apollo/Marsyas split her own sense of her self-importance, as if she and history, or she and Stalin, were not only equals, but the force of Good ranged against the force of Evil.

This kind of confidence borders on self-parody: why would the officials at Kresty Prison unbolt the doors to an "old woman" (and, by extension, to Akhmatova herself) who "howled like a wounded animal"? And isn't there something faintly absurd in asking for a monument, as if she were angling for the honor? Beware of what you wish for: a statue of Akhmatova was erected there, a statue that, in its distortions of line suggestive of heroic suffering, borders on kitsch. No doubt it will add a touch of scenic melancholy to the hotel/entertainment complex.

But again, this courting of absurdity is one of the poem's triumphs and provides the key to Akhmatova's own sense of her persona—at times ironized, as in her wish for a monument, but overwhelmingly direct, grave, sincere. You can see this clearly in how the poem begins with an oft-quoted anecdote, titled "Instead of a Preface," in which she casts her persona as tragic rather than ironic or absurd. She insists on her own singularity, her superiority even, granted to her by her poetic gift. In that sense, she writes as if she herself, and her experience, were representative of history. Or to use Yeats's phrase, her poems provide an example of poetry's ability to hold reality and justice in a single thought:

Instead of a Preface

Once someone "recognized" me. Then a woman with bluish lips standing behind me, who, of course, had never heard me called by name before, woke up from the stupor to which everyone had succumbed and whispered in my ear (everyone spoke in whispers there):

"Can you describe this?"

And I answered: "Yes, I can."

Then something that looked like a smile passed over what had once been her face.

This story has been repeated hundreds of times by American writers, most often as an example of what used to be called "the poetry of witness"—and as far as I know, always in a heroic context, such that the poet is presented as an exemplary figure, almost a kind of knight or Joan of Arc doing battle with an evil villain. But what interests me here isn't so much the poet, but how she characterizes the woman with bluish lips: in keeping with the anti-Romantic nature of toilet-paper-roll blowguns, what would have been the woman's reaction if the poet had refused the challenge and said, "No, I can't"? Or if the poet had described the woman's face, instead of saying that the woman had no face until the poet's affirmation of her art brought back the woman's smile out of limbo? And what if the poet's focus had been on finding out the woman's name as opposed to the poet's assertion of her own name? In other words, what if Akhmatova had abandoned the heroic pose and picked up a blowgun to blow a message not to the "hundred million" who scream through her mouth but to one person?

Poetry and poets can't be expected to do everything—record atrocity as well as dignify each person in the photograph with a living name. At first, the tacit egotism of the poet, her assertion of her own power against the massive power of the state, may seem oddly pitched—but if you're being crushed, isn't the flaring of the ego a survival instinct? And couldn't the woman's face becoming a face again be emblematic of the egos of both the poet and her questioner? So poetry summons up faces when they've been lost.

Yet doesn't the story also hint at how the role of the witness might equally well result in the faces of others being erased? In its self-seriousness, its almost stagy conviction that a hundred million can indeed scream through one mouth, Akhmatova's limited subjectivity becomes the subjectivity of an entire people. The poem asserts poetic privilege as being unlimited, almost divine, in which the poet's identity overbears history through what Osip Mandelstam once called "the steadfastness of speech articulation." But when Marsyas is screaming, he isn't being ironic or prophetic or displaying virtues like steadfastness: he's simply screaming the way an animal in pain screams. And while the choice to scream or not to scream is, according to Nadezhda Mandelstam, the last assertion of our individual humanity, no poetic gesture can fully compensate or restore the symmetry of a face contorted into a scream. Screaming, after all, is prehistorical, precultural, predialectical.

This is perhaps why Emmanuel Levinas's concept of the Other as being prior to history, psychology, discourse itself, becomes so important in a contemporary understanding of the word *witness*, in which a media-saturated age makes everyone an inadvertent voyeur, if not a witness, to global suffering. Through the revelation of what Levinas, in *Totality and Infinity*, calls "the primordial phenomenon of gentleness," the transcendent fact of the Other's face gives the appetitive ego ethical coherence as a self—a coherence around the need to preserve the Other: it makes the absolute demand on the self, "Do not kill me." A voyeur, on the other hand, lacks any ethical commitment: whether someone is killed or not becomes secondary to the watching.

Maybe Levinas's formulation is a luxury, though, for someone in Akhmatova's psychic extremity. In fact, her obsession with her own self-image—as she attempts to overcome the split in it and make it an emblem for other sufferers' self-images—becomes not only a canny means of survival but also a primal expression of her desire that she and others survive with dignity. Isaiah Berlin, in his visit to the poet in 1945 (a visit that may have set off a chain of disasters in bringing Akhmatova to Stalin's attention so that he had a bug placed in her ceiling, had her work banned, ordered the ongoing imprisonment of her son, and oversaw the public and private humiliations she suffered later in life) recounts a conversation with Akhmatova in which he comments on her sense of self-importance and how she deeply believed in the larger historical importance of her fate:

> we—that is, she and I—inadvertently, by the mere fact of our meeting, had started the Cold War and thereby changed the history of mankind. She meant this quite literally; and . . . saw herself and me as world-historical personages chosen by destiny to begin a cosmic conflict . . . I could not protest . . . since she would have felt this as an insult to her tragic image of herself as Cassandra—indeed, to the historico-metaphysical vision which informed so much of her poetry. I remained silent.

What Berlin calls her "historico-metaphysical vision" and his tactful silence seem partially attributable to what Berlin's own modesty and self-skepticism might call a paranoid delusion. In his account of her poetics, she chooses to be Cassandra, the prophetess doomed never to be believed: but this is hardly how Akhmatova casts herself in life or in "Requiem." Cassandra is helpless, her gift ignored. But in "Requiem," Akhmatova seems almost to connive with fate to be both Apollo and Marsyas, to be both the singing sufferer and the god who plays—or flays—Marsyas like an instrument. But a sense of destiny that Berlin regards as out of scale for himself—after all, he is protected from Stalin by working for the British Embassy— may have been Akhmatova's way of holding on to her own identity, poetic and personal. Perhaps the pressure of Stalin's day-to-day murderousness made her cast herself as his equal on the stage of world events so that she could see herself and Berlin as titans too—titans of the spirit if not titans of power, like Stalin. But the point here isn't whether Akhmatova was deluded or had lost perspective: the point is her faith in the power of art as embodied in the actual events of her life. Whether or not Stalin understands it, whether or not her self-dramatizing insistence on her own life as ushering in a whole epoch of political and historical conflict is accurate, Stalin's nightmare, at least in Akhmatova's mind, is to look in the mirror and see his condemnation staring back at him in the lineaments of her poetry. And why shouldn't Akhmatova and Berlin's meeting be the catalyst for the Cold War? As a metaphor for Stalin's own paranoia, what cause could be more apt?

But while Right and Wrong, Good and Evil, are stable terms in "Requiem," the poet's self-division engendered by her suffering is anything but: the fluctuations between pronouns in which she addresses herself in second and third person; the ferocity with which she ironizes her pre–Yezhov terror self; even her absurd demand for a commemorative statue, are all examples of how unruly her emotions are, despite her conviction that she is on the right side of history, and that history will justify her as having shown what Auden called "an affirming flame."

2

On YouTube, you can watch a video of Colonel Muammar Gaddafi being dragged by a group of militiamen firing machine guns into the air, his desert camouflage shirt being ripped off, his body thrown across a jeep hood, his head bloody, his eyes glazed, his face puffy and bruised. It's hard to know what to feel when you watch such a video. Gaddafi, the author of *The Green Book: The Social Basis of the Third Universal Theory*, which explains all questions of government, society, and relations among all beings, not to mention sports and horsemanship; he of the crazy hats—brown, black, purple fezzes, a Russian-looking fur bonnet, a peaked military cap with more gold braid, piping, and badges than any general in history, a hammered gold diadem, a kofi, a kufi, a ushanka; he of the all-female bodyguard, "the Revolutionary Nuns," though they don't look particularly holy; he whose moniker was "Murshid, Guide, Brother Leader," in which he wasn't a dictator since the People ruled (albeit with his advice); he of the murderous disposition, assassinating anyone suspected of being politically opposed; he who promoted himself to Colonel (in homage to Egyptian leader Gamal Nasser) after his coup in 1969, when he could have named himself Generalissimo, Commander-in-Chief, Emperor, His Highness; he whose fashion sense was so outlandish that it's hard to compare him to anyone, expect maybe Liberace; he of the unceasing oratory about pan-Arabism, pan-Africanism, the Great Man-Made River, the Great Socialist People's Libyan Arab Jamahiriya; he who supplied arms to the Black Panther Party, the IRA, the Red Brigades, the Japanese Red Army, ETA, and half a dozen more: when you see him getting his face bashed in, and then a still photo of him with a small bullet hole in the side of his head between his left eye and sideburn, you can't help but be appalled by what his ruthlessness and cruelty would seem to have merited him.

When I visited Libya in the spring of 2014, three years after Gaddafi's death, wherever I traveled in Libya there was an immensely hopeful feeling in the streets. It was as if Marsyas had overthrown Apollo in the person of Gaddafi, and what Akhmatova longed for, and realized only in her poetry, had actually taken place in Tripoli in the renaming of Green Square (after *The Green Book*, of course) to Martyrs' Square. Libya was like being in a laboratory and watching the creation of a civil society from whatever modes of political and cultural life Gaddafi hadn't destroyed or co-opted. The international poetry festival I was invited to was part of that experiment. Its founder, Ashur Etwebi, one of Libya's best-known poets, is also a highly regarded oncologist and professor of medicine. Etwebi barely escaped being murdered by the Brother Leader: after the dictator was killed, it was discovered in the files of the secret police that the poet's name was on a "kill list."

With Ashur as our guide, three other poets (one from Spain,

Greece, and Italy) and I gave readings with local Libyan poets. As we went from town to town in a poetic caravan, we traveled by Land Rovers and SUVs instead of camels. We read in tiny hamlets and major cities, and spent hours crossing hardpan dirt tracks through miles of desert. Beneath a huge canopy on giant carpets, Ashur had arranged for us to sleep out under the stars just like the Bedouin did fifty years back. He had us spend one night underground in a house carved out of rock, and then in an oasis surrounded by date palms. Of course, he took care to expose us to modern Libya as well. We stayed at the Hotel Corinthia in Tripoli, a Western-style hotel that the website promises will provide "unrivalled comfort and impeccable service"—the same hotel where, in January 2015, the Islamic State in Tripoli killed ten guests. So while we were in Libya at a relatively hopeful time, wherever we traveled outside Tripoli, we were part of a convoy guarded by a militia. Our movements were at the behest of the militia leaders as we drove from one militia's territory to the next.

Yet even before we arrived, the signs were ominous. The country is awash in weaponry, and the day we were supposed to fly to Tripoli from Rome, a rocket-propelled grenade blew a couple of holes in the runway. We had to wait a day for things to return to normal (nowadays, given that the country has been torn apart, such incidents wouldn't be worth mentioning). And one afternoon, when we went to the souk in downtown Tripoli, rival militias were having a shoot-out by the waterfront next to Martyrs' Square. The Square was crowded, and it was hard to see, but I glimpsed a man crouching down, firing a machine pistol. We craned our necks for a while until the gunfight moved off down the waterfront, and then, like the rest of the crowd, we went back to our shopping. Gunfire went on day and night in Tripoli: sometimes it was a shoot-out, sometimes a wedding or a birthday, and sometimes it was just a trigger-happy youngster shooting off a machine gun. One of the local poets joked that anybody with a gun likes to shoot it into the air because you always hit your target.

When the country came apart a few weeks after we left, and Apollo and Marsyas began battling it out again, Libya's warring factions, anti-Islamist as well as Islamist, seemed bent on destroying the work of people like Etwebi. Since he is resolutely anti-authoritarian and pro-democratic, neither side has much use for him. His house has been burned down and blown up, people in his village executed and arrested, and the egalitarian society that he and others like him envisioned has turned into rubble, just like his home. As of now, he has been forced to flee with his family to Norway, which granted them political asylum.

As to what life under Gaddafi was like for Etwebi and his compatriots, this little story, in all its idiosyncrasy and small-bore humor, sums it up better than the big journalistic/political/historical cymbal clash. A young Amazigh poet (Berber, but the name is frowned upon in Libya) told me that when he was a boy there were something like two or three TV stations that you could watch, all controlled by the Brother Leader. Over many months, he'd been watching the episodes of a cartoon show in which a baby bee goes in search of his missing mother, and at the climax of the entire series, just as it looks like the baby bee is about to be reunited with Mom, the program is interrupted by the Guide addressing some revolutionary congress or other. So he never got to see what happened to the baby bee. And when he was a little older, he was again watching the climactic episode of a cartoon about a boy who wanted to be a soccer player, and just as it seemed that the boy was going to make the team, again! THIS PROGRAM IS INTERRUPTED TO BRING YOU THE BROTHER LEADER, gassing on about Pan-Africanism or some other hobbyhorse.

Which is why the Amazigh poet found Gaddafi's murder on YouTube as savagely ironic as it is savage.

Given Gaddafi's weird persona, I wonder how Akhmatova would have approached a character like him—he isn't exactly a World Historical Villain, or the embodiment of Evil. His flamboyance and theatricality were just the opposite of Stalin's cultivation of secrecy, though Gaddafi's secret police assassinated exiled Libyan dissidents whenever they could. But how can you confront, as an artist, a dictator who isn't quite, well, a bad enough "baddie" (to quote Tony Blair)? Not because Gaddafi wasn't as ruthless as Stalin, but because of how his brutality and his public buffoonery went hand in hand. And in a country where there was no real functioning civil society because Gaddafi habitually undermined it, fearing that his own institutions might one day come back to bite him, you could say that Gaddafi, unlike Stalin, was an extremely elusive target. The Guide was only the Guide, not the Iron-Fisted Ruler. And as the Guide, he could position himself outside his own government's deliberately sketchy formal institutions so that if need be, the Brother Leader could turn on his ministers and align himself with the People if a policy proved particularly unpopular.

This, of course, is a radically different set of conditions than the centralized state terror that Akhmatova faced. In a sense, all she needed to do was lower her head and charge. But for a Libyan poet, a target like Gaddafi, who was always moving, was harder to hit. Besides which, he was so calculatedly ridiculous that to see in him Evil Incarnate would be a form of artistic self-demeanment. (President Trump comes to mind.) Of equal importance, how do you land a blow on such a murderous clown, but without playing into his cult of personality?

In "A Hymn from the Seventh Century B.C.," Etwebi devised strategies radically different from Akhmatova's. He locates the poem in a long-past heroic age, but unlike the usual heroic conventions, he commemorates the losers, not the winners in an ancient battle between warring kings of the Nile delta.

A Hymn from the Seventh Century B.C.
to Muhammad Al Faqih Salih

On the backs of men whose feet don't touch the ground,
who look up at the temple steps they climb and climb back down,
the bows on their backs gleam and stiffen—
the bow strings tighten at the specter of a mountain goat, a lion.

They don't put down the bow
except to piss, to fuck.

The women take the bow,
they rub its back and belly,
they oil it and strengthen it,
they whisper in the bow's ear.

The chief of the horsemen who fought the armies
from the southern plains,
who fought and died in Heliopolis, said:

We were ninety men,
the best the earth gave birth to:
Not one came home but me.

In their prowess the bowmen are almost supernatural, seeming to float above the ground. But the focus isn't on the imperial powers, but on this select group of individuals. And since Libyan militias are primarily local, and the men choose to fight with each other in bands that are often less than a hundred, the mention of the ninety men could be seen as a gesture of mourning toward friends and comrades killed during the Libyan Revolution. Rather than a poem that laments the passing of empire, it focuses on the individual grief of the only survivor of the campaign. And then it amplifies that grief by shifting to an old man's voice, presumably a man of the chief horseman's tribe or village:

An old man, eyes filling with tears,
draws lines with a stick in the sand:

You were out there on your own for forty days and nights.
Where are your men and your rearing horses?
Why did you come back all alone?

The starving men cover their eyes,
behind them the young boys carry an iron scythe.

The Celeo bird rising through the palms
cries its cry of dry thunder.

Falcons, wolves, elephants wreathe their trunks
and sweep the earth in mourning with their tusks.

In the courtyard where heat waves waver
and feed themselves into the air,
hatred twists the sweating faces,
the men shout and curse:

How did the bull get to the mountaintop?
How did the bull lower its horns and charge at the free man?
How did the man twist away from those horns
that gored the air?

When the bull charged, a rope
of words, syllable by syllable, tightened
round its neck and yanked it back.

The deliberate vagueness of who this old man is or what community he represents—if he's a fellow tribesman or a villager or the father of the one of the dead bowmen—suggests a desire to step away from the particulars of history in order to instantiate a myth. This isn't done in the service of the poet's ego, but in the service of what ordinary people feel when someone they love has been killed in war. And the fact that the poem feels progressively more mythic, and so less aligned with a time-bound political stance, makes me wonder if Etwebi isn't coming at his own grief for the fate of his country, but coming at it slant. Gaddafi may be the agent who brings about this grief, but he's nothing more than a catalyst. The poem seems to want to keep Gaddafi and his buffoonishness at arm's length because it would cheapen the pathos of the poem in its sorrow for individuals. There will be no ten million sufferers screaming through this poet's voice, only the old man's eyes filling with tears. The animals in procession are mourning not so much the defeat as the fact that the men were killed. Gaddafi is an annoyance in comparison to this sorrow.

So rather than dignifying Gaddafi as a titanic opponent that a heroic poet must do battle with, Etwebi disappears into the fabric of his poem, displacing himself and the history of conquest in favor of something much more local, homely, and in this poem at least, on a more human scale. But lest the poem seem too modest, the last two stanzas reverse the poetic terms the rest of the poem would seem to accept. Suddenly, emerging out of the tropes of mourning elephants is the free man who twists away from the horns of the bull that has managed to charge its way to the mountaintop, which is where the free man resides—high above the men of hatred who, lower down the slope, shout and sweat and curse. And what peculiar quality of freedom does the free man possess? The power of language as a check on the bull's power to do harm—a rope of words that when the bull charges holds the bull back.

Etwebi's modesty, couched as it is in a scenario of myth and displaced agency, is every bit as responsive to his peculiar conditions of tyranny as Akhmatova's insistence that her voice will weigh more than Stalin's on the scales of ultimate Justice. But for Etwebi, there is no Justice with a capital *J*. There is only the counterforce of language to hold back the bull, there is only the agility of the free man to twist away from the bull's horns, there is only the sorrowing knowledge that all your comrades have died and you alone are left to tell the tale.

Under this scenario, the poem relies on no tragic gestures, no discourse about "witness," neither of the variety proposed by Levinas or Akhmatova's version of poet as hero. Apollo's notes would sound a little flat, a little outsized in this stripped-down song of the free man's private grief. Nor is he much interested in blowing a message through the bars of history in the hope of some redress. The words themselves are sufficient reward in their power to yank the bull back. But even in his much quieter way, the free man's faith in language as a restraint on brute force is every bit as strong and convincing as Akhmatova's.

3

If ever there was a poet who could play Apollo's notes and blow an artful message through the bars of history, it is the Swedish poet Tomas Tranströmer. Unlike Akhmatova, who sees Truth as a means to bring down Stalin, for Tranströmer the truth only becomes true in the process of telling it. The stripped down YES/NO of courtroom evidence—and in Stalin's case, it doesn't matter if the evidence is true or not, just as long as it serves his purposes—has to be rendered back into a full-fleshed story. Otherwise, Stalin's most famous aphorism (possibly a misattribution)—"One man's death is a tragedy, but a million men's death a statistic"—becomes the only epitaph for the disappeared million. But by focusing on the ones forgotten or overlooked by history, Tranströmer's poem "Codex" devotes itself to memorializing these "men of the footnotes," rather than the world-historical personages through whose mouths the otherwise inarticulate "hundred million scream." In that sense, "Codex" is a kind of anti-"Requiem," more concerned with those who have escaped not only "the morality of power" but also "the black-and-white checkered game where the corpses' stench is the only thing that never dies"—a stench, of course, that hangs heavy over "Requiem," and would hang heavy over Etwebi's "A Hymn from the Seventh Century B.C." if the free man had concerned himself more with the heaped dead of massive armies than with the bodies of close friends.

Like Etwebi, Tranströmer's focus on "the men of the footnotes" implies a sense of proportion about what Berlin called Akhmatova's historico-metaphysical stance toward experience. While Akhmatova is interested in showing how personal history shades into myth (and not only a myth, but *the* myth that will hold true in the titanic struggle between Good and Evil), Tranströmer makes myth shade into the particulars of history. But in both his and Etwebi's poems, *good* and *evil* are written with small letters, and the outcome of the struggle between the two feels provisional, at best a temporary reprieve (no lasting cease-fire has taken hold in Libya) in which "the men of the footnotes, the unplayed, the half forgotten, the deathless unknowns" are the paradoxical standard bearers for artistic achievement as well as humane behavior. Rather than depending on Akhmatova's myth of poetic genius, of the poet as representative sufferer elected by Fate and granted poetic privilege by Apollo's touch, Etwebi's "free man" transforms into Tranströmer's "deathless unknowns" through the act of making themselves even more anonymous, as these lines from "Codex" so beautifully illustrate:

> But the ones who really want to be taken off the list . . .
> They don't stay in the territory of the footnotes
> they go into a declining career that ends in oblivion and peace.

In these lines, you could accuse Tranströmer of a radical form of quietism, even a complete lack of political engagement. But what is so moving about this oblivion is that it comes across as a choice: I can hear the reader rejoining, *Some choice—about as much choice as asserting your humanity through screaming.* And while that overtone is strongly present, the agency Tranströmer gives his oblivion seekers seems like a subtle repudiation of what in the first line of the poem he calls the men "of the headlines," the ones who revel in "swallowing the morality of power," and who think they control "the black-and-white checkered game" that results in Stalin's grim little bon mot.

But these murdered unknowns aren't statistics because the poet explores the corridor, not for the sake of the judges, but to find, in Jean Genet's words, that place of "lightness from which he can speak the truth"; a place that at first seems like the realm of myth, but then resolves into the world of history:

> . . . I find myself in the deep corridor
> that would be dark

if my right hand weren't shining like a flashlight.
The light falls on something written on the wall
and I see it
the way the diver sees the name on the sunken hull flickering
    towards him in the streaming depth:
ADAM ILEBORGH 1448. Who?
The one who got the organ to stretch its clumsy wings and rise—
it kept hovering almost a minute.
What a successful experiment!

In this passage Tranströmer, like a deep-sea diver exploring a mythic wreck, grounds his exploration in the fact that Adam Ileborgh was an early composer of organ music, and that his experiments succeeded in making the organ "stretch its clumsy wings and rise." It may not seem like much in comparison to Akhmatova, but Tranströmer's excitement transforms Ileborgh's successful experiment into a triumph over gravity: that such an unwieldy, cumbersome thing as an organ can hover for almost a minute borders on the magical.

Despite such magic, Tranströmer recognizes that the men of the footnotes, the Adam Ileborghs, may only speak in whispers in comparison to the world-historical personages. But as individual efforts like Ileborgh's gain momentum, "whisper upon whisper" adds up "to a breaker that rushes along the corridor / without knocking anyone over." The tactfulness of that wave exemplifies a different kind of artistic and cultural virtue from Akhmatova's poetic grandeur. However great a poet Akhmatova is—and given her historical circumstances, her courage, her verbal artistry, and her endurance, she exemplifies one form of poetic integrity that is truly heroic—I suspect she would want her words to be more of a tidal wave sweeping away everything in its path: Kresty Prison, Yezhov, Stalin himself.

Of course the historical conditions that have pervaded the West since the end of World War II are radically different from Akhmatova's. The Cold War era's eerie nuclear security among well-defined superpowers, as well as the creep in our post–Cold War period of what Christopher Hedges calls corporate fascism, in which democratic values are subordinated to economics, makes it difficult to pinpoint just who the Stalins are. Or else there has been such a proliferation of little Stalins all across the globe—the Gaddafis and Joseph Konys and Charles Taylors and Slobodan Miloševićs, the Interahamwe of Rwanda, the "devil on horseback" of Sudan, and, in some political circles, Benjamin Netanyahu, Henry Kissinger, and Donald Trump—that to speak from the vantage of one country, one history, seems somehow inadequate. The image of Stalin as evil incarnate has shattered into our current paranoiac's dream of terrorist cells everywhere you look—though one man's terrorist is another man's freedom fighter, such that, in Lowell's words, "small war [follows] on the heels of small / war." Perhaps Akhmatova's heroic stance isn't flexible enough to capture our relentlessly shifting, kaleidoscopic vision of world conflict in which the world at war isn't a World War but the sum total of hundreds of smaller conflicts. In our era, the murdered and unknown, as well as "the deathless unknowns," forge an uneasy solidarity with the Unknown Soldier. Imagine a monument to the Unknown Collateral Damage that the Unknown Soldier both slaughters and defends. Under such conditions, Tranströmer's celebration "of the almost rubbed-out names of the artists" is just as much a heroic undertaking, but without the heroic stance, as Akhmatova's "Requiem."

   In contrast to Akhmatova's insistence that she can describe what she sees in the shadows of Kresty Prison, Tranströmer insists on the work of humane culture as a collective seeing, a nonhierarchical effort. It's not so much that Tranströmer is hostile to the myth of isolated genius; it's just that it's inoperative in the particular corridor of history in which the poet happens to find himself. His role is more Genet's witness in search of a place that will allow him to describe the way in which the "why" of the truth gets revealed under the subtle colorations of the "how." And as that coloration deepens his understanding, the corridor transforms so that it "isn't a corridor anymore":

Neither burial place nor market square but something of both.
It's also a greenhouse.
Here is plenty of oxygen.
The dead of the footnotes can breathe deeply, they are included
    in the ecological system just as before.

While these lines would seem to refer to dead musicians, Etwebi's
free man can also find his place in the poem's well-oxygenated spaces
in which even the dead are "rehabilitated. / And the ones that can't
receive any more / haven't stopped giving."

Tranströmer's use of the word *rehabilitated* subtly conjures the
post-Stalin thaw of the vindicated dead, in which Akhmatova's first
husband, as well as thousands of others who made up the millions of Stalin's grim statistic, were cleared of their so-called crimes.
Tranströmer's canny expansion of the term to include all the dead
who, even though they are dead, "haven't stopped giving," suggests
another way out of Akhmatova's embrace of her own singularity,
or the endless wrangling of victims who vie with one another over
whose grief is greater, whose grievance more justified. Even after
death, whether we die in our sleep or are slaughtered, the work of
a humane world goes on among the men and women of the footnotes just as certainly as it does among the world-historical personages. Ileborgh may be dead, but nearly six hundred years later his
organ can still fly.

Yet as the "light falls on name after name" so that the "walls are
covered with scribbles," the names are slowly being erased:

Some are anonymous, they are my friends
but I don't recognize them. They are like those stone people
carved on grave slabs in old churches.
Mild or severe reliefs on walls that we brush against, figures
    and names
sunk into the stone floor, being rubbed away.
But the ones who really want to be taken off the list . . .

They don't stay in the territory of the footnotes
they go into a declining career that ends in oblivion and peace.
The total oblivion. It's a kind of examination
that is taken in silence, to walk across the border and no one
    notices . . .

In this form of communal anticommunion, in which everyone equally must suffer the forces wearing away their scribbled names, Tranströmer suggests that even in death our responsibilities—and culpabilities— toward others don't come to an end. In his subtle way of casting light, this uncanny vision of the afterlife of death means that we are all bound together by our desire for "oblivion and peace"—but an oblivion and peace that each of us must choose by crossing that border between remembrance and absolute anonymity. No matter if our names are historical or not, Tranströmer makes it clear that none of us can exist forever in the leaves of the codex: not the Akhmatovas, the inmates of Kresty Prison blowing messages through the bars, not the free man whose freedom is always threatened by the rampant bull, nor "the deathless unknowns" hidden away in the "territory of the footnotes."

III

Disappearing Act

1

I remember having dinner with a journalist, a decent enough guy, afflicted with The Danger I've Been Through Is Bigger Than the Danger You've Been Through disease. It's a pretty common form of one-upmanship, but since he thought of me as a poet—a dude who gazes at his navel, and then, for a little variety, asks his other poet pals if he can gaze at their navels—he was a little surprised when someone else at the table mentioned that, in addition to my being a poetic navel gazer, I'd also done some journalism. There was maybe a touch of scorn in his voice when he said, "You? About what?" I said that I'd just finished a long piece about Somali refugees. He gave me a blank look and said, "Oh, you mean you look stuff up and write it here in the US." And when I said no, I'd been to Mogadishu, I could see him recalibrating what he thought of me.

And I have to admit, the surprise in his voice is a surprise I share. Given my age and my unpredictable health, why would I choose to go to places like Somalia? Why run the risk? And people often ask me, Aren't you afraid? The short answer is Yes! . . . but only beforehand— when I'm actually out in a refugee camp talking to people, I'm so focused on listening that there's no room for fear. And anyway, fear wouldn't help me do my job.

Of course, it's more complicated than that: there's a difference between the rational fear that you are deliberately putting yourself in a situation where everything is OK until it's not OK, and then it's too late; and the overpowering fear of thinking that you're going to die, not at some distant date, but right now, right here. But since the circumstances aren't usually so dramatic, and because all of us have our own ways of being afraid, I'm going to come at this question of fear in a way that's roundabout. I'd like to be more straightforward, but trying to tell the truth slant is what I know how to do.

2

So let me turn the clock back to the 1970s, when I was in my twenties and on my way to southern Mexico, to San Cristóbal de las Casas, to become an anthropologist. I went down by train from San Diego, across the Sonoran Desert and the high plateau of central Mexico, to the southern uplands and mountains sloping down to *tierra caliente*, the hot country, where the Usumacinta River basin in the extreme south borders on Guatemala: a brutal sixty-hour trip on a wooden bench in which my seatmate slept for what must have been forty of those hours; in which I forgot my camera in a bathroom somewhere at a whistle stop; in which I ate mango and papaya and tamales from vendors who held up their wooden trays to the train windows; and in both a comic and terrifying incident at 3:00 a.m., helped a group of federal Mexican police unload fifty or so kilos of marijuana, which somehow or other had been hidden behind my seat. Reflected in the glass, my hair stood on end like a cartoon character's, my face looked exhausted, grimy, and in shock, as my seatmate, by now wide awake, handed me kilo after kilo that I passed through the window to some bored-looking Federales. All the while a soldier, just for form's sake, stuck his rifle in our faces and flicked the safety on and off.

These Mexican adventures (or misadventures) came about in the most random way: I'd been studying anthropology as an undergraduate, and while hitchhiking between San Diego and LA, where my school was, I got picked up by a truck driver who had just returned from Chiapas. When I told him about my interest in anthropology, he took me back to his house, had his wife fix me a sandwich, showed me some of his loom-woven and hand-embroidered textiles from around San Cristóbal, and gave me the name and address of Gertrude Blom, the Swiss photographer and anthropologist, doyenne of Casa Na Bolom, House of the Jaguar, an anthropological research center. He told me that if I wanted a job, I should write to her. And when I did, a few weeks later I received a note from her assistant, Laura, saying, yes, they would be delighted to take me on, provided that—and I should have paid better attention to this part of the note—I was "willing to work under any conditions."

Casa Na Bolom, in addition to being a research center, also doubled as a hotel; and Trudi, as everybody called her, combined the irascibility of Basil Fawlty of the British comedy *Fawlty Towers*; the grandness of a duchess; the mischievous honesty that needs only a little prompting to tell you to your face what she'd just said behind your back; and a passionate advocacy for the local Mayan tribes, and especially the Lacandones, a jungle-dwelling group of a few hundred Maya who managed to isolate themselves from the modern Mexican state and the incursion of technology until the 1950s.

When I got Laura's note, the art school I was studying at was on the verge of eliminating my department, Critical Studies. My professor, Beryl Bellman, who had done his fieldwork in west Africa, had assigned me the usual canonical British works: Malinowski, Boas, Evans-Pritchard, Leach. I wasn't much of a scholar, but he tolerated me: kind, attentive, he told wonderful stories about the bush. He said it took time to get used to working in the jungle in hot weather, but once you got used to it, the sweat would pour off you in buckets, and it was exhilarating. He described cutting wood with a machete and building his own hut to live in. I was immediately hooked on the idea that a life of adventure, of meeting people radically different from me, could also be a way to use my mind. I confess I never really took in the scholarly part of the discipline—the elaborate mapping of kinship systems, the linguistic analyses, the cosmological mapping—but I loved the idea of living with what were then called "native informants" as a way of coming to a better understanding of the human race in general.

At least that's how anthropology billed itself in those days. All this, of course, was before Clifford Geertz came along and blew the whole idea of a stable cultural anthropology, either of the universal or historical or scientifically systematic type, out of the conceptual water. The pose of objectivity, the ability to get outside your culture and inside another culture, the ideological uses that anthropology could be put to, the coercive nature of the abstract paradigms that supposedly sprang out of the cultures themselves, and not the anthropologists' cultural biases—all of that came to light a few years later. Long story short: when I told Beryl (in the hip spirit of the 1970s he encouraged me to call him by his first name) about my plan to drop out of school (I still don't have a BA) and go work for Trudi, he told me he thought it was a great idea. He then told me in a hushed voice how he himself was leaving the art school in order to take a real job at a real university where his research would be understood and respected.

Anyway, after working at Casa Na Bolom for several months, I'd met a lot of anthropologists. I loved some of them as personalities, especially Robert Bruce, whom I helped bandage a baby monkey's paws one evening in Robert's room after supper. The little fellow had lost his mother in a bush fire down in the Lacandon jungle, and Robert was taking the orphan back to his daughter in Mexico City as a pet. I held the monkey behind the head so it wouldn't bite Robert, a huge man who, as he smeared salve on the monkey's paws and wrapped them in clean bandages, talked in very precise terms about the Popol Vuh, the Mayan sacred book. But except for Robert, who spoke several Mayan dialects fluently, and shared a sense of the absurd in his joking with Don Antonio and Don José (what their Mayan names were, I don't remember), two Lacandones who came up from the jungle in Pepe Martinez's little bush plane to get tested for TB and treated for worms, the other anthropologists I'd met seemed a little distant, stiff, abstracted: they were like cardboard cutouts set alongside a live human being.

But then, Robert's magnetism was hard to compete with: he was a huge man, but despite his giant frame, he looked completely at home next to Don Antonio and Don José, neither of them any taller than five and a half feet. Broad-faced and sturdily built, with long black hair hanging down to their waists, they wore knee-length white tunics made from tree bark. The three of them sat together, along with Trudi's other guests, in high-backed mahogany chairs at an oversized trestle dinner table as if we were extras in a faux-Elizabethan, Adventures of Robin Hood mead hall out of a 1950s MGM movie. Robert, Don Antonio, and Don José spoke Mayan together, laughing uproariously at times, and as far as I could follow it, trading jokes about some evangelical missionary. Trudi, in a floor-length, green brocade gown, sat at the head of the table. We all chowed down on chicken and battered, fried squash blossoms, while she threw chicken bones over her shoulder to the narrow-headed, neurasthenic Russian wolfhounds that sat at attention behind her. To know those dogs was to hate them—whenever I took them for walks, they invariably got into fights with all the half-starved mutts that trotted our way. I remember hauling back on their leashes while they snarled and snapped at a small brown cur who seemed to be grinning a little buck-toothed grin at them, taunting them as they strained against me. I suppose if I'd had my wits about me I could have come up with some kind of ethnographic take on the severely limited cultural adaptability of purebred wolfhounds in comparison to that little brown dog, whom I thoroughly admired for sticking it to them. But I was too much in awe of the scientific-sounding mumbo-jumbo the other anthropologists opined in, as they sipped hot chocolate and settled down into the oversized, overstuffed chairs in Trudi's excellent and extensive library.

Which is another reason why I admired Robert Bruce. He didn't talk jargon, or pretend to objectivity, or try to pass himself off as more native than thou. And in comparison to him, most of the other anthropologists reminded me a little of those wolfhounds—a little too intense, a little too high strung, a little too aggressive to prove some theory. Of course I was much too cowed—and cowardly—to openly admit my doubts about "the discipline," but it was Robert's un-spoiled enthusiasm, his immediate feeling for the Lacandones and the pleasure he derived from visiting the Lacandon jungle, that inspired me. Robert represented the adventurous spirit of going out to meet people much different from you and doing your best to learn about them, not on your terms, but as much as possible on theirs.

But then life intervened, and I was to become so radically changed that there was no possibility of my indulging that spirit—a spirit that I loved and still do love, a spirit of taking risks because only through risk can any of us grow beyond ourselves and come to know the world on its own terms—the world as it appears, according to Wallace Stevens, when it's been "cleared of its stiff and stubborn, man-locked set."

3

The change I'm speaking of was my transformation from a young man who took for granted that he'd have plenty of time to make his way through the world, to a young man who, with a potentially fatal bone marrow disease, sometimes doubted that he'd make it past next week. In medicalspeak, I'm referring to my "hemolytic crises" sparked by my unpronounceable illness, paroxysmal noctur-nal hemoglobinuria—PNH, for short—or in cats and dogs English, blood in urine at night. A relatively benign translation for my symp-toms that more often than not were a stop on the way to leukemia or, even more fatal, aplastic anemia. But with PNH, when I have a crisis, my red blood cells break down so quickly (*hemo-lytic* means "blood breaking") that I can lose more than half my red cells in just a few days, turning my urine thick and black with exploded red cells. All through my twenties, thirties, and forties, my illness ran on something like six-week cycles of destruction and replication of my red blood cells. And because my cells were defective, the destruction part of the cycle, if it were complicated by a bad flu or some other common infection, could pose life-threatening consequences— blood clots, thromboses, strokes. All that really needs to be said is that when I was first diagnosed at twenty-four, the median life expectancy from diagnosis to death was ten years, and I've been lucky enough to live well beyond that. But as a matter of record, my illness has brought me near death three times.

Of course, I doubt very seriously that I would have lasted as an anthropologist, no matter the state of my health, given my antipathy to abstraction and my skepticism about "fieldwork"—trying to pass as a "native Chamulan" by donning one of their white wool tunics and slipping on a pair of huaraches while hauling around a tape recorder? It all seemed a little dubious. This feeling was bolstered by Ruth Benedict's remark (another anthropologist Beryl told me to read) that the best anthropological document of the twentieth century was Proust's *Remembrance of Things Past*. Of course I hadn't read Proust when I read Benedict—but because I'd become so lonely for the sound of English during my time with Trudi, in which I spoke Spanish most of the time, I too had begun to write: little sketches of what I'd seen or done; or of certain anthropologists like Robert; of Don Antonio and Don José; or of the eccentric community of expats in San Cristóbal, including a shy bachelor sculptor whose entire house was filled with life-sized carved mahogany nudes in all kinds of bizarre, at times anatomically impossible, Kama Sutra–like positions.

But if Proust's novel could be counted as anthropology, then maybe my sudden passion for writing (I turned to poetry pretty quickly, again because sequential logic was never as appealing to me as thinking in images) could become a way of doing it—and without all the onerous theorizing.

But that still doesn't explain why, in the past decade, I would choose to go to a place like Mogadishu, where I could run far more serious risks than not having access to a high-tech hospital. Is it simply compensatory, a way to prove to myself that my illness doesn't rule my life the way it once did? I am, after all, according to my blood tests, clinically improved. I don't break down nearly as often as I used to, my blood counts are more stable, I have more physical stamina, and when my blood disease does kick in, the recovery isn't nearly so arduous. So maybe my decision to take these kinds of risks is a way to forge a truce between the well self and the sick self.

Or maybe my going to a place like Mogadishu is just me trying to fool myself into thinking that I'm once again physically normal. Or perhaps I'm just trying to make up for lost time, cramming into the years I have left what I couldn't do during those years of sickness, in which the defining adventure was the adventure of staying alive.

But regardless of my compensatory impulses, the journalism has become its own passion—a passion for the people I meet, for the need to forget myself in order to do my job. I remember the young Lebanese man who took me to Qana and told me the story about the little girl whom he found in the rubble, thinking she was alive, but who in fact was dead. He looked as if he were about to tear up, so I told him he didn't have to go on with his story. But he looked me in the eye, and said, "I'll tell you what happened, but you must promise to tell my story." I'd never felt such a sense of responsibility, almost a kind of commission, in all my life. As to how a cultural outsider can tell the story, that's a different question. One thing I think is crucial, though, is to find a way to acknowledge the limits of what you can know, and to be honest about what it is you don't know.

And just because a writer is borne into a situation doesn't mean that person has the linguistic or emotional gifts to tell a compelling story about those circumstances. Among the best books I've ever read about the Palestinian uprisings is Jean Genet's *Prisoner of Love*. By the same token, the notion that the writer gives voice to the voiceless seems to me like self-delusion. I wonder how many of these writer-spokesmen ever stopped to ask the so-called "voiceless" how they feel about being called that. Besides, no one is voiceless if you really stop to think about it: people express themselves in how they dress, by what they eat, by the music they sing or listen to, and in a thousand other ways. In accord with the way we express ourselves in our daily lives, Frost has a beautiful statement about our impulse toward form:

When in doubt there is always form for us to go on with. . . . The artist, the poet, might be expected to be the most aware of such assurance. But it is really everybody's sanity to feel it and live by it. Fortunately, too, no forms are more engrossing, gratifying, comforting, staying than those lesser ones we throw off, like vortex rings of smoke, all our individual enterprise and needing nobody's cooperation; a basket, a letter, a garden, a room, an idea, a poem.

I love how Frost views the impulse toward form as one of the basic sanities that we all live by. Even something as simple as blowing a smoke ring is a formal gesture, an expression of your place in the world. So if you say you're speaking for "the voiceless," you're negating that common impulse toward formal expression: in fact, in all your well-meant political fervor, yours might be just another voice drowning out the voices you think you're speaking for. At least the "let's play dress-up" ethos of my era's anthropology—no matter how naive or unconscious or culturally arrogant it was—expressed a desire to see another person's world from the inside.

But not for one second do I believe that I'm ever going to understand what the young Somali woman was feeling as she sat outside the perimeter fence of the refugee camp in Dadaab, her two young boys sitting quietly beside her, her baby daughter asleep in her arms as she told me how first her goats died, then her crops dried up, then her husband was killed by a militia—and so she walked across the desert from Mogadishu to get to the camp.

All I knew about her was what she told me, and what I observed. To pretend to know more would just be me projecting my feelings onto hers. As Thom Gunn writes about the limits of empathy, "Save the word / empathy, sweetheart, / for your freshman essays. / Doesn't it make / a rather large / claim?" In Gunn's canny understanding, "empathy" is way too overweening. The best we can do, in our isolated selves, is the more modest "sympathy." So sympathy, rather than empathy, has become for me not only a poetic and journalistic principle but a rule of thumb in dealing with people in general.

And within those more modest bounds, I wonder if the intensity of illness and of being in a place like Mogadishu vibrate on not dissimilar wavelengths. Just as my disease has led me to out-of-the-way mental places, and made me feel solidarity with the guy in the hospital bed next to me, a drain in his gut, a port for blood in his upper chest, the tube of the implanted catheter faintly outlined by the skin above his right nipple, so has my journalism led me to places and people I couldn't come across in any other way—a camel seller, the sister of a suicide bomber, a tank mechanic who loves his tanks the way other people love their dogs.

And in these people's presences, maybe my journalism is a way of transforming the self-absorbed drama of being ill, in which you pay obsessive attention to the back of your own hand on the rumpled sheet, as if it held a clue to the course of your sickness, into a more outwardly directed act of attention. This kind of intense focus is similar to what Clifford Geertz once called "thick description," in which you render through careful and meticulous detail what appears to be going on, rather than assuming you know. So the traumatic self-absorption of sickness transforms into the hyperalert awareness of my role as journalist, in which my personal concerns vanish into what other people are wearing, saying, eating, into the expressions on their faces, into the way their gestures reinforce or undermine what they're saying. Without meaning to, by paying close attention, I render myself faceless so that their faces can come more clearly forward.

It's as if this little disappearing act that I'm calling journalism helps me balance out my years of illness with the person I am now. And now that that person has achieved a little more breathing room, and even though who he was before he became ill feels so distant that that young man might as well have been living in another dimension, the sick person inside me gives a little shove to the well person to get out there in the field and keep my concentration focused outward. And while I might feel afraid before putting on a flak jacket and getting into an armored vehicle, when I'm actually out on patrol all I can think about is taking notes, and trying to record with as much accuracy as possible what's right there in front of me.

Of course, we've all been bludgeoned by the Right and the Left into thinking that every act of perception is in the service of some ideology that we, wittingly or unwittingly, are subservient to. And however true this may be in some ultimate sense, since none of us can escape our backgrounds and our histories, nonetheless, this isn't what I experience when I'm scribbling notes. No matter what barriers of perception or culture may block my way, and all my personal and perceptual baggage aside, there's something truly freeing about noting down exactly what it is you're trying to see. I'm so immersed in doing my job that there's really no room for fear, or trying to neaten things up to fit some abstract paradigm. And as for taking risks, as a documentary filmmaker pal once put it, "Look, man, if you're doing this kind of thing, you do it because that's just what we do. It's no different than working in a hardware store. You need a nail, you find a nail. You need a shot, you get the shot."

4

But there's another level to all this that goes beyond my, or anyone's, limited perspective. I once spent a day interviewing refugees from all over east Africa, and as they told me stories of almost unimaginable suffering—never once breaking down, telling the most terrible things in dead-level voices—there were so many common threads that by the end of the day they wove together into a tapestry of dread and fear, but also of human endurance. Always there were gunmen, sometimes mutilation, sometimes severed heads, arms, legs; or slow starvation; or bombs falling on a house, killing a mother or a father or a child; or sometimes wiping out at random, between breakfast and a trip to the market, an entire extended family, except for the one who told the tale. And as I listened, I became acutely aware of each person's physical presence, and of just how fragile our bodies are—arms, legs, heads scarred, bruised, beaten; or just subject to normal aging in sagging, slackening muscles so that no matter how protected or insulated we are from the world's violence, all bodies in time are damaged bodies. And I came to realize that what I was trying to do with my journalism, and of course with my poetry, was to find a way, which wasn't phony or sentimental, to connect with all that suffering, and to add my slender thread to all the others.

As Adrienne Rich once put it in her sequence "Contradictions," the problem is how "to live in a damaged body" and yet find ways "to connect, without hysteria, the pain / of any one's body with the pain of the body's world." She writes that she has "longed to live on this earth / walking her boundaries   never counting the cost." And yet her whole life as a poet and as an activist has been devoted to examining how the boundaries imposed on "the body's world / filled with   creatures   filled with dread / misshapen so   yet the best we have" can also deform us. Her husband's suicide, her crippling arthritis, her difficult path to the love of women and men made more complex by her passion for justice, all these "costs" that she would prefer not to have counted and yet she counts nonetheless, make of her longing to live in this "best world that is the body's world" a profound imaginative gesture across those boundaries. And yet our vulnerable bodies, which constitute "our raft among the abstract worlds," can't escape the large-scale hysterias of some hectoring, reified abstraction like Freedom or Jihad.

And because, as Rich puts it, we live "in a world where pain is meant to be gagged," there will always be those who will want to twist that pain to serve their cause. I once met in Nairobi a suspected Rwandan *génocidaire* who told me that because Tutsis had killed Hutus in previous pogroms, the Hutus in massacring the Tutsis were only doing what had to be done. He said, with an air of sadness and aggrieved outrage, that the worldwide publicity generated by the genocide was in fact an attempt to gag the real victims. And yet the man's pain was real, just as the massacres on both sides were real. The contradiction isn't one I know how to live with, resolve, or dismiss. And yet I don't wish I'd never met this man: my journalism has brought me into far more intimate contact with the body's world, both the misshapen and the beautiful, than if I'd never gone out of my way to meet such a man.

At the deepest level—and I have a hunch this is the same wellspring that poetry comes from—my need to see things for myself is a way of cutting through the haze of media-spawned fantasies. I used to feel like I lived in a hell of abstractions, of canned images, of jabbering, competing ideologies. What journalism has done for me is to help ground my experience in what Seamus Heaney once called the "primal reach into the physical." So now, when I think about Iraq, I know what the Tigris and Euphrates Rivers look like. In Mogadishu, I see the green sea, the red earth, and the half-destroyed cathedral, the ceiling caved in, the glass blown out of the rose window, but the walls still soaring upward. In Lebanon, I see my tank mechanic on his back in the dirt reaching up inside his tank and doing something to it that looks intimate, private, while his tank, as he gently raps on it with his wrench, talks back to him in little pings and clangs.

5

On that night when I first met Don Antonio and Don José, before sitting down to dinner, Trudi had asked me to catch them up with polite table manners. I worried that in doing so they would see this as a symptom of unconscious Western privilege, but they seemed completely unfazed by my instruction. Perhaps Trudi—and for that matter, Don Antonio and Don José—knew that to survive the relentless destruction of their native mahogany forests, the Lacandones were going to have to learn how to move in many different worlds at once. And so my attempt to teach them how to use a napkin, or the proper way to grip a fork, which they handled very sensibly like knives, no longer seems quite so ridiculous as it did back then.

Of course, since those days, the Lacandon rain forest has been overrun, and the Lacandones' concern for cultural purity, which they deeply cared about—though not with the virulence or self-consciousness with which certain anthropologists wanted them to care about it— has necessarily adapted to the deluge of technology they've been exposed to. But when Don Antonio and Don José signaled that they needed to use the bathroom, and when I proceeded to show them the flush toilet in the library, and was dumbfounded as to how to explain to them the basics of washing waste away by pulling on the overhead tank's pull chain, let alone the purpose or proper technique of using toilet paper, realizing all the while that they must have been puzzled indeed by my leading them in the first place into a room in which there was nowhere to squat, but a strange-looking white chair mounted over what looked like a little fountain or well, is it any wonder that eventually I thought better of the whole doomed enterprise, and led them outside to the very back of the garden that sloped to a ravine—which is where I habitually went because the toilet was so often occupied, plugged up, or broken.

When we returned to the library, I'll never forget how Don Antonio and I sat in silence for a while, and then he got up, and went over to the wall where a bow and a set of arrows were mounted above the fireplace. As I learned many years later, Don Antonio eventually did die of TB. It was one of the leading causes of death among the Lacandones in those days, so it wouldn't be surprising. However, I found his death notice on some missionary's website, and who knows how accurate it is—there is so much misinformation on the web about the Lacandones, that if you look up the best-known Lacandon, Chan K'in Viejo, Robert Bruce's teacher, the age of his death ranges from the mid-90s to 109. But as to Don Antonio, there were absolutely no details. And yet I can still picture him in his knee-length tunic of white bark, and later on, wearing a pair of large glasses, with very thick lenses to correct what I guess was a serious astigmatism. But on that night, he took the bow and arrows down, and beckoned me to join him in front of the fireplace.

He showed me how the stone arrowheads were flintknapped, as has been done for many thousands of years; and then how the bow, which was almost as tall as Don Antonio himself, was shaped from ironwood, one of the hardest of the hardwoods. *Lignum vitae*, "wood of life," is its Latin name, so-called because of its use in treating syphilis and other like ailments brought to the New World by the Spanish colonizers.

Then he strung the bow, placed it in my hands, and encouraged me to draw back the string. I never did find out what the string was made of, but possibly it was henequen, the same fiber that the Lacandones use in weaving hammocks. I drew back the string and let it twang. It twanged all right, right against the unprotected skin of my forearm. I winced, we both laughed, and then I handed the bow back to him. He positioned the bow and arrows on their hooks in the wall, and then we pulled up two chairs to the fire.

Even in that companionable silence, I still felt a little mortified at having been asked to play Miss Manners. I worried that Don Antonio and Don José would think I was being condescending, that my "metropolitan way of conceiving the Other's experience"—or some such pompous formulation—was dehumanizing to them. But my anxiety to appear sensitive to "the other," which was really my desire to look virtuous in my own eyes, made me almost miss what was really being asked: that I appreciate the beauty of what Don Antonio was showing me—how the bow tapered toward the ends, and was a little thicker in the middle; and how the arrows were tipped with parrot, buzzard, or hawk feathers, two feathers each, almost always of the same kind.

The arrows were as much works of art as the bow and, as I learned from Alfred Tozzer's book on the Lacandones, possessed different functions: a blunt-tipped arrow, very light in weight and made from a hollow reed, was used to stun birds for capture, rather than killing them for game; a sharpened wooden-tipped arrow was for shooting fish or small birds; and a stone-tipped arrow, with a barbed foreshaft, was employed in hunting monkeys.

Of course, Don Antonio was a lot more successful in his efforts to show me how to use the bow than I had been in showing him how to use the toilet. And not simply because I'd used a bow and arrows before. I was a little overawed by him, and if I saw him as a sort of wise man of the jungle out to teach the city slicker a thing or two, what I now see is that he was just trying to share with me a moment of pride in his craftsmanship, both in the bow's utility and, if it's not too fancy a word, in the aesthetics of what was truly a beautiful object. Of course his gesture may have been ironic, but only gently so. It wasn't so much to put me in my place, as to signal that both of us had places—but places we could move beyond, provided we could look past ourselves to "the best world" that is "the body's world," a world filled with creatures, misshapen or not, filled with dread or not. And at least for those moments when we were looking at the bow, we didn't need to count the cost.

"Where's the football?"

If everything isn't black and white, I say, "Why the hell not?"
—JOHN WAYNE

It is said that the camera cannot lie, but rarely do we allow it to do anything else, since the camera sees what you point it at: the camera sees what you want it to see.   —JAMES BALDWIN

My father is off in the projection booth running the projector, my mother is working the snack bar, and the other cars parked in the drive-in movie theater lot have the look of large sleeping animals, the whole of east Texas sprawled around. Beneath me, my older brother is asleep on the back seat of our old green Plymouth. And my twin brother, asleep in the left half of the rear window ledge, reaches out his hand and, dreaming, pats my shoulder, the two of us sleeping head to head, our feet pointing toward the darkness just outside the doors.

There's the Milky Way overhead, the warm night humming with crickets, a cat in heat yowling off behind the drive-in fence, the faint whirring sound of the projector from the projector booth, the beam of white light momentarily illuminating moths swarming up in front of it. My mother is tucking a light blanket around me just before she goes off to attend to the customers—and naturally there's a screen, a huge white screen that dwarfs the whole horizon.

Or it's intermission, and looking through the back window, I can see my mother standing on top of the little cinderblock bunker that houses the office, the supply room, the projector booth, and the snack bar. She's climbed up the back of the building on an old wooden ladder, and with a microphone in her hand, she's reading off ticket stubs for the raffle—tonight it's a dozen Chop-o-matics, the precursor to the Veg-o-matic. Whenever somebody wins, they jump out of their cars, and wave their hands to the crowd, their shadows expanding and shrinking in time to the high beams flashing on and off, while horns honk, and people lean out of their windows to laugh and yell congratulations to their fellow townspeople, the lucky ones, the winners.

Or on really special nights, my parents manage to book one of the actors in the movie to make a guest appearance and autograph black-and-white photos of themselves. And in one great coup, they even get Robert Preston to come and sing for half an hour up on the roof while everybody cheers and honks and flashes their lights.

Or it's my twin brother's and my birthday, and we've invited some of our friends to sit with us in lawn chairs right in front of the snack bar—the best seats on the grounds—which we then get to raid, stuffing ourselves with hotdogs, guzzling Cokes, and wolfing down Snickers, while Bob Hope and Bing Crosby sing and dance and make us laugh.

But on most ordinary nights, I'm up on the rear window ledge, hearing, through the metal grille of the speaker, the voice of a woman singing, "Zing went the strings of my heart!" Or on another night, the sound of a monstrous talking crab about to eat a mad scientist; or an old man thinking to himself as he sits in a boat trying to catch a marlin; or a goony guy who trips and falls a lot and makes odd noises with his nose and gets pies hurled in his face and who reminds me in a creepy but also humorous way of that kid who always smells like catsup and onions and who breathes so loudly through his mouth and nose.

And of course there are bombs exploding, and rain and windstorms and sandstorms, and the more disturbing and thrilling sounds of the cavalry's bugles and the Comanches' pounding drums, elemental with war and weather, and strangled, jeering voices of soldiers or a lynch mob, and huge orchestras cascading in my ears as I drift in my dreams, the music weaving all through them, the voices of the dead telling me things I was afraid to know during the daytime: what that moaning and shouting is up in my parents' bedroom; who the monster is on the stairs that keeps stalking me at night; why my mother takes away Mr. Potato Head when I get into a scuffle with one of my brothers over my pocket knife. And all through this orchestral swirl of voices and music and human and animal cries, I can feel a vibrating restlessness on the other side of sleep, just like a hair on the projector lens quivering across the bottom of the screen until my father swipes the lens clean.

My mother says that we were outsiders: when she and my father first took over the drive-in, they didn't give a thought to where people should park. Whoever got there first got first choice. But after several weeks of this . . . well, I was going to write "policy," but as my mother told me, "The closest we came to knowing anyone who was different than us was a Russian fellow—someone said he was Jewish, but I had no idea what that meant." So anything like a "policy" would have been beyond them. They grew up in the most provincial of towns—a tiny Kansas town on the High Plains prairie that you can walk across in five minutes. The closest she'd ever come to people different from her town folk would have been the shackled German POWs cleaning up, and keeping the grounds, at the University of Kansas campus in Lawrence, where they'd both gone to college. "We just didn't know siccum," she told me. But since she'd grown up dirt poor, in the worst years of the Dustbowl, she wasn't naive about money.

After my father came home from fighting in China in World War II, he finished college, and they traveled around in a trailer caravan for a year, my father stringing signal wire for the Southern Pacific Railroad while my mother kept house as best she could in the trailer. They'd been on the lookout for a business, and when they came across the drive-in in their travels, they decided to approach my father's parents for the money. "We were excited," my mother said, "because it would give us a chance to have a family on our own terms. Little did I know about the grind of keeping it going. Not to mention being beholden to your in-laws." So my grandfather loaned them forty thousand dollars to buy the drive-in—a lot of money in those days. "We had no thought," she said, "but to pay back that money. And failure to pay—well, your dad wouldn't think of it: and so we worked seven nights a week, winter and summer, for ten years to pay it all off."

So at first, the people who came to the drive-in for a quarter a person were just customers—black or white, if you paid, you were a customer.

During the first few weeks in that town, my parents, who knew next to nothing about the South, let alone Texas, except what they'd gleaned from cowboy movies, were surprised to see Colored Only and White Only signs posted on the separate grocery stores and in various businesses. They were so ignorant of Jim Crow that my mother tried to convince Osie, a man whom they'd hired the week they arrived to help them clean up the grounds, to sit in the front seat with her when she picked him up and they drove to work together. But he was visibly disturbed by this, she said, looking deeply uncomfortable each time she joked with him to sit up front with her, and eventually she let him sit in the back seat: she had no idea of the danger he might be running, but she was sensitive to his desire not to share the front seat with a white woman.

And then one day, a soft-spoken, well-meaning, well-dressed man came to the drive-in during the daytime, a restaurant owner whose restaurant was, as my mother put it, "one step above a beanery." He was an older member of the Kiwanis Club that my father had just joined as a fledgling newcomer to both commerce and the South. He found my mother and father doing the books in their little cinderblock cubbyhole of an office in back of the snack bar and where they kept their supplies. My mother said he spoke to them in a friendly, courteous manner, and told them that this wasn't how things were done; that if they wanted to continue in business, they would have to restrict where "the coloreds," as he called them, could park.

She says they were both thunderstruck, and didn't know what to say, and so they said nothing, except for the required small-town pleasantries when the man left. And that night, as usual, they allowed anyone who bought a ticket to park wherever they liked. But this didn't go unnoticed, because two days later, another, different man came in, with the same friendly, courteous manner, but with a kind of determination that they both understood meant business. Again, they were nonplussed—they didn't know how to respond—and the man left without them saying much of anything.

But now they were worried: about the business failing, about failing "you kids," as my mother put it, about letting down my father's parents. But they still persisted in allowing people to park where they liked. Then a third man came by about a week later, and they knew: again, he conducted himself in that quiet, courteous, butter-wouldn't-melt-in-his-mouth manner that my mother said she now recognized as the veneer of white hatred. At that moment, she felt build inside herself a bitter hatred of that man and toward the South—an anger that later fueled her rebellion against the Mormons, and the Mormon Church, as a high school English teacher in a small Mormon town in Utah—but that lay a decade in the future. The man said his piece, left, and then my mother and father had a decision to make.

My mother, who is now ninety-two, said, "No doubt I talked a lot of high and mighty bombast while your dad just listened . . . and then we both looked at each other and knew—we'd have to come up with 'a policy,' as the man put it. And so, we decided to give our black customers rows ten and eleven."

That night, when each one drove up, she said she had the most awful feeling. "I was utterly humiliated in humiliating them—but I asked them to park in the back of the theater. All this happened over sixty years ago, but you can see how it's stuck with me. But we did it because we had real poverty staring us in the face, and we couldn't afford to fail—we had to pay your Grandpa Bob back. . . . And of course we had you kids in mind."

———

What was remarkable about those years, as she later told me, is that never once, except occasionally between themselves, did they *ever* have a discussion with anyone else, white or black, about racism. There was nothing but silence—and everybody knew exactly what that silence meant. "Except us," she said. "And then we learned."

When I asked how she felt about the dailiness of such injustice, she said it was horrible—separate bathrooms, separate water fountains . . . as if the blackness would rub off. She said she didn't know what our black customers did when they needed to use the bathrooms, since they weren't allowed to use ours. She told me that once a car of young black men from Dallas drove up to go to the movie, and when she told them they had to sit in rows ten and eleven, they looked at each other, then looked at her—nobody said anything, but the anger in their eyes stirred up anger—and fear—in her. "So we had a stand-off," she said, "them glaring at me, me glaring back. Nobody said a word. And then they finally got out of line and drove away." I asked her how it made her feel, and she said, in a low voice, "Dirty."

How did they stand it for all those years? She shrugged, and simply said: "Things were different back then . . . no TV, no way to talk about these things. It's awful to say, but you got used to it, stopped thinking about it, stopped noticing it until there was something so awful or stupid that you couldn't ignore it any longer. There was one town near us that had an iron arch over the entrance that read in big letters, *The blackest earth, the whitest people.*

She told me how, after a few years, my God, she hated Texas . . . she was afraid we boys would grow up to be provincial yahoos, as racist as the rest of the town—and the kind of movies we showed, lots and lots of Westerns—well, that didn't help, either. On a Saturday night, for example, we'd show a B Western for the first feature, and then a D Western for the second—it made her wonder what it would do to us to see such stuff. Of course, we loved it—for me and my two brothers, playing for hours outdoors in the little playground, sliding down the slide, digging in the sandbox, swinging on the swings, we lived hermetically sealed in our little world.

But for my parents, after the first couple of years, it must have felt purgatorial: never a vacation, always working working to make money to pay off their debts to their family in order to escape. "Some escape," she laughed—"more like the frying pan into the fire. First Texarkana, then those crazy Mormons."

Here, I hesitate: when my mother told me these things about the drive-in, I was more than a little dismayed: always I had imagined them—witnessed them in daily life—as people who would never do anything, consciously at least, to demean anyone. And later, after Texas, and during the ten years we lived in Utah, my mother, in her very public, dramatic way, and my father, in his quiet, more private one, were radical liberals among the Mormons. So how could they behave like racists too? What might the camera see, if it were focused at another angle, that I have yet to see?

The white customers behind the Dallas car were getting restless, so my mother went to the car in the other lane and took their money, and took other customers' money. "I didn't know what would happen," she said. "It was like that first job I had, you know, the one in that Mennonite town where the kids tried to run me out of school on the first day. It was me or them—and it wasn't going to be me."

A chrome fender glinting, a headlight flickering, the sun just going down, someone swearing under his breath, looks exchanged—and then the car wheeling out of line and pulling away: then dust drifting across the lens, dust settling on the other cars in line. Mouths moving, but no way to hear what they're saying, faces grimacing—in anger? Maybe even laughter at some choice expletive? Then a pan of white faces staring out of their windshields, a pan of black faces in the back rows?

So yes, they depended on the good favor of their white customers; yes, they were under the yoke of financial and familial obligation. *It was me or them—and it wasn't going to be me.*

I see them as young marrieds, my mother standing by an old model Ford with a running board, staring into a fire built under some trees, while my father, on the other side of the fire, stares into the flames. For some reason, it seems significant that they peer into the fire together, rather than at each other.

This cookout, if that's what I'm remembering, must have occurred at the drive-in, probably behind the screen, since I still see quite clearly the creaminess of the marshmallow I've impaled on a stick, beginning to shrink up and wrinkle, its skin toasting brown, black, then finally turning molten and slithering like a live thing into the flames. So why do I recall that, but not Osie, or his wife, Mamie, who occasionally babysat my brothers and me?

In Utah, the place of their long-deferred rebellion, my mother became a high school teacher, and my father used his engineering degree to get in on the ground floor of the space race. My mother said she felt a kind of righteous rage fueling her actions. "I was goddamned if I'd be quiet any longer," she said. "The Mormon teachers in the high school nicknamed my classes 'Rosie's Remedial Religion' because we talked about things the Mormons wouldn't allow: abortion, drugs, drinking, whether or not there was a God. And all that crap about Cain being black: I had a lot to say on that one. But it took its toll, that kind of fighting—it made me a hater—it hardened me." And part of that hardening was the strain on my parents' marriage: the just man or woman isn't always easy to live with. Anger becomes a habit, as my mother knew full well. "Let's just say," she told me, "it didn't make things any easier. But your dad was kind and gentle and took up the slack."

My father, too, when he went down to Florida to Cape Canaveral to observe rocket launches, refused to eat in restaurants or stay in hotels where his fellow black engineers weren't welcome. If the restaurant owner gave them any trouble, he'd say, "If you're not going to serve him, then you won't serve me." And then they'd walk out.

But here's the rub: there have been plenty of racists in my family; and not in some distant, antebellum past, at a safe remove, but all through my growing up and adulthood. My grandfather was racist in how he treated the black nurses who so kindly nursed him during his final illness, calling them "blackbirds." My father's brother had a streak of it in him, as did my father's father. My great-aunt, an old-style liberal Democrat, nevertheless had a fierce hatred of blacks. Whenever I went to visit her, she'd tell me in language that shocked me, for a woman as genteel as she was, how much she hated the black heroin users in her Newark apartment complex. Of course, they terrorized her and robbed her, so she felt she had good reason. But as she got older, she eventually lost the ability to take people one person at a time, and this hate spread to anyone who was black.

But it's also important to tell this other part of the story about how my parents behaved in Utah, because if a story is going to matter, then something has to be revealed. Not resolved as in a plot, but revealed as in the unfolding of a life story. Plot, as Baldwin tell us in an essay on the movies, proves a point, answers the questions it proposes. But revelation means telling a story that, consciously at least, has nothing to hide. And whatever resolution comes in a story "must occur in us, with what we make of the questions with which the story leaves us."

So what does the camera reveal? My parents fell into line behind Jim Crow. Based on their actions, our family was no different from the rest of the white people in that town. But that's the problem, isn't it? To restrict people to their actions is to reduce their lives to a plot. And none of us lives life like a plot, not even a racist. All of us live out stories. We may bury these stories under landslides of plot, and lie to ourselves and others, behave cruelly and unconsciously, or cruelly and consciously, subjecting our fellow human beings to our brutal inquisitions out of the utmost refinement of our consciences in the grip of some plot that we mistake for a story. But that's not a story—stories don't resolve in themselves, they resolve in us. I can't tell you what to think of my parents, or my relatives, or me.

As my mother put it, "So we compromised, Tom. We felt we had to . . . it was all we could do to put one foot in front of the other. If we were in a tight spot for money, we had to hope that you boys would grow up OK, in spite of your having to watch John Wayne movies for a month—but he could bring the cars in, boy—the parking lot was always overflowing for John Wayne."

When I asked my mother why she thought Wayne was so popular, she said that people in Texas saw Wayne as one of their own. "He was larger than life, we were romantics back then. He represented to us that you can overcome adversity, no matter how bad. We'd come out of the Depression and the war. Wayne was like the promise that we could go back to the good times of the twenties." When I asked her if that was as true of the black customers as well as the white ones, she said, "Oh yes, I think so. Of course, I can't say for sure, but back then he made you feel more powerful, more like you were in control." And then she said, in a little slip of the tongue that revealed a more complex truth, "He was a demagogue—demigod, I mean. Well, I guess you could say he was both. Of course we knew that life wasn't like it was in the movies, but at least for the time that the movie was playing, we could forget how things really were and get lost inside the dream. That's something that goes back all the way to the Transcendentalists. You remember how Alcott in Concord wouldn't grow potatoes because they were root vegetables and he only wanted to grow inspiring vegetables? Well, it was like that. Wayne was an inspiring vegetable."

In light of my mother's understanding of Wayne's appeal, when I think of the quote from Wayne that begins this essay—*If everything isn't black and white, I say, "Why the hell not?"*—it becomes a real question, and not mere redneck bluster: Why aren't things black and white? Wouldn't it be simpler if they were? And no matter how sophisticated we fancy ourselves as moralists, wouldn't all of us like to find repose in some large-scale Certainty? After all, our desire for clarity is a genuine emotional need, even if Wayne's bellicose way of expressing it makes it mean something more like, *Everything is black and white and I know which is which.* Of course, this was back in the 1950s, and Wayne wasn't quite so controversial a figure. But by the 1980s, the macho public figure, the archconservative who supported Ronald Reagan, and whose racial views were at times deeply repellent, sparked off one of Public Enemy's most famous lyrics in "Fight the Power": "Mother fuck . . . John Wayne." And as James Baldwin says of Wayne's oversimplified sense of reality, "A black man who sees the world the way John Wayne, for example, sees it would not be an eccentric patriot, but a raving maniac."

Of course, there's a difference between John Wayne's views and John Wayne the actor. But whatever scars my mother was afraid of inflicting on us, whatever backward or unjust attitudes I'd pick up from the movies, wouldn't compare with what daily life in Texas had to offer. Still, I can't resist telling what she said were the worst, the absolute worst, movies we ever showed. "Anything Ronald Reagan was in," she said. "Nobody came if the movie had Ronald Reagan. Bad actor, worse president . . . But I wonder what you must think of your pusillanimous parents?"

I am eight, maybe nine years old, when I first see *To Kill a Mockingbird*—just a year or two older than Scout, the little girl who tells the story. The scene that most clearly stands out in my mind is the moment before the jury delivers the verdict. I can see before me on the screen the courtroom, and in the center of the courtroom, the tall figure of Tom Robinson, the black laborer accused of raping a white woman, facing into the camera, so that his body and face are surrounded by a field of white faces. Their eyes drill into his back, but into my eyes in the audience.

I also remember the black faces up in the gallery, where Scout is sitting. They stare down into my face from an angle high above my level in the audience. The camera angle (talk of camera angles would have been beyond me as a child, though I still remember with complete visceral recall the effect of those angles) exaggerates both the height of the gallery, and the absolute separateness and distance between white and black. (At the church where my mother played the organ, signs pointed white worshippers to the downstairs pews, black worshippers to the ones in the balcony.) And then the camera narrows in on Tom and Atticus, the genteel, gentle, humane Southern lawyer, played by a genteel, gentle, humane Gregory Peck—I mention this because Peck's persona on screen reminded me very strongly of my own father.

Tom was more of a stretch for me, though I also connected with him because we shared the same name . . . that, and the fact that, when he was on the stand, telling his side of the story, he began to cry—or at least struggled to keep tears back. I was shocked that a grown man, and a powerfully built one, would break down that way. More than anything I didn't want to be a crybaby, even though I often did cry . . . and here a grown man was almost bawling. But that also served as a bridge between the Tom up on the screen and the Tom in his seat.

No, this wasn't at the drive-in—we'd sold it a year or so before because of the advent of television—but my parents took me to the movies almost every weekend. We now lived in a tiny town in the Rocky Mountains, but I still had the flat, taffy-stretched vowels of a Texarkanan accent. And as Tom told his story about a white woman asking him to come into the house, and then throwing herself at him, his speech felt deeply familiar to me, even as the story he told made me feel a little squeamish: anything to do with sex would have in those days.

Oddly, I don't remember thinking anything, or anything much, about the fact that he was black. So in a way, I'd missed the entire import of the movie. But what did register was that the white girl was lying about Tom. And I could see right away that Tom was telling the truth. But since I lied too to get out of punishments that I'd happily have visited on my brothers, I wasn't so different from the white girl. I felt sorry for her—there was so much torment in her face, and such rage and shame when she accused Tom of raping her. But I didn't know what to do with any of these feelings, except to get lost in the tension of what the verdict would be. Both Tom and Atticus were tall, quiet men, and as they stood for the verdict, I watched the black faces above looking down on them, the white faces staring up from below.

When the foreman of the jury said, "Guilty," I was bewildered—who was guilty? Tom or the white girl? Or was it her father, Bob

Ewell—his name was Robert E. Lee Ewell, and I'd just read a book about Lee, a heroizing book that made almost no mention of slavery, but focused on Lee's personal qualities as a leader. I was amazed that such an obviously evil character as Bob Ewell could be named after the virtuous Lee. And not only that, but this Robert E. Lee Ewell was going to triumph over an obviously good character like Tom—like Tom and Atticus both. It just made no sense.

As for the girl, well, girls were largely unaccountable in my moral universe, partly because we were a family of boys, and partly because I was way too shy to speak to any of them in school—except when we were forced to square-dance with them in assembly hall. But I remember seeing a girl crying at a school dance, a girl named Jenny Fish whose father wouldn't let her dance with anyone but him. Behind her thick glasses fastened to a chain around her neck, tears ran down her cheeks, and she seemed in the grip of some dreadful shame. But up on screen, I felt a seamless connection to Scout: she was a girl I could comprehend because she fought like a boy, ran around like a boy, hated wearing dresses, and even asked to be rolled down the street in a tire, revolving round and round until the tire, gaining speed, collided with the wooden steps of Boo Radley's house, the crazy young man who'd stabbed his father, and never came out of the house, ever. All that made sense: Scout, Tom, Atticus.

But Ewell and his daughter felt inexplicable. In the movie, Atticus proved that Tom, because of his arm crippled by a cotton gin, couldn't possibly have beaten up Ewell's daughter, let alone left bruises around both sides of her throat by choking her with both hands: how could he choke her like that if he only had one hand?—and if I could see that at my age, then the grown men of the jury surely could understand it. And yet Tom was guilty. But guilty of what? That's when it dawned on me that he was guilty of being black. I didn't pick up at all on the innuendo, much subtler in the film than in the book, which makes it explicit, that the real violator was Ewell—that he'd beat up his own daughter, and possibly raped her. Nor did it occur to me that the girl was trying to shove off her shame and fear of her father onto Tom. But maybe my instinctive revulsion for Jenny Fish's creepy father made Bob Ewell more comprehensible as a character than my bewilderment in the movie theater suggests.

However that may be, Ewell's daughter's disgrace became Tom's disgrace became the father's triumph: a morally perverse Möbius strip. So no matter how strong a case Atticus builds, the larger framework of Jim Crow renders that evidence irrelevant. So when Tom Robinson is taken into custody by the sheriff after he's been pronounced guilty, it's no wonder that the look of despair and anger in his eyes shows just a hint of contempt for Atticus's naïveté. This is the only moment in the entire film when Tom Robinson has a moment of his own that isn't mediated in some way by Atticus: either by asking him questions when Tom is on the stand, or by visiting his family during the trial. But never once do we see Atticus on film talking to Tom's wife. Or children. Or any other black character, with the exception of his black housekeeper, Calpurnia, who could be viewed as nothing but an updated, far more dignified version of Butterfly McQueen's Prissy in *Gone with the Wind*. It's as if the segregation the movie so publicly deplores is still working behind the scenes to keep the black characters mute, little more than ciphers for white pity. And while the movie is far more ambiguous, and far less limited as a work of art than the book—still, what the camera sees is what Scout sees.

The book, in that sense, is deeply problematic. Flannery O'Connor— who refused to meet James Baldwin in her hometown, though she would be willing to meet him in New York, wrote to a friend, "Might as well expect a mule to fly as me to see James Baldwin in Georgia"— called it "a children's book." O'Connor's unwillingness to go beyond "the traditions of the society I feed on" says something as well about the limited angles that the filmmakers let the camera see. So when, in the movie, Atticus tells Tom that they'll appeal, that they must expect to lose in this courtroom but that the outcome will be different in another courtroom, Tom's anger shatters the frame of the movie, and, for one brief moment, he emerges as an independent character.

In fact, the only adequate response to the verdict would be for Atticus to join a revolution like the one in *Battleship Potemkin*, and help the mutineers turn their guns onto the tsarist ministries and blow them to pieces. The only way Tom Robinson will get justice is if the Maycomb courthouse is blown to kingdom come. And even though Atticus is the best shot in town, and proves it by shooting a mad dog, he's no revolutionary. It's as if the movie's remorseless logic wants to reduce Atticus to the liberal aspect of Jim Crow—the just man that Jim Crow relies on to go through the motions of a fair trial, even though a "guilty" verdict is a foregone conclusion.

Given that Tom's fate is sealed, it's revealing that the piece of evidence that affects the jury most is Robinson's testimony that he felt sorry for the white girl, that she must have been lonely. Up until this moment, it seems as if Atticus still has a fighting chance. But you can see on the prosecutor's face a look of hate, as well as triumph: what Tom has just confessed to is a terrible crime—as bad as, if not worse than, rape: a black man who is so uppity as to feel sorry for a white woman! Oddly enough—or maybe not so oddly—this made complete sense to me at the time: of course the white people hate that: doesn't Tom know that he's the weak one, and that the white people are the strong ones? If your mother or father or older brother yells at you to do this or that, what can be more infuriating than to feel sorry for them for their outburst—and then have the temerity to tell them so?

And the way the prosecutor calls Tom "boy," the vindictiveness and pettiness of his behavior after Tom expresses his pity for the white woman, shows that the deepest wound in the white male psyche as it's portrayed in the film is to have to admit that the womenfolk are unsatisfied, lonely to be kissed—that in fact their menfolk are nothing but carbon copies of Robert E. Lee Ewell—overgrown, brutal children, inadequate as lovers and husbands. When Atticus insists that Tom Robinson was subjected to Ewell's daughter's attentions against his will, that he is a decent, hardworking man who should not be on trial for showing kindness, or held responsible for Ewell's daughter breaking white-enforced taboos, he goes much further than the jury—or even the movie—is prepared to go. Even with his one crippled arm, Robinson still poses a serious threat to white male superiority. He has more moral and spiritual integrity in him than any white man can stand to contemplate.

So of course he's shot down trying to escape, running away, as the sheriff states, "like a madman." But if I'd been in Tom Robinson's shoes, I would have run too—unless, of course, he was simply pushed out of the car taking him to another jail, and shot down in cold blood. So I was shocked but not surprised by his murder. I wouldn't have known at the time the exact logic that required it, but it's clear enough to me now—from the lynch mob early in the film that Atticus and Scout had stood up to, to Tom's quiet dignity in the courtroom in comparison to Ewell's ignorance and meanness, to the moment on the stand in which Tom lets slip that he felt sorry for Ewell's daughter. And yet Atticus presents such a strong case, and with such passionate conviction, that Jim Crow can't afford to take chances: and so Tom Robinson is shot down to avoid a second trial. The irony, of course, is that what would really make Tom a madman would be for him to place any hope in Atticus's woefully idealized version of justice—admirable, courageous, generous, and even noble, as Atticus is.

And yet for all its shortcomings, I greatly prefer a movie like *To Kill a Mockingbird* to a repetition compulsion of a movie like Quentin Tarantino's *Django Unchained*. When I saw it, I felt nothing except adolescent anarchy trying to get a rise out of me, even as I admired the sophistication of the movie's often hilarious, hipper-than-thou, wised-up savviness in manipulating the audience to accept, even revel in, being splattered by boatloads of movie blood. Race and slavery were only the excuse—not a lame, but an expertly deployed, excuse, given Tarantino's technical expertise—but an excuse nonetheless. Furthermore, the movie turns the legacy of slavery into an absurdist trope, something we've all seen through or gotten beyond.

Whereas *To Kill a Mockingbird* embodies what I think art should do, no matter how badly it falls short—in Atticus and Scout, and to some extent, Tom Robinson, I feel the full range of our faculties being engaged—the movie doesn't just moralize, or reflect, or imagine; it's not some single faculty "moving and fanning the air," to quote Robert Lowell. It attempts to show not just some cartoonish sliver, but the whole human being in action. And in that action it reveals the ugly, even the tragic nature of trying to act decently inside a system that won't allow it.

But I'm not just talking about movies. I'm talking about what I realized as a child in the humiliation and murder of Tom Robinson. I'm talking about the injustice that occurred in rows ten and eleven at the drive-in, and how that injustice is never far removed from my fundamental sense of what we ought to strive to look at in art and life—no matter how painful or irreparably harmful the damage may be. It's one of the deep motives behind this entire book. Of course, when a friend said to me, "Tom, why go halfway around the world to see injustice, when all you need to do is go to Scranton," I immediately took his point. But even if many of these essays deal with events happening elsewhere, I think that those events have everything to do with how Americans conceive of their freedoms and responsibilities to one another here at home.

But again, I hesitate: the image of my parents humiliating their black customers can't be wiped away by good intentions or stirring statements. So I want to return to my mother's question: just what do I think of my pusillanimous parents? Or is that question simply "plot," my trying to manage, and answer for you, what only you, the listener to this story, can manage, and answer? But if I'm going to write beyond plot, that's a risk I don't see how I can avoid.

Now, what the camera sees is a blank: it doesn't see them appealing to the sheriff for protection against their three visitors. You don't see them sitting down to write an editorial to the local paper, full of "high and mighty bombast," as my mother put it. They don't stand on Main Street, passing out leaflets, or make stirring speeches in people's doorways about racial equality and universal brotherhood. They have nothing to say, pro or con, about "the traditions of the society" they "feed on."

Meanwhile, up on the big screen, their customers watch the courageous sheriffs and cowboy loners, those gunslinging heroes who stand up, night after night, for the Right. In order for my parents to assume those heroic proportions, as wide as the sky, they would have to be revolutionaries—the way, a decade later, the Black Panthers were revolutionaries, or the members of the Weather Underground, or the Symbionese Liberation Army. For the sake of revolution, my parents would have to be in earnest that Good meant killing people "who needed killing," as John Wayne, playing Sheriff Rooster Cogburn in *True Grit*, so succinctly put it—but with perhaps a touch of self-mockery?

My mother tells the story that after a few years in Texas, she joined a singing group called the Euterpean Music Club—named after Euterpe, the Greek goddess of music—and she and the other women would get together to sing the lyrics to musicals such as *Oklahoma!* And when they weren't doing Rodgers and Hammerstein, they sang some classical—Handel's *Messiah*.

One day when they were practicing, the Queen of England's coronation was broadcast on TV—one of the first TVs in town, and the harbinger of the end for not only the drive-in but also much else: Jim Crow could not stand the light of day—the murders of Chaney, Goodman, and Schwerner, black schoolchildren being roughed up and screamed at, Bull Connor letting loose his police dogs on demonstrators—the little cathode ray that lit up, with a soft blue light, the windows of dark houses, helped to overcome the dreadful isolation in that little town that my mother said was one of the worst deprivations of her life—and showed Jim Crow in an increasingly unflattering light. Not that the racist underpinnings of Jim Crow are over with—in fact, many would say that Jim Crow is alive and well, only his clothes are a little more subdued. Or are they? Trayvon Martin, Freddie Gray, Eric Garner, Michael Brown Jr., the Charleston church shooting—the list goes on and on. But at least the white-sheeted version of Jim Crow was revealed, not in the romance of a burning torch, but in the harsh focus of a camera's spotlight.

My mother said that if it weren't for her loneliness, she would probably not have joined this particular group of women: they were all well off, certainly a large step up from her hardscrabble life at the drive-in where she and my father never took a day off, ever. Not only was there a black–white divide, there was a class divide: rich white, middle-class white, working-class white, poor white: and then white-trash white—an ambiguous denomination for whites like Robert E. Lee Ewell. Okies, hillbillies, rednecks were made so by their lack of education, whereas Bob Ewell, no matter his noble-sounding namesake, was seen as lazy, shiftless, morally degraded.

Except for my mother, the other Euterpeans were fairly well off and could afford to employ black women as full-time maids and domestics. My mother said that the Euterpean who hosted the club that day treated this woman who worked for her—well, certainly not in the way that Atticus treated his housekeeper, Calpurnia, as an equal treats equals who, in fact, aren't equals, but out of sufferance and daily necessity pretend they are—that her hostess tended to treat this black woman as a person of no culture, with an unconscious condescension that was hard for my mother to bear. And so when the hostess called in her housekeeper to see the queen, the housekeeper said something that the other white women seized on, and mocked her for, laughing mercilessly at the woman's expense, their unthinking mocking laughter horrifying my mother at their cruelty.

"And what did you do?" I asked.

"Nothing," she said. "I did nothing. I tried to speak with her, but she left the room, confused, not knowing what she'd said that everyone had thought was so funny. The worst thing about it was that the women were unconscious: they seemed not to know that they were being cruel."

"So, Ma, come on, tell me, just what did she say?"

"Well," said my mother, "when the woman who was her employer called her in, she said to her, 'Look, look, there's the queen.' And the woman looked at the TV for a little while, and said—it was just awful the way they laughed at her—the woman said, 'I see the queen. But where's the football?'"

As Baldwin cautions us, the camera lies because it sees only what you point it at. And while I have no reason to doubt my mother's account of the queen's coronation, the camera, quite clearly, was pointed at the Euterpeans, at my mother, and me through my mother—but only tangentially at the housekeeper. So let's pull the camera back and see what else there is to see.

What none of the women could have known is that the coronation of the then young Queen Elizabeth, which occurred in 1953, was filmed not only in full color, but in 3-D. But because the American women were watching a one-dimensional, black-and-white TV set, they couldn't see full color, or 3-D; all they could see on a black-and-white set was one dimension in black and white.

Now let's suppose that a color, 3-D camera from 2017, over sixty years after this incident in which my mother felt shame in this woman's humiliation, focuses back down the years on this particular woman's face. How do we know, how do I know, that she doesn't know perfectly well the difference between homecoming queens and the House of Windsor? So let's give her a history and a name that she alone knows, and let's study the film more closely: is that a touch of subtle mockery in her face? By talking of queens, by talking of football, is she in fact mocking these white women? Their supposed superiority? Their Euterpean airs?

But of course I'll never know, in 2017, what she was feeling in 1953.

The camera sees only what you want it to see—unless it slips—or you let it slip—and then you might see something different, something outside the frame, something more.

Momma's Boy

I feel as if I've always worked. In our household we were three boys, and we did all the chores: laundry, dishes, housecleaning, yard work. When we moved from a small town in Texas to a smaller town in Utah, we had to rake up rocks in the backyard in order to prepare the ground for planting grass. We put in rose beds, spent endless hours pulling weeds, cutting out dandelions with a knife, and watering cherry trees. And when the cherries bore fruit, we picked the cherries and helped my mother can them and make jam. I'll never forget the smell of melting paraffin. We'd pour the hot liquid wax into the top of the jars to seal them off, and then screw on the lids. Once, the wax spilled on my hand and gave me a dome-shaped blister that I longed to lance with a sharpened pencil. Somehow, I resisted the impulse, and the wound healed. And I have other scars from those days: one above my forehead from the blade of my twin brother's shovel; and a little pit of scar tissue at the base of my palm where I managed to jab myself with a nail when I was building a rabbit hutch—a woeful, rickety, odd-angled disaster of chicken wire and plywood. The hutch's frame was like looking at yourself in a funhouse mirror and was as shoddy as could be—a kind of rabbit gulag where Clarence, our completely uncuddly, not to say thuggish, rabbit crouched in sullen wariness, malignantly eyeing the world through the wire. If you tried to pick him up to pet him, he'd claw at your arms with his hind legs and leave you scraped and bleeding. We'd let him out to run from time to time, and the only way we could capture him and not get scratched was to net him in a butterfly net—no wonder he hated us. Still, there was tacit thanksgiving all round when he escaped! I'm sure Clarence must have left his mark on my hands among the other almost invisible nicks and scars—reminders of mishandled hammers, screwdrivers, pruning shears, knives, and saws. And yet I loved tools, the feel of the handle grips, the galvanized brightness of the various blades.

There was no lazing about in our house during the summer break from school: you either went to summer school or got a job—and you were encouraged to do both. I learned how to type in summer school—the clatter of forty typewriters punctuated by pings when it was time to sling back the carriage was like listening to the obsessive, broken talk of a room full of mentally disturbed people during visiting hours. I'm not being "inventive" with this detail: it was a part of my growing up. I remember going with my father and two brothers to the asylum one bright Sunday in midsummer, and waving at my mother standing in front of the hospital's glass door. She stared blankly in front of her, without the slightest look of recognition on her face. We held badminton rackets, and were knocking a plastic birdie around on the asylum lawn sometime after lunch. We'd been told by some other kids that they didn't allow nets, because the patients might steal them and use them to escape or even try to hang themselves. Playing badminton without a net—it's always seemed weirdly right, an emblem of what my mother was going through. In the same way, I guess my typing class gave me an image of her mind clattering away, the pinging like the shocks being administered to her poor brain. Many years later, she told me how these treatments were done communally—that is, you weren't in a room by yourself, but in a large hall with other patients on gurneys who were all undergoing shock at the same time—quivering, jerking, biting down on a stick? At least that's how I imagined it. She told me that they put some kind of gel on your temples to make your skull a better conductor of

electricity. The shocks, which were supposed to render you highly sug-
gestible, left a blank space in your head for the doctors' suggestions to
fill. Anyway, that's the theory as she explained it. "Once the shock
hit you," said my mother, "you went out, as if you'd been knocked
unconscious. But as I was lying there, waiting, the woman next to
me, who'd already been zapped and knocked out, was being told
over and over, in a mild, reasonable voice, 'Now, Rose, don't go to the
barn and try to hang yourself. Don't go to the barn and try to hang
yourself. Rose, don't go to the barn.' The odd thing, Tom, is that we
had the same first name." My dear, brilliant, vivid, volatile, passion-
ately changeable mother—her voice when she got angry wasn't shrill
or hysterical or any of the other clichés that women get stuck with.
My older brother put it best in a letter he sent me years later: "her
voice-weapon" was what he called it.

A few years after her hospitalization, when I was fourteen, we
moved to Del Mar in Southern California—in those days, a low-key
beach town on either side of Highway 101. My mother had found a job
in the local high school, after having taught school for ten years in a
bitterly contentious and conservative district in a tiny Mormon town.
My mother had conducted a one-woman renaissance, in that she encouraged her students to question any form of doctrine—including
Mormon doctrine. There were far worse battles, of course: the church
was anti-homosexual, anti-drugs and alcohol, anti-premarital sex.
And in spiritual and intellectual matters, Mormonism was just plain
anti-complexity. She told me how one boy came to her about his
homosexuality (*gay* wasn't a term that had reached Utah in those
days), and told her he was going to kill himself because he felt evil.
And despite her efforts to convince him otherwise, he did try to kill
himself when he went on his Mission a year or so later.

It was death by a thousand cuts—and year after year, it began to
take a heavy toll on her. But in that decade-long struggle, she gave
no quarter. "When the school district came after me," she said, "for
teaching *Lord Jim*—*Lord Jim*, for God's sake, it wasn't even *Lady
Chatterley's Lover*—I wasn't going to lie down." But Utah is where the
cracks in my mother's psyche began to appear. Her deep and abiding

hatred of the church pointed to a deep and abiding wound in her own mind. And how could that wound not be felt by her family?

So it was a huge relief to all of us to escape that town in which, from a selfish point of view, I could see my social fate was going to be relegated to the "uncool kids," partly because I wasn't Mormon. To be released into Southern Cal was almost paradisal: this was the mid-1960s, and there were still no freeways, malls, or suburban sprawl. There were the coastal hills backing the low cliffs above the beach where much of the town was built, and there were the stables and the grandstands of the famous racetrack in Del Mar. After the horses worked out, the trainers and grooms rode them down to the beach through an underpass beneath 101. The horses loved to swim, and roll on their backs in the sand. After a workout, the cold seawater was good for the overheated tendons in their fetlocks: you could watch them canter and even gallop down the beach all the way to the next town, Solana Beach.

Of course, as soon as we arrived, my mother started bugging me to get a job. I suppose this is because she grew up dirt poor—and when I say dirt poor, I mean dirt poor: she'd grown up in Tribune, Kansas, as a dry-land wheat farmer's daughter during the Dust Bowl. The first house they lived in had a dirt floor, which they'd made smooth and hard by pouring water on it, then stamping it down, repeating that process over and over, until it became dense as concrete. Then they put gunny sacks down as a kind of wall-to-wall carpet. As a family of four, they lived on half a dollar a week. Later, when they were a tiny bit more prosperous, and could afford wooden slats for a floor, one night the half dollar slipped through a crack in one of the slats, and her father had to crowbar them up in order for them not to starve. He was something of a binge drinker, and could fly into rages, once going so far as to yank the tablecloth off the table— along with the Thanksgiving Day feast—so that everything, dishes, gravy, water pitcher, turkey, all of it flew up to the ceiling before smashing down onto the floor. But he could also be immensely affectionate when he was sober, and when he saw how passionate she was about playing piano (my mother learned to play by practicing on the church piano after school) he somehow managed to buy her one—trading his labor for money he didn't have. So always she had worked to supplement the family income, starting when she was eight as a housekeeper at other women's houses, and when she was older, driving a tractor in the fields.

When she went away to college at KU—the first person, boy or girl, ever to go past high school in Greeley County—she put herself through college by playing in a dance band she christened Rosie and Her Four Thorns: "The club we played in," she told me, "was aptly named: the Bloody Bucket. The boys would get out of hand from time to time, and so to discourage their attentions, I took to wearing a bowler hat, and pretending to smoke a cigar. But I liked the taste of them after a while, so it worked out pretty well—the boys stayed away, and I got to smoke." Nothing if not flamboyant, she had a flair for self-dramatization. Despite her illness—or maybe because of it— when she was feeling well, or well enough, she loved being thought of as a "character"—and I'll never forget how excited she was when, years later in Texas, instead of being assigned to play one of the female roles, she performed Curly in drag in *Oklahoma!*—jangling spurs, black boots, red bandanna, stetson, right down to a sequined cowboy vest that must have given some members of the audience a little gender-bending start.

Given how poor she was, her insistence that I get a job seems inevitable. Of course, I dreamed of becoming a groom at the racetrack, but you had to know somebody, and anyway, it was much easier finding work as a gardener: jacaranda, ice plant, agave, bougainvillea, manzanita, honeysuckle, acacia and eucalyptus trees, palm trees, umbrella and Torrey pines, and the usual gardener's domestics grew everywhere. I started working for a swimming pool company that also did landscaping. I'd later learn how to spray gunite over steel pool ribs, carry a hod, operate a jackhammer (a miserable, nerve-destroying job), and put in PVC sprinkling lines (though I was hopeless at adjusting the electric timers). From time to time, I'd drive down with my boss into some back canyon, wrestle a log into the back of the pickup, spray it with insecticide, shellac it, and then plop it down poolside for that "natural look" that was just coming into fashion: we charged outrageous sums of money for these special touches, but the clients, mainly wealthy La Jolla businessmen, loved them.

In many ways, the job was a blessing. I was an edgy sixteen-year-old, and it got me out of the house, out of my burgeoning drug use, which was soon to include heroin, and away from that unacknowledged, clattering pinging that grew louder in our house about this time: it didn't require hospitalization, but it was always there in a tone of voice or look or sudden mood swing. And of course it wasn't the only reason why I resolved to run away from home: all my life I've had an incurable romance with experience. And long before I took up journalism, I believed in testing myself: drugs were a way of doing that, a way of stretching who you thought you were. I believed with Keats, before I'd ever read Keats, that if we're really going to know the world, we have to prove "it on our pulses." I've never understood the attraction of the virtual, though I'm as mired in it as anyone else. I'm certain that was one reason why I took drugs: everything was intensified, the voltage coursing through me freeing me for an ecstatic but sometimes scary journey round the insides of my own brain. But at the best moments, I completely forgot myself. What Keats called negative capability—"when man is capable of being in uncertainties, Mysteries, doubts, without any irritable reaching after fact and reason"—was brought home to me by my ability to become waves breaking in front of me, or the whirling blades of a windmill, or the blurring and clarifying of a changing stoplight, red, yellow, green, the colors amplifying and flowing through each other. Keats described the "poetical character" as having

> no self—it is every thing and nothing—It has no character—it enjoys light and shade; it lives in gusto, be it foul or fair, high or low, rich or poor, mean or elevated.—It has as much delight in conceiving an Iago as an Imogen. What shocks the virtuous philosopher, delights the camelion poet. . . . A Poet is the most unpoetical of anything in existence; because he has no Identity—he is continually in for—and filling some other Body.

And you might say that that ability to connect with all forms of primary experience has been the best training I could have for the kind of journalism I aspire to. The politics of negative capability is to immerse yourself as fully as you can in what you're observing, to take it in in all its sensory immediacy. Only afterward comes judgment, even if that judgment occurs a split second after the immersion.

But all that was years in the future. And in the meantime, my drug use—which would eventually bottom out in appalling behavior, like swiping stuff from my friends' parents' medicine chests—was a continually unfolding revelation. Heroin and I were still in our honeymoon phase.

All right, not exactly a honeymoon—my mother and father had taken to searching my clothes for drugs, and one morning, my father and I ended up in the bathroom wrestling over a fix that he'd found in my jeans pocket. I'd been taking a shower, and the room was filled with steam drifting, so that as we grappled, and I rose up above my body, watching it all happen, the fight seems to take place in slo-mo, me grabbing at my father's hand as with his shoulder he pushes me away, flushing my fix down the toilet while shouting, *This is hard drugs!* to which I shout lamely back, as if the *Boy Scout Handbook* were in effect, *You shouldn't steal stuff from my pockets!*—and as the Baggie swirls down the drain, and I stand there horrified at the waste, calculating how many hours I'll have to work to buy back what I've lost, he reaches out to touch me gently on my arm, as if his touch could fix what is unfixable.

But in 1969, during the summer that climaxed in Woodstock, when I finally made up my mind to leave, I saw my running away as more of a romantic gesture than a desperate one. I couldn't face the facts of what my life was becoming, nor did I see how selfishly oblivious I was to my mother's suffering. But I also must have known, in a way that I had no words for, that my rebellious streak came directly from my iconoclastic mother. Didn't she take risks? So why shouldn't I? Of course it was more muddled than that—the adventure in my head that starred me smoking dope, me dropping acid, me shooting up, often had little to do with what I was actually feeling.

This disconnect extended to my love life, if you could call it that: I'd had a girlfriend, sort of, who, as soon as I left, would take up with my older brother. I think I knew that that was going to happen, no matter if I stayed or ran away. I remember dropping acid with her and an older friend of my brother's, and I got the creepy feeling that if I'd turned my back for even a second that they'd have ended up in bed together—not that I could blame her! He was a good-looking, beautifully muscled young man, a surfer who worked construction and was going to San Diego State. Anyway, when I finally came back home, I was shocked but not surprised when my older brother sat me down and told me, in the parlance of the day, that he was balling Robin. Well, useful to get that learnt! I was hurt, of course, but in a way relieved. At least I knew the score, and rather than being angry with my brother or her, I pretty much shrugged it off: in the time I'd been away, I'd toughened up a lot.

All this would be easy to dismiss as mere adolescent confusion, and I suppose a lot of it was. But maybe the oddest thing about my behavior was this constant tale I kept telling myself about myself, in which I needed to cast myself as a rebel, an adventurer who'd do anything once. Of course the role I created for myself was only part of a larger generational story that included assassinations, race riots, Patty Hearst, Huey Newton and Bobby Seale, Vietnam, my upcoming physical for the draft. And then there was the sexual revolution that Robin and my brother seemed a part of, but whose liberating influences never seemed to reach me. In the end, I have to admit that I was pretty unconscious of my own motives for making such a break with my family. The film running in my head told me that I was just another free spirit. In fact, all the cultural chatter of risk and adventure—which paradoxically I loved, and believed in, and to a great extent still believe in—kept me from having to look at some of the knottier reasons for my leaving. But however short-lived or delusory, the spirit of optimism that was abroad at that moment in 1969 helped me shut the door on our tract house in a new subdivision a little north of San Diego, and enter into a life where I learned no end of things, both pleasant and unpleasant, about myself and others.

Unlike the exodus of California runaways who had started hitch-hiking across country in anticipation of Woodstock, I was on my way to join up with its polar opposite—a paramilitary organization called Quest International. What a strange bunch we turned out to be! I sometimes think we were Woodstock turned inside out, the dark B-side to that weeklong party-hearty saturnalia. Sure, we had long hair, and were interested in sex drugs and rock 'n' roll. But whatever ethos we shared wasn't the peace-and-love kind, but more the military kind, the displaced Vietnam vet kind, the kind whose so-called brotherhood was due to military discipline, not the amativeness of communes. Out of work, out of money, no family to fall back on or, like me, in flight from family, at bottom most of us were misfits, romantics, drifters, hustlers without a hustle. In addition to ex-military, we were petty thieves, bikers, jacks-of-all-trades moving from job to job, even a guy who claimed to be a rodeo clown. My only distinction, if you can call it that, was that I was the youngest, the least experienced.

But once I'd decided that home life was intolerable, I began looking for opportunities—and to my vast surprise, the help-wanted section of the *San Diego Union* ran an ad that read something like:

Wanted: Quest International is looking for unattached single people to serve as crew for salvage operations in the Caribbean. We will train you to dive for sunken treasure. Room and board included.

The address for the interview turned out to be a sleazy motel in El Cajon. I knocked on the door and was welcomed by a man with long hair and a beard, and a young woman named Shelley dressed in jeans and a halter top. Neither looked all that savory—the man was a natural salesman, with just the right touch of steel in his manner, as if I were a younger brother who needed considerable wising up. He could spot a rube like me a mile away. He called himself something theatrically piratical, like Rogue. (It wasn't Rogue, for Rogue was the name of the officer who ran the base I ended up at, in a sleepy coastal town called Summerland, just outside Santa Barbara. Our other base was in Lemon Grove in east San Diego County.) But it was something like that, a sort of *Pirates of the Caribbean* moniker: so let's call him Long John, though Johnny Depp's kitschy, you-know-that-I-know-that-you-know-that-I-know self-consciousness couldn't have been further from his edge of smooth-talking menace.

As to Shelley, I would later learn that she was a perquisite restricted to officers. Not that she was a prostitute—she and Long John could have been childhood sweethearts, for all I knew—but only officers were allowed to fraternize with women. For, as Long John explained to me, Quest was organized into ranks, like the navy. Certain privileges went with certain ranks. Shelley didn't smile or talk, but simply sat there with a faintly amused look on her face, as if to say, *My God, is this kid green* . . . And I was green, shy around girls my age, self-conscious to the point of being tongue-tied, if not mute. And as to women like Shelley—older, knowing, with a kind of wary watchfulness that I found intimidating but exciting—my mind simply shut down. Nor did I look at skin magazines, even when my older brother thrust them on me as a kind of joke. It amused him to see how shy I was. But there was nothing mean in how he did it, and probably in his mind he was only trying to help me get past my inhibitions. But I found the pictures too provoking. In fact, they frightened me a little. But as I sat there trying not to look at Shelley, most likely she wasn't thinking of me at all—except maybe to notice my acne. She must have witnessed hundreds of these same interviews, and hippie types like me, at least until you'd proved yourself, were pretty much interchangeable.

Long John told me that Quest's leader was a man named Captain Nashe, and we were called "Captain Nashe's pirates." (I never actually met the Captain, who was away, wheeling and dealing, the entire time I was a pirate.) As the ad stated, our dream, our goal, our delusion—it partook of all three—was to go salvage diving in the Caribbean and look for sunken treasure. To pay for this adventure, Long John told me, we fixed up old cars, trucks, buses—any piece of junk you could buy dirt cheap at auction—and then sold them in the hope of amassing enough cash to buy a salvage vessel.

Long John also told me that pirates were expected to work hard, and adhere strictly to the disciplinary code. In return, we got our board, and lived in what Long John said were "very comfortable barracks"—that is, if you think of comfort as living in a rusty old school bus fitted out with metal bunks. Of course you were free to leave at any time—"run the road," as he put it—and many of the recruits in my group did after the first two or three days. There was a man named Vern, big, well muscled, ex-navy, who ran afoul of one of the officers, a petty thief named Joe who had a Jekyll–Hyde personality. He was usually jovial, even easygoing—but if you ran afoul of him, he could be overcome with homicidal rage. Not the loud shouting profane kind, but a rage so quiet it was like that time I heard a pin drop in the Mormon Tabernacle in Salt Lake City: at first you heard nothing, but then echoes began reverberating and literally filled the hall. You didn't want to be anywhere near Joe when that happened.

A few days into my trial, I remember Vern standing at the edge of the yard littered with old engine parts and random stacks of tires, his sea bag in front of him, his arms folded so you could see his bicep tattooed with an anchor wrapped in a chain. The anchor rippled when his muscle rippled, giving it the look of a set anchor glimpsed through the rolling swell. I don't know why he and Joe were so pissed off with each other, but Vern, who'd decided to run the road, was taunting Joe—nothing too inventive, just the traditional string of epithets: if Joe wasn't such a goddamned little pussy, mother-effing this, mother-effing that—you get the picture.

If Vern had had the sense to leave it at trash talk, he might have got away with his insults. Joe just stood there, his face expressionless, staring at Vern across the yard. But in his eyes, you could see a quiet rage building. Vern must have thought Joe was too scared to fight, so he dared Joe to step off the effing property and fight it out. Vern's fists matched his biceps, but Joe's restraint wasn't fear—he was an officer, after all, and there was a code of discipline he had to adhere to as much as the rest of us. But then Joe's eyes seemed to cross, and he flipped—he ran upstairs to the fo'c'sle (the attic of Captain Nashe's house, where he and the other officers slept), grabbed his shotgun out of the gun rack, and came back down to the yard. Vern had shut up by now, while the rest of us stood there, silent, cowed—but also eager to see what Joe would do. Joe aimed at Vern, who stood there, stupefied—and then the hollow blast of Joe's gun exploded. We all jerked back into ourselves, like turtles jerking back into their shells. A huge hole blossomed in Vern's sea bag and blew his clothes into the street. I'm sure we all felt relieved that Joe had chosen to aim low . . . but didn't we also experience just the thinnest edge of disappointment? Heartless as it no doubt is, it's not every day you get to witness a murder.

Any sensible person would have run the road right then, but I was more than a little thrilled: this was real life, this was what I'd come for, this was what my romance with experience had long promised me. I can't be too hard on my naïveté, since that teenage self seemed to know what he was doing in a way that I've come to admire, and to a certain extent emulate as a journalist. But even so, I'm a little astonished at how he managed to come through such experiences with all his body parts intact. But Vern, who now knew Joe meant business, hoisted what was left of his bag over one shoulder, and ran down the street while Joe stared at him, his long hair hanging to his shoulders, his lips curled in a little smile.

But all that was a few days off. Right now, I was trying not to look at Shelley, or at the mussed bedcovers she was lying on, or at the glass-faced diving helmet on the table. The first month, Long John explained to me, you were on probation, restricted to base until you proved your trustworthiness. After that you could apply to the officer in charge for leave in the evenings once you finished work. Surfer boy though I was (I was never all that good, too tall and uncoordinated to really adjust to the hotdogging short boards that were at that moment coming into fashion), and a fledgling druggie, I was also a bookish kid. I loved Robert Louis Stevenson and had seen the movie of *Treasure Island* several times. As I listened to Long John's spiel, maybe I could be like Jim Hawkins: this would be my trial by fire, fitting for an organization called Quest.

What I didn't know at the time was that if you screwed up, mislaid a tool, say, or worse, managed to break it—then you got demerits that you worked off by the hour. Of course, demerits were inevitable for someone like me, who up to then had done mainly unskilled labor, picking fruit in orchards, or gardening and landscaping jobs. In a way, my inexperience was my best piece of luck—it kept me from rethinking the whole nutty enterprise. Long John, who must have noticed my eyes wandering away to look at the dented diving helmet, could see that I was hooked. So he explained that on Monday morning at 9:00 a.m. two trucks would come to take anyone who showed up to either of Quest's two bases. When I asked Long John how long it would take to raise enough money to go treasure hunting, he told me that Quest already had a contract to buy an old Coast Guard cutter that we'd fix up. Then we'd sail it through the Panama Canal to Galveston, where we'd exchange the cutter for an even bigger ship. We'd repair it, and sail it up to some East Coast shipyard—maybe Hampton Roads in Virginia, maybe New York City harbor—those details are hazy to me now—and sell it. With the profit from the boat, and what we made fixing up old machinery, we'd buy the salvage vessel—a deal that, even as we spoke, the Captain was off arranging. And while all this went on, Quest would teach us how to dive and run a salvage operation. If all went well, we'd be off to the Caribbean in just a few short months to search for Spanish gold. It sounds ridiculous writing it out in cold blood like this, but I knew it was exactly the adventure I was looking for: at least I thought so at the time.

So I went home, packed up a pillowcase full of clothes, including a dictionary, and a doorstopper edition of Shakespeare's complete plays that is still my go-to Shakespeare, managed to convince a friend of mine to take me back to El Cajon, and slipped out of the house next morning a few minutes after my mother and father left for work.

I'll skip over most of how I ended up in Summerland, as opposed to the base in San Diego. All I'll say is that when we got to Lemon Grove in the back of an open truck, the compound looked like redneck heaven—or hell, depending on your point of view: busted machinery everywhere, dirt dirt dirt, an incomprehensible scatter of junk and spare parts. Long John told us we could change our names, and that nobody asked questions about our pasts. So I'd be harder to track, I volunteered for Santa Barbara and was told to climb back on the truck. I felt relieved as the engine growled into gear. My tension in running away dissipated in the warm spring weather as white and red fields of commercially grown flowers nodded along the roadside in full bloom. The guys around me were all older, but they seemed friendly, jokey men, including Vern—and with the truck's slipstream blowing my hair around my face, I felt grown up in a way that was exhilarating.

The memory of that day proved crucial in buoying me up over the weeks that were to come, for our routine, which was about the same at both bases, wasn't for the lazy or faint of heart: you worked dawn to dusk out in the machine yard, you lived in the aforesaid school bus fitted out with bunks, and you ate US government food bilked from the Welfare Department. My story was that I was an out-of-work fisherman with two kids and a wife to feed. I remember having an interview with a woman at Welfare who kept looking through her glasses at me in a cross-eyed sort of way, as if I were an unknown specimen of coleoptera that she couldn't quite classify. Anyway, we got a few weeks' worth of food out of my scripted lies, enough for four people—cans of chicken, sacks of flour, rice and beans, powdered milk, all stamped USDA—and loaded it up in the pickup for the cook's pantry back at base. There were twenty or so of us at any one time, and we all took turns going in to Welfare to help replenish the pantry. That's just one of the scams we went in for. My personal favorite was the pie racks scam: in exchange for left-over pies, we steam-cleaned pie racks—though of course we never let on to the bakeries that we were the ones who'd placed all those unclaimed orders.

Since I'd never worked on machinery before, I was constantly making mistakes and accruing extra hours of work. But I got accustomed to working very hard, on very little sleep, seven days a week. I learned—slowly—about carburetors, brakes, pumps and hoses, machinery of all kinds, and how to fix them—or fix them well enough so that whoever bought one of our Frankenstein creations could at least drive it off the lot before it malfunctioned and began to wreak havoc among the villagers.

About my second week, I fell under the command of a Vietnam vet I'm calling John (was that his name?—again, I'm not sure), a true martinet. He was none too fond of me, or of anyone else, as far as I could see. He wasn't like Joe, whose native temperament, for the short time I knew him, was basically friendly—until he flipped. Of course, after the shooting, the officers held a council, and Joe was expelled from the pirates. Nobody wanted the police looking into our various scams, not to mention our unlicensed weapons. And of course the appeal to a lot of long-term pirates was our Don't Ask, Don't Tell policy—many of us were on the wrong side of the law, and it wouldn't do to have the cops probing into our sketchy pasts. Of course, I was a runaway, a minor, and so when Joe left before dawn, I too was relieved. I didn't want to get dragged back home.

But now I was being bossed around by John—he took an immediate dislike to me, I'm not sure why. Maybe it was my bookishness, which he somehow saw as pretentious, for I remember him staring at me in disbelief one evening when I was sitting on my bunk in the bus, absorbed in reading *Romeo and Juliet*. And I have to admit, John had a point: I must have looked ridiculously out of place, in jeans so dirty and grease-stained they could have walked away on their own, propped on one elbow, blissfully absorbed in Mercutio's duel while the guys on the bunks around me were huffing toluene from a plastic bag—an infraction John ignored, since drugs and women were both off-limits. But where I really ran afoul of him was when we played chess one night. I was nothing if not deliberate, and to a good chess player like John, maddeningly so. We hunched over the board for what seemed like hours, the little library around us, which was full of technical manuals, travel books, and a scrapbook of Quest's dodgy history, the one place where I felt truly comfortable. The chain lamp hanging from the ceiling beat down on our drawn-up armies, and despite my intuition that winning would be a disaster for my future relations with John, I stubbornly resolved not to give in, no matter what the consequences. Thus I took so much time in considering my moves that at last John got impatient, and began making rash moves, until, much to my surprise and John's chagrin, I checkmated him. John never got over the shock, since he prided himself on his chess playing, and all I had going for me was John's bungling.

After that, things got pretty nasty: John yelled at me constantly, particularly during my second week when we had to pull an all-nighter in order to meet a deadline for fixing up a school bus that we'd sold to a church group. We were putting in a transmission, and for most of the time, I'd been working with a small but well-knit man named Carlos—a quiet, easygoing, ex-military guy. He was patient, fair, low-key, and a good teacher. He never yelled at me, even when I screwed up, which was pretty often. Nor did he give me demerits. Instead, he took the time to explain how this fit this way, and that fit that way, and if I used a little lubricant here, then that would make unscrewing that thing over there a whole lot easier. I loved working with Carlos, and whenever I could, I tried to get myself assigned to whatever work detail he was heading up. And for some reason, Carlos seemed to like me too: there was a gentleness in his manner when he showed me how to do things, the feel of his callused hands on mine as he taught me the proper use of a tool making me that much more eager to please him.

But Carlos was assigned to some other project, and the bus and I were both handed off to John, who was now in charge of installing the engine, transmission, and wiring, and hooking up the exhaust. And as day dragged into night, and night into day, we were both stupefied with exhaustion. John had been ragging on me constantly, and though I was feeling beaten down, I was completely dependent on him in the somewhat tricky business of handling a winch to lift the engine and transmission back onto their respective mounts. And that was when he decided to take his revenge for the chess game.

The tripod we were using to lift the transmission was a rickety affair, three steel pipes slotted in a metal head, with the winch attached to the head by hex bolts. I didn't know any of this lingo at the time, and I drove John crazy by calling the bolts the screws, the tripod the "thingy," the winch the "lifter." We wrapped a chain around the transmission, and fastened it to the winch hook—then John twisted the crank, and when he'd succeeded in lifting the transmission off the ground about an inch or so, he told me to get down on the ground and keep the transmission from swinging around. When it was something like six inches off the ground, the tripod gave a lurch, and we could see one of the pipes sinking into the soft ground. So John began to winch the transmission down, shouting all the while, "Jesus Christ, do I have to do everything? Put some feet under those pipes." I scrambled up to find some blocks of wood and brought them back. John's normally pallid face flushed a deep angry red, like the bulb in a thermometer, and he glared at me while I tilted the tripod up one leg at a time and slid the wood under each foot. Then he started winching again, and I knelt down beside it to steady it as it rose. He'd cranked it up again to about twelve inches, when the winch handle looked like it was binding just a little. And so he told me to slip under the transmission and push up on it from underneath. I got down on my back and wiggled my way under, and began to push—but instead of the chain rising upward, it began to sink down toward my chest. The harder I pushed, the less good it seemed to do. And then I heard the winch click, and when I glanced over at John, he was cranking the chain down, not up—which was when the transmission settled on my breast bone. I began to arch my back, pushing with all my might, terrified he was going to crush me. I felt the weight gathering on my chest as my breathing sped up. At first I didn't feel pain, but then I began to pant—which was when the metal began to bite into my skin, the weight making my ribs feel as if they were breaking. I looked over at John, but all he was doing was smiling at me, his hand on the winch, his other hand fiddling in his pocket for a cigarette. "Smoke break," he said cheerfully. He rolled a cigarette from a pouch in his pocket, eyed it appraisingly, as if there were all the time in the world, pinched the end a bit, then licked it. "Want me to roll you one?" he asked. It was all so stupid, so stagy—but what wasn't stagy was the pain in my chest, and how I was pinned to the ground. If the chain slipped, or John let the winch go . . . of course, if this were a Dickens novel the chapter would break off, and we'd go to a different scene entirely. And something like that did happen: when I should have been most focused on the dirt under my back and the metal pressing into my chest, I suddenly floated up out of my body and, just as in the fight with my father, saw the whole absurd business from about twenty feet in the air: a dirty boy pinned under a transmission, a dirty young man striking a match to light a cigarette, a dirty, fenced-in compound spreading around them, and off in the middle distance, the beach, and beyond the beach the R-boat, a kind of dive boat, that I'd paddle out to in a dory or on a surfboard to clean every couple of days, and beyond that, an oil well platform set in the middle of the ocean, where at night when one of us got up and stumbled out into the yard to take a piss, you could see the platform lights burning against the blackness, like a low-hanging constellation. "What a little momma's boy you are," said John. I didn't know it then, but my momma had actually been to the base the night before. My parents had managed to track me down through the boy who'd given me a ride to El Cajon. I'm not sure if they'd been to the police, but if they had, they'd decided to see for themselves where I'd gone.

My mother later told me that she'd been up in the foc's'le while I was downstairs at mess. "He's in boot camp," said Rogue, the officer in charge during Captain Nashe's absence. "If you want to see him now, then he's done—you'll have to take him home with you."

I see my mother and father sitting on the back seat pulled from an old Chevy that served as a makeshift couch. Rogue, his long brown ponytail neatly braided and secured at the braid's end with a skull-and-bones roach clip, sips coffee straight from a thermos and stares out the window, not at them, since it wouldn't be his style to show concern about a recruit's fate. My father would be silent, his eyes lowered, his fingers interlaced over his right knee. He stares at my mother expectantly—despite her illness, in big decisions about her children, she's always been the one to make the call. And something about her face at that moment, the way her expression keeps shifting between anger and relief (and even an ironic smile at having tracked me down, only to leave me in the fell clutches of pirates?), brings back two other opposed images from boyhood that have long haunted me.

The first is of the drive-in theater we ran back before my mother started teaching school. I'm helping my mother wash the dishes one night after supper. Standing on a stool next to the sink, I watch the water roil as the soap bubbles hiss, her invisible hands scrubbing and scrubbing reminding me of the "creature feature" we've shown the night before: up on the screen that stretched horizon to horizon, the huge tentacles of a giant squid are rearing up from the deep and coiling round and round the trestles of a bridge. I say to her in a way that's both wounding and confiding, "Mom, I'm afraid of you." To which she mutters, "You little pissant, you'd better be."

The other image is of her reading aloud to me from the ant-war section of Thoreau's *Walden*—red and black ants are gnawing each other's legs off; a severed black ant's head still lockjawed to a red ant's half-bitten-through antenna. She's entranced by the book, she and the book seem to be talking together, this isn't like reading for book reports—who is this woman I've been mistakenly calling "Mom"? There's such joy in her voice as she reads to me. I love that it isn't some stupid kid's book, I'm thrilled and horrified that the more gruesome the details, the more delighted she seems. And then I realize it's not the crazed behavior of the ants—it's what the words are doing to her, with her. Behind her on the dresser, five styrofoam heads sport the wigs she wore in those days—long-haired Mom, beehive Mom, French twist Mom, bouffant Mom, updo Mom. . . . Their faces are frozen, their pupiless eyes give nothing away. But the intense pleasure she gets from Thoreau's words makes me want to find my way to this not-Mom and share in her delight.

Our whole messy relationship crystallizes between the catatonic lineup of those styrofoam heads and the squid's enormous eyes filling the screen. Which one would show up—the mom who was thrillingly exotic in her strangeness? Or the one whose voice-weapon could cut right through you? I've tried to live my life between these two extremes, while taking risks my mother might well have taken herself, had she been born twenty years later. And as to those huge, unblinking eyes staring at me in a wholly unknowable, wholly alien way, whether you think of those eyes as the eyes of fate or contingency or chance, what is it they see down in the lightless zones? The bottom, after all, is a long, long way down.

My mother said Rogue was neither friendly nor unfriendly and that she was on the verge of making me come back home. But then she overheard me joking and laughing downstairs at dinner. And so, after Rogue had explained the rules to her, and when she heard about the discipline, she decided to let me stay.

Was it out of delicacy for my feelings, her feelings, or both our feelings that she insisted that Rogue not tell me about her visit? (Or maybe feelings are beside the point. Who would want to live with an unruly teenager who'd gotten into a fight with his father over a heroin fix?) Of course the other men heard about her visit, and John calling me a momma's boy was his way of letting me know just what he thought of me. And I suppose he wasn't far wrong. After all, I always have been a momma's boy: not in the sense of running to momma to make the hurt go away, but running away from momma, only to become that much more like her.

So yes: I was and am and will forever remain a momma's boy.

I don't know how long John left me pinned under the transmission—probably no more than thirty seconds—but when Carlos came by, looking for some tool, John immediately winched the transmission off me, glaring at me as if he were daring me to say something. But I kept my mouth shut, despite the bruises on my chest that were in the exact cylinder-inside-a-rectangle shape of the transmission body, with blacker bruises for the pressure of the bolts where they'd pressed deeper down into my chest. I learned a lot from that moment: I saw how much John hated me, but I also understood how part of his hatred was envy. I was just a kid and could always go home to momma. But John was an adult, and this was home. I recognized immediately the disparity that separates those whose options in life are narrowing from those whose options still seem wide open. I guess you could say that John taught me two valuable lessons: how to handle (or not handle) a winch and, of equal value, the limits of empathy.

But that didn't mean I forgave John. A week or so later, when we were forced to work together again—and by this time, I was calling a hex bolt a hex bolt, a winch a winch, a spanner a spanner, and I knew the difference between a screw thread and a threaded screw—we had to charge a dead battery. Somehow, I don't know how, the jumper cables just seemed to slip from my hands and give John a nice little jolt. He jerked the way my mother might have jerked—and as I apologized, consciously laying it on a little too thick so that he'd know exactly what I was really thinking, and reading in my eyes just how much I hated him back, a look of respect flickered across his face. And then he sentenced me to an hour of latrine duty, which I carried out after work that day, cursing him the whole time under my breath, but with the momentary conviction of feeling myself at home, which I've seldom felt before or since.

A Man of Care

I do *not* intend to write about Seamus Heaney the Nobel laureate icon, or "famous Seamus," as he was sometimes called behind his back, especially by other Northern Irish poets. Instead, I want to give a more oblique view of him, and what he cared about as a poet and a man. Seamus struggled as much as anyone "To strike it rich behind the linear black," and in the thirty years I knew him, he had long dry spells, when either the springs had subsided underground or he couldn't find his way to them. In the letters he wrote me from time to time, sometimes including poems, sometimes not, he would mention this, not in a desperate way, but as something patiently to be endured. He spoke of it often enough in a machine age metaphor: a drive belt no longer slipping but taking hold, the rope of a windlass going taut as it hauled up a bucket from the depths of a well.

I thought of him as a streak writer, but that isn't entirely accurate. That implies a certain brute faith in knowing when you're at the right spiritual pitch to write, and Seamus was always more of a self-skeptic. And even though, like Rilke, poems would sometimes pour from him in a torrent, he would have looked askance at a self-dramatizer like Rilke, always intent on nursing his talent toward poetic speech— that kind of self-absorption would have struck Seamus as precious, and a little nonsensical. "But to hell with overstating it: / 'Don't have the veins bulging in your Biro,'" he once wrote. (And from that point of view, Berryman was certainly right when in one of the *Dream Songs* he says, "Rilke was a *jerk*.") Besides, Seamus was far too practical a man, and too loyal to his upbringing as a farmer's son, to court poetry with a capital P. It was more that he had to find a way to care about the images that would go beyond literature and spill over into life before language would invest him. As Proust once said, the cause of literature was a terrible reason for a person to write anything. For Seamus, the relation between words and images had a sacral, incarnational element, such that the first priority of language was to embody the world before making it say something about the world.

You might say that Seamus, who did a lot of tidying up around the house, was a careful man, as well as a man of care. And taking care of the world through his use of language was as fundamental to his vocation as a poet as it was to his sense of what it meant to be a father, a husband, a friend, and a human being. I remember visiting him once at his old Georgian-style house on the Strand Road in Dublin, and I was touched and amused to find him wearing an apron as he placed on the stairs a book or a sweater or a pair of shoes to be carried up later. "I do this as an experiment, just to see if the children will actually take these things upstairs," he said. When I asked him what the results of the experiment were, he shrugged, shook his head, and smiled, "It's an ongoing experiment."

Robert Lowell, a good friend of Heaney's and a poet he hugely admired, once began an essay on T. S. Eliot, "I wept when T. S. Eliot died." When Seamus died, I found it hard to weep—and I still don't think of him as dead, only hovering just out of sight on the borders of vision. On the eve of his birthday, when he would have been seventy-five, I felt like a twenty-first-century necromancer, trying to talk to a dead pal who certainly would have preferred sharing a whiskey and a Guinness to "literary criticism." Well, as Lowell once said, the problem with criticism is that it makes points. I will try to keep the points to a minimum, and instead fly fast and far and wide in a mode more speculative than critical. And in doing so, I'll hope to conjure him up again in the still bright lucency, the present absence, of the newly dead. As Seamus put it in one of those miraculous twelve-liners in "Squarings," little fluttering kite tails of poems, "Perhaps / As we read the line sheer forms do crowd / The starry vestibule." And then, in a hardheaded recognition of the limits of poetry, "Otherwise / They do not."

But despite Seamus's stricture, I found myself face-to-face with him in, of all places, the Libyan desert. When I went to a literary festival in Libya, I took Seamus's poems with me. The festival was accompanied by as much gunfire as applause—and I couldn't help but think how Colonel Gaddafi, as Seamus once told me, had given the IRA most of their weapons, including several tons of Semtex, the plastic explosive that helped kill over thirty-five hundred people, wounded over a hundred thousand, and terrorized hundreds of thousands for much of Seamus's lifetime.

I remember how finely tuned Seamus was to impending violence, like a sixth sense he'd acquired through the decades of killing. Several years ago, on our way to a Jewish poetry festival at Boston University, I noticed his walk slowing, and a kind of hypervigilance taking over, a tightening and a hunkering down into himself— another aspect of both his care, and his carefulness—and he said, in a level voice, as if commenting on the weather, "There's been a bomb scare." And indeed there had been: police cars fumed under the trees, a bomb squad was standing by, and a moment later an ambulance, with its lights flashing, drove up. After the event, which went ahead as planned once it became clear that there was no bomb, I asked Seamus how he'd known. "Ah, well," he said, "you get a sense for these things: and then I saw that the police weren't moving in, but standing back."

In Libya, especially in Tripoli, where gunfire goes on night and day, I too felt that hypervigilance coming over me as we drove in a convoy, protected by a local militia carrying AK-47s. In the little snatches of time I had, I'd read a few lines in Seamus's poems about the Troubles, poems which seemed weirdly parallel to what was happening outside his poems in the Libyan realities of militias and sectarian and clan rivalries. And then, one day after many hours of bouncing over a remote stretch of open desert in an SUV, I found myself scrambling up a steep slope to crouch down before a small engraving of a gazelle incised in a limestone outcrop some nine or ten thousand years ago. It had been engraved at an angle just under the top of a mesa, so that the gazelle, drawn in three-quarters perspective, seemed to turn one eye toward me, as if staring at me warily from across that vastness of geological time. Its wariness was part of what made it so lifelike. It was both a picture of life, and possessed of a kind of numinous life in itself.

That same kind of wary animal alertness was a quality I'd observed in Seamus many times, at the bomb scare of course, but in meeting people for the first time: under his kindliness, which was as genuine and reflexive as his wariness, you felt yourself undergoing a quick radar scan, as he took your measure and sized you up. I'd experienced just that same penetrating stare the first time I went to see him at his apartment at Harvard, where he offered me a drink. After a few minutes, I could feel the scan's force field being switched off. And then the immense jubilation of conversation with Seamus, in which you felt smarter, funnier, happier for being in his presence, took hold full force as we talked at ease for close to two hours.

I loved the colloquial eloquence and ease and the "damn all, this could be the best night yet" aura that came over him when the whiskey warmed and the talk was congenial. In speaking once of some Portuguese sausages set aflame, he said, "Now those are sausages of the mind!" There was the Connor Cruise O'Brien game, a game that Seamus played with his kids, and that he sometimes played in a more sophisticated version with his friends. *Question*: Who is the famous Irish chimney sweep? *Answer*: Connor Flues O'Brien. *Question*: Who is the famous Irish narcoleptic? *Answer*: Connor Snooze O'Brien. Or the dead poets game, in which one poet would use his hand as a finger puppet to act out some poet's famous death: two fingers staggering to the edge of a tabletop, woozily balancing on it for a moment, and then leaping over the edge . . . ! Hart Crane, of course.

But it wasn't all self-mockery and roguish good humor. I remember speaking to him about the death of my father, in which my dad's body—and long after my father wanted to keep on living—simply refused to give out. Seamus nodded and said, with great accuracy of feeling, "Oh, I know, I know: the hateful strength of the dying." And on a foggy morning when we were out walking in Dublin, he said, "It's a soft day." But despite Seamus's openheartedness, trust for him was also an intimate conspiracy—at least until he got to know you and his vigilance relaxed. After all, during the Troubles, neighbors murdered neighbors, and it was survival information to get a line on who you were meeting for the first time. "Now, what do you know about X?" he'd ask. And after listening closely, and if the report was good, he'd nod and say, "Ah well, then, that's OK."

Just because a friend dies doesn't mean the friendship ends—and like all my connections with the dead, my relationships with them are at least as volatile and changeable as those I have with the living. So in those miles and miles of empty, hardpan desert that we'd been crossing for hours on end without seeing a single living thing, suddenly his presence was before me, refreshed and renewed in the way the gazelle lowered its long graceful neck to drink from a hollow in the stone, as if that hollow were a spring pool, an emblem of the waters of life—and at the same time, an emblem of the fragility of the soul. For a crack in the stone slanted right across the heart line from the curve of the gazelle's neck to its belly. Another hard rain, or a sandstorm, or a freeze followed by a sudden thaw could be enough to break it apart, and those nine or ten thousand years of human and geological history and prehistory would fall to the desert floor and be lost.

As Seamus wrote in one of the poems I kept coming back to, about an engraving of Christ's baptism on the facade of a cathedral, the water "Where Jesus stands up to his unwet knees," is only carved stone incised with "Lines / Hard and thin and sinuous." Like the gazelle, those lines were steadily eroding away in wind and rain. And yet that carved stone representing the waters of baptism was, in the poem at least, "Like the zig-zag hieroglyph for life itself." For Seamus, describing a sign of the sacred was as close to the sacred as one could credibly get as a poet. Thus, "Description is revelation!"

was Seamus's plighted troth to the world of soul and sense, just as the image of the gazelle, where I felt Seamus's living presence restored to me, had been another human being's attempt to capture the zigzag essence of the gazelle's indwelling life. And so I stood there looking at the rock, having sweated my shirt through from scrambling up the slope, and shivering a little in the spring desert chill. Facing the gazelle was like facing Seamus for the first time all over again—in death, as in life, I felt his invisible presence scanning me and testing me and moving on.

It's as if his radar-like alertness to the world of the senses as harbingers to the soul made description as a major poetic mode for him not only inevitable, but inevitably right. And yet Seamus once told me that shortly after he met Robert Lowell, Lowell said to him about his penchant for natural imagery, "There are a lot of trees in your poems, Heaney." A remark that Seamus relished, even as he was quick to point out that Lowell had said it "in a not altogether commendable tone." A barb wrapped in gauze, its aspersion of rural nature poetry, of premodern escape into pastoral, served in Seamus's mind as a styptic reminder of what he should never let his gift for description succumb to: a sort of rural theme-park Ireland in which nature redeems Ireland's bloody history.

But I want to go back behind the issues of description and what it's used for to the more fundamental issue of inscription. And here Lowell's remark is revelatory in quite another way. As Heaney writes in "Alphabets," a poem about learning how to write as a way of possessing knowledge of the wider world beyond the local "Smells of inkwells . . . in the classroom hush":

> The letters of this alphabet were trees.
> The capitals were orchards in full bloom,
> The lines of script like briars coiled in ditches.

Language and the trees are coterminous. They overlap and interpenetrate. They don't suffer from what Eliot called "dissociation of sensibility" in which feeling is separated from thinking. They rebuke

semioticians, who see language as an arbitrary system, for not understanding how words in the mouths of individuals are private, protected, wholly personal things—as if every word, as soon as it's spoken
or written in a poem, receives its incarnation not only in the life of
the one who speaks it but also in the life of the one who reads or hears
it, as if words in poems refuse to be separated from their immediate
human purposes just for the goal of reducing them to a system.

When Seamus wrote "Alphabets," he was teaching every spring
semester at Harvard, and living at Adams House in a nondescript
little one-bedroom apartment that he called his "bolt hole." He told
me that he wanted nothing more permanent or grand. "It keeps the
balance between my two lives," he said, meaning his home life with
Marie and his children in Ireland, and his life that was a constant "on
the go" hurry in the United States. He handed me the poem almost as
soon as I walked in, and while I read it, he poured both of us ice-cold
vodkas from a bottle he always kept in the freezer. It was only one of
two poems that he finished at Adams House in the twenty-odd years
he taught at Harvard. When he taught, he was living what he called
"my executive life"—not in the sense of a CEO, but in the sense of
executing utilitarian teacherly tasks. "I put my poem life on hold
here," he told me. He was a devoted teacher, deeply invested in his
students' progress, and he once said to me, in concern about a student,
"Well, the fellow tries, but you can't squeeze blood from a turnip."

But despite his teaching duties, and his demurrals about not writing, from time to time he would show me a draft that, as often as
not, came to him at three or four in the morning, just after waking
from a deep sleep into the still, dream-drenched wide-awakeness of
a poem announcing itself to him. "Alphabets" was just such a poem.
As I read it, it seemed bedrock Heaney: sprung from childhood in
that it was "adept / at dialect," but asserting its rights to the English
lyric. It makes that moment of childhood, when you first pick up
a pencil and make the stick figure drawings of block printing, followed by the big whirling, lead-smeared Os and loops of cursive,
resonate with the mysterious excitement of taking possession of the
word hoard one letter at a time.

In "Alphabets," Heaney's relation to language is like the necromancer's relation to his "figure of the world with colours in it" that he hangs from his house's domed ceiling "So that the figure of the universe / And 'not just single things' would meet his sight // When he walked abroad." The trees in the poem aren't simply trees, but "shape-note language, absolute on air / As Constantine's sky-lettered IN HOC SIGNO." For Heaney, words were charged, and in charge of both spiritual essence and an undeniable materiality—the materiality of Milton's angels, say, who have sex with one another by completely intermingling their ethereal substances. I'm not saying he worked at this relation to words, or thought of it as anything out of the ordinary. It came naturally to him, as naturally as bending a paper plate that once held a piece of watermelon on it, so he could slurp up the leftover juice that much more efficiently. The juice was a kind of bonus, and when poems came to Seamus back home in Ireland, sometimes writing as many as forty or fifty in a streak, he didn't second-guess what language brought to him, just as you don't second-guess the sweetness of watermelon. He trusted it as a bounty that would lead him where he needed to go, even as he revised them, often extensively. Yet the big whoosh of arrival of such "binge writing" bore out his faith in poetry as a ratification of the impulse toward transcendence.

You could say that Seamus's faith in language paralleled Giordano Bruno's faith in words as sacred signs. The seventeenth-century Italian mystic, burned at the stake by the Inquisition, thought that if you concentrated on a particular image derived from *spiritus mundi* (the spirit world), the star demons would shed their influences into you via the image in your mind and transform you into a divine mage. The star demons were celestial guardians that shed influence from the stars, which Bruno thought of as roving sentient beings that made up the superbeing of the universe. Once, when Seamus and I were on a junket in Vermont, including a fishing trip in which we could see brown trout hovering in the current, but couldn't get them to bite, we stopped on the way home from dinner to take, as Seamus called it, "one of life's great pleasures—a piss *en plein aire*." Standing

by the road, the headlights switched off, the peepers behind us cho-
rusing in orgiastic overdrive, we looked up at the Milky Way while
Seamus quoted the opening of *The Prelude*: "Fair seed-time had my
soul, and I grew up / Fostered alike by beauty and by fear." The wash
of stars and the pattering piss and the Wordsworthian invocation
came together as both a goof and a communion with the elements.
It seems to me now an emblem of how poetry in our daily lives surpasses mere "information," and irradiates the mind so that bodily
pleasure and "intimations of immortality" are one. But then we got
back in the car, and we let that moment slip from us in the onslaught
of executive life. As Seamus writes in "The Mud Vision":

> experts
> Began their *post factum* jabber and all of us
> Crowded in tight for the big explanations.
> Just like that, we forgot that the vision was ours,
> Our one chance to know the incomparable
> And dive to a future. What might have been origin
> We dissipated in news.

Vision and canned explanation—those are the poles our world runs
between, with the canned verbiage wildly predominant. The vision
that belongs to each of us gets drowned out by the "big explanations"
of the experts' "*post factum* jabber."

It would be wrong, though, to think that Seamus was an anti-
digital Luddite, hostile to mass media. He was as adept as anyone
in front of a TV camera, and there's no question that his ease on
screen played a part in his public career. In fact, "The Mud Vision"
is a wised-up poem about the relation between private revelation and
media exposure. After all, Seamus worked for a time for RTÉ as a
radio reviewer and commentator.

But when it came to the role of poet, he wrote in an essay on
poetry and politics, "'pure' poetry is perfectly justifiable in earshot
of the car bomb, and it can imply a politics, depending on the nature of the poetry. A poetry of hermetic wit, of riddles and slips and

self-mocking ironies, may appear culpably miniaturist or fastidious to the activist with his microphone at the street corner, and yet such poetry may be exercising in its inaudible way a fierce disdain of the activist's message or a distressed sympathy with it."

Seamus once took me to Glasnevin Cemetery to show me the memorial to the IRA hunger strikers, including Bobby Sands, who starved himself to death in the infamous Maze Prison, while Margaret Thatcher refused to intervene. It was a misty day and both of us stood in front of the memorial, saying nothing. All through the Troubles, Seamus walked a tightrope between his Catholic sympathies and his love for a figure like Osip Mandelstam, who died in Stalin's camps for upholding what Seamus called "his essentially subjective, human- ist vision of poetry as a kind of free love between the auditory imagi- nation and the unharnessed intelligence." Unharnessed, that is, from the socialist realist cogs of the revolutionary machine, just as Seamus resisted the Northern Irish groupthink about the arts being subser- vient to the nationalist cause. He then took me to see where Father Gerardus Hopkins was buried in an unmarked grave in Glasnevin's Jesuit plot. Hopkins's name, engraved in tiny print with a host of other Jesuits at the base of a granite cross, seemed, in its nearly anony- mous condition, to bear out the contradictory pressures that Seamus lived under for many of the years I knew him. The activist Sands, and the priestly singer, Hopkins, were both part of his makeup.

When Seamus wrote "I have no mettle for the angry role," he didn't simply mean planting and detonating bombs made of Semtex in Belfast shopping centers. He meant, quite literally, that anger was a blunt instrument, suitable for the "anvil brains of some who hate me," but not for his feeling that the poet was "stretched between poli- tics and transcendence and is often displaced from a confidence in a single position by his disposition to be affected by all positions, nega- tively rather than positively capable." And this negatively capable ability to sympathize with conflicting viewpoints meant that his re- lation to language had to retain that primary Adamic freshness of verbal play that would not lie down before dogma, whether religious or political or philosophical or literary critical. Heaney's insistence on

poetry as an independent category of human consciousness, not beholden to worldviews of any kind while of course partaking of them,
was central to how he understood language as a form of care.

And one of the ways of caring about the world was how he submit-
ted himself to the discipline of observation. As he wrote of Elizabeth
Bishop, but equally of himself, "Observation was her habit, as much
in the monastic, Hopkinsian sense as in its commoner meaning of
a customarily repeated action. Indeed, observation is itself a mani-
festation of obedience, an activity which is averse to overwhelming
phenomena by the exercise of subjectivity, content to remain an assisting presence rather than an overbearing pressure." Thus Seamus in
his apron, placing his children's things on the stairs, as a means of
assisting those things to find their rightful places up the stairs. As he
observes in the ending of "Alphabets" about not just seeing "single
things" but "the figure of the universe" in the homely details of our
world, the O of the planet nests inside the O of language which hatches
from the ovum of generation:

> . . . As from his small window
> The astronaut sees all that he has sprung from,
> The risen, aqueous, singular lucent O
> Like a magnified and buoyant ovum—

"Alphabets" then shifts from the macro to the micro, and shows us
Heaney as a child observing with a wide-eyed prereflective wonder
the mystery of his family name being written out by the plasterer:

> Or like my own wide pre-reflective stare
> All agog at the plasterer on his ladder
> Skimming our gable and writing our name there
> With his trowel point, letter by strange letter.

So in this act of close observation, the child comes into contact with
the primal power of naming. In a rural down-home way, Heaney observes his local universe with the same agog attention of a Giordano

Bruno fixated on the star demons. By paying attention to the skimming trowel point writing out the family name, the astronaut's macrocosmic view of the planet is instantiated in the homely act of plastering a gable. So the astronaut observing the planet in the first stanza morphs into the boy's mind agog in the second. In Heaney's poetry, the act of observation is so vital and powerfully transformative, that it has the effect of embodying the macro in the micro while quietly blowing our minds through lightning shifts in scale.

In the face of advertisers, propagandists, and the ubiquity of mass media, poetry's insistence that images are full of living power that can irradiate the human soul like "sun / In a pillar of radiant house-dust," is predicated on language being available to write a poem at all. Seamus was like a champion diver on the high board who has to keep limbering up, waiting for just the right linguistic lift to carry him up, over, and under, in order to reach the proper spiritual heights before plumbing the depths. It was a measure of his artistic integrity that he always kept the bar for poetic utterance very high, which sometimes meant enduring long silences. As he once said to me during a dry spell, "I don't know how to work at poems unless the words are there to give me something to work on."

2

Given the notion that poetry retains its rights, as well as the rites, to lyric pleasure in what Seamus once called "the temple inside our hearing," I want to home in on his use of language as a language of care, and suggest how that language might be salutary to contemporary poetry. Again, this feeling for words wasn't something Seamus worked at. I remember driving to a friend's house together and, as we stopped at a stop sign, we looked over into a bay window where a harp shone behind the glass. "It looks like a seahorse," said Seamus, merely noting it as we drove on. And the curve of the harp, its burnished gold color, and the wash of streetlight it was bathed in, did indeed make it look like a seahorse swimming behind the transparent walls of a child's aquarium. As a practical matter, Seamus's image has inscribed that harp forever in my mind. And if one of the properties of poetic care is to preserve what vanishes from the inertial void and heat death of space, this single instance is, for me, talismanic of the kind of care poetry takes of the evanescent world. As I get nearer the apogee of my mortal orbit, the crucial importance of language as a way to keep that harp lit up, or afloat as a kind of seahorse, keeps pressing against the g-forces of death.

Seamus's preternatural gift for description didn't just happen, though. As he says in *Stepping Stones*, an extended interview with Dennis O'Driscoll that turned into a sort of unintended autobiography, "I'm devoted to Pound's early work. I love that first 'Canto.' He was important to me from the start as the author of the imagist principles." Pound's strictures—"the natural object is always the *adequate* symbol"; "Go in fear of abstractions"; don't use phrases like "dim lands *of peace*" because it mixes "an abstraction with the concrete" and dulls the image—confirmed Seamus's sense that Adam, the first poet, named the animals not because he wanted to subdue them but because naming would help them remain rooted in their bodies, regardless of their symbolic role in God's creation.

But just as a piss en plein aire can lead to an appreciation of the stars, so our body's open-eared and -eyed attentiveness to the world can be a springboard to revelation. Pound's interest in the Chinese ideogram as a concrete language in which the sign for *integrity* would be a character of a stick figure man standing next to an oval-shaped mouth—a man literally standing by his word—dovetails with Seamus's conviction that poetry is "verbal icon." Throughout Seamus's writing life, poetry's mind pictures, broadcast through the tongue to the ear, achieved density and definiteness by rooting in home ground—"Quagmire, swampland, morass: / the slime kingdoms."

By contrast, early in our friendship, Seamus and I discussed at length a notoriously abstract and disembodied poet whose work he described as "a centrally heated daydream." Similarly, we once attended a reading in which the poems evaporated into vatic maundering. Seamus leaned over and whispered, "Methinks there is something wrong with our Tennyson." I think his animus wasn't so much at the poets, as how their work lacked what he called "the primal reach into the physical," and reflected "the uncannily insulated, materially comfortable, volubly docile condition of a middle-class population on the move between its shopping malls and its missile silos." Harsh as this sounds, I think he only meant it as a way to explain his preference, at least in the 1980s, for poetry that came out of historical conditions more like Ireland's, stuff by Czeslaw Milosz, Zbigniew Herbert, and Miroslav Holub—all veterans of the Cold War's Iron Curtain. On another, more personal level, he once told me that in Ireland, as a matter of self-protection, the collective antennae were always up. And I've wondered at times if his devotion to fine-etched detail wasn't in part hypervigilance to the threat of sectarian murder.

However that may be, one of the *Don'ts* in Pound's essay that came up in several of our conversations was "the definiteness of Dante's presentation, as compared with Milton's rhetoric." In Dante's version of hell, the naturalistic treatment of surreal details—sinners with their heads on backward or cloven in two or frozen into ice or who morph from human forms into reptilian demons and back again—contrasts with Milton's conventionalized description of hell: lakes of fire, flames, hissing serpents; there isn't a single original observation in the entire poem that isn't gilt in Milton's rhetoric, which achieves its effects primarily through the ear rather than the eye. This fact wasn't lost on Seamus, for whom the sound effects of Hopkins were a bellwether of his own musical gift. He once said that reading Milton was like watching a master mason at work, laying courses of brick— each line was so firmly in place that it would take a stick of dynamite to unseat it. But what Pound and Seamus both admired in Dante was his imagistic precision leading to revelatory experience.

The *Purgatorio*, Seamus once told me, was his favorite book of the *Commedia*—and I'd be hard put to overstate how much he loved Dante, how deeply Dante's example had inspired him, and how crucial a poet Dante was for him as both a touchstone of what he wanted to achieve, as well as Dante's luminous dedication to homely Florence as the means of achieving it. The Troubles, the Iron Age,

and the internecine politics of twelfth-century Tuscany come together in three of his most powerful books, published in succession:
North, *Field Work*, and *Station Island*. The homage to Dante is obvious in the latter two. *Field Work* ends with an Ulsterized version of
the Ugolino canto, and the central sequence of *Station Island* derives
directly from the mise-en-scène of the *Inferno*, in which a pilgrim
meets up with revenants in an act of contrition and renewal—much
of it composed in a simulacrum of terza rima. And *North*, while
superimposing the time of the Troubles on the revenge cycles of the
Viking raiders, shows a man in the middle of his life, the way ahead
in the *"selva selvaggia,"* the savage wood, *"rugged and harsh."*

   The Troubles had another twenty-five years to run after the publication of *North*, and when Seamus left Northern Ireland for Glanmore
cottage in the south, there were many in the north who thought
he was a traitor. Seamus understood the reason for the animosity:
however backstabbing it might be, it was, nonetheless, an intimate
gesture between one member of the tribe and another. As such, it
conferred a kind of distinction. And in conversation at least, Seamus
was inclined to take a wry view of the matter. As he once said to me,
"You know, Tom, the ancient Irish warriors wore their shields upon
their backs." And after a long deadpan stare, with just the hint of a
smile, he said, "Which was the proper place for them." In fact, *North*
ends with an affirmation that he is neither "internee nor informer,"
but "an inner émigré," living a life of self-imposed exile while weighing his responsible *"tristia"*—an echo of both Mandelstam's and
Dante's exiled status.

   Heaney's fellow feeling for Dante's situation in internecine Florence
extends to the *Divine Comedy*'s imagistic methods. In canto X of
the *Purgatorio*, Dante has progressed downward through hell, and
is now climbing up the slopes of Mount Purgatory. Along the way,
he sees some low reliefs carved into a cliff face: they depict scenes
of humility—the annunciation of Mary, the transit of the ark, and
the Roman emperor Trajan being confronted by a poor woman who
demands justice for her son's death. Dante describes these carvings
as *"visibile parlare"* (speech made visible), and the sculptor is none

other than "He who on no new thing hath ever looked." Dante says that these reliefs, in their astonishingly lifelike detail, surpass nature so far as nature surpasses any human sculptor. So God, the supreme sculptor who uses the Word as his chisel, is an ekphrastic maker dedicated to Pound's ideal of "definiteness of presentation."

This dovetails with how the English philosopher T. E. Hulme, a friend of Pound and a fellow imagist, thought poetic language should be "a compromise for a language of intuition which would hand over sensations bodily. It always endeavours to arrest you, and to make you continuously see a physical thing, to prevent you gliding through an abstract process." Which of course doesn't mean that poetic language needs to be tethered to an image in order to earn its poetic keep. Tone of voice, rhythm, and patterns of sound are all ways of grounding abstraction in subtle vocal maneuvers.

And that's true not only of the language of poetry; in the reading of it, when you say a poem out loud, you embody the words in your lungs and belly and breath, and speak them out to the world. Poetry reembodies its readers by restoring our bodies to us. And a version of this also happens when we read a poem to ourselves, insofar as we have to embody the speaker of the poem in the voice in our mind that the poem helps create.

Seamus would point to the sensual immediacy of Keats's "Ode to Autumn," or Hopkins's "The Windhover," as examples of poetry that come close to creating an ideographic experience, if not an ideographic idiom. This attitude depends on Keats and Hopkins very patiently attending on nature, observing it closely, so that the images of the outside world embody the emotions on the inside. What gives this ideographic experience its special poignancy is how insistent both poets are on doing justice to the subjects they are observing. For Keats and Hopkins, paying attention to the surfaces of the world is one way of honoring those surfaces. Heaney would have agreed with Simone Weil, who said, "It is better to say that I am unhappy than that the world is ugly."

So in "speech made visible," the poet doesn't gesture at, or editorialize, or think around emotions; he embodies them. You could say that this mode of paying attention instantiates an ethos of linguistic care as a means of preserving infinitely rich but fragile moments of sensation and experience. Equally important, that gesture of preservation overleaps what it preserves, and creates an alternate reality in which vanishing sensations not only continue to resonate but also surpass and transform the originary experience. For an act of poetic preservation to achieve its fullest potential, the language has to break free of the gravity of the pertaining historical conditions that in part determine it, but also keep it earthbound. As Seamus says about the imaginative powers conferred by sitting in the basalt throne of "the wishing chair" at the Giant's Causeway, not only should the rock make "solid sense" against the small of your back, it should also freshen "your outlook / Beyond the range you thought you'd settled for."

Now let's take a sudden swerve to what I'm loosely going to call the contemporary surrealist temper, so as not to get bogged down in arid debates over whether it's Breton's surrealism or someone else's version. This was a kind of poetry Seamus respected, but at first had little affinity for. It's a mode dedicated to hassling and chafing the surfaces of the world, that requires great rhetorical skill and range of reference, as well as a willingness to let language leave ordinary signification in the dust as it rides at a furious gallop toward the bounds of sense. Of course, I'm talking about a poet like John Ashbery, but in a more crucial way, about his predecessors, Baudelaire and Rimbaud—Baudelaire for his subject matter and Rimbaud for his linguistic invention.

Critics like to say that the Frenchmen were symbolists who made it possible for Breton and others to practice surrealism, but the surrealist temper as I'm defining it is something different from either surrealism or symbolism. It means the desire to be free of natural law and make a mental landscape, a verbal landscape whose referents float free of the surfaces of the world, instead of conforming to a physical one. Under that definition, Baudelaire and Rimbaud were pioneers of the surrealist temper, wrote great poetry out of that feel for experience, and did it about as well as it can ever be done. I can well understand the appeal of that temper: unlike Keats or Hopkins, or Heaney for that matter, you no longer have to think about nature, or patiently attend upon it. Images in your head don't have to follow the laws of nature, which govern what's outside your head. You can construct your inner landscapes without reference to outer ones. Those landscapes can be seen from many different perspectives, but you yourself are always at the center of them. Besides which, there's no more waiting on nightingales or observing the seasons or worrying about getting the details of a turnip snedder right. There's just you, your mind, your images, your arrangement of those images.

Perhaps this is one reason why fewer and fewer contemporary American poets seem interested in writing poems that come out of direct observation. Plus, the ethos of care that Keats, Hopkins, and Heaney embody may seem hard to arrive at when such streamlined methods of arranging mental landscapes have become for many artists an unconscious norm.

But I wonder if such a norm doesn't have a crack in it. What Breton intended as a way of getting in touch with the nondiscursive realities in dreams overlooks Heaney's kind of insistence on honoring the surfaces of the world. There is, after all, something in the discipline of patiently attending on those surfaces that can lead you to an informed interest and reverence for them. As Donald Davie notes, these modes of human perception aren't worth losing "just for the sake of a more streamlined poetic method."

So yes, the surrealist temper is a huge gain, but it's also symptomatic of a grievous loss. The tenderness toward existence that can come from watching an actual bird build a nest is quite different from hatching birds in your own mind. I remember when I almost died of a chronic illness that what I felt more than fear was grief: grief that I would no longer be able to experience something as simple as watching light and shade playing over the face of an immense sunflower. The medical imaging of my body that brought me such relentlessly bad news began to displace my own sense of the pleasure in perception that my body formerly brought me. As Wallace Stevens once wrote, "The greatest poverty is not to live / in a physical world."

Against this creeping sense of disembodiment, I am asking that an ethos of care, like Heaney's, but adapted to the exigencies of contemporary American life and speech, find its way back into our many-lensed perspectives. I see it at the center of a language that, like Dante's speech made visible, would pour itself out like honey and create, like honey, whatever forms would spontaneously emerge.

This image comes from Osip Mandelstam's idea of Dante as a supreme improviser, as opposed to Eliot's magisterial idea of him as a universal writer sealed off behind wax in his status as a classic. Heaney loved Mandelstam's version of Dante as a mercurial creature caught up in the spontaneous buzz and hum of composition as tercet by tercet his terza rima unfolds. Dante's speech made visible isn't a quest for divine knowledge, or a form of social control via Christian orthodoxy, but the result of an instinct for what Mandelstam calls "form creation":

> We must try to imagine . . . how bees might have worked at this thirteen-thousand-faceted form, bees endowed with the brilliant stereometric instinct, who attracted bees in greater and greater numbers as they were required. The work of these bees, constantly keeping their eye on the whole, is of varying difficulty at different states of the process. Their cooperation expands and grows more complicated as they participate in the process of forming the combs, by means of which space virtually emerges out of itself.

This emerging space is what for me, a secular person to the bone, would be a form of speech made visible well worth caring for.

One of Seamus's poems that I most love tells the story about Saint Kevin and the blackbird. Saint Kevin has his arms stretched out in imitation of the cross, but because his cell is so narrow, one of his up-turned palms sticks out the window. A blackbird lands on his palm, lays its eggs, and settles down to nest there. The poem goes on to speculate, not about Saint Kevin's spiritual state but about his physical one: Does his arm hurt? Is Kevin in a state of self-forgetfulness or in agony?

But between Kevin and the new life in the eggs, another conversation is going on—one that bypasses both his holiness and his achy shoulders. That conversation has to do with care, and how care is based on an awareness of the other's body. And bodily fellow feeling, how we experience it in ourselves and others, has pervaded Heaney's work from first to last. From his poem about the death of his little brother in "Mid-Term Break," to his revisiting of that same subject forty years later in the "Blackbird of Glanmore," bodily pleasure and bodily harm have been the secular equivalents of the Crucifixion and the Resurrection.

Perhaps the most remarkable instance of Heaney's devotion to the care of, and for, the body has been the way that he's taken Catholic tropes of sin and redemption that target the body and transformed them into psychological categories that cut free of the need for orthodoxy. The bedrock of that transformative power is his devotion to securing what he calls "the bastion of sensation." Book after book elaborates an informal somatic politics, almost a carnal politics, as in a poem like "Oysters," in which the erotics of oyster eating runs head-on into the imperial power of Rome—a conflict that can only be resolved in the conditional tense by translating Rome's imperial brutality that "ripped and shucked and scattered" into a lyric overleaping such that the poet is quickened "into verb, pure verb." In the realm of language, then, the government of the tongue can hold sway over the violating legions. Not in the sense of keeping the legions from fire and pillage, but in poetry's tendency to "place a counter-reality in the scales—a reality which may be only imagined but which nevertheless has weight because it is imagined within the gravitational pull of the actual and can therefore hold its own and balance out against the historical situation."

So in the politics of care, language devoted to the preservation of the actual, means that poetry must be vigilant at this moment and this moment and every succeeding moment, so that Kevin's eggs will be kept safe as the blackbird incubates the life inside. Of course, they are notional eggs, and not real ones. But as Heaney says in the poem:

And since the whole thing's imagined anyhow,
Imagine being Kevin. Which is he?
Self-forgetful or in agony all the time

From the neck on out down through his hurting forearms?
Are his fingers sleeping? Does he still feel his knees?
Or has the shut-eyed blank of underearth

Crept up through him? Is there distance in his head?
Alone and mirrored clear in love's deep river,
"To labour and not to seek reward," he prays,

A prayer his body makes entirely
For he has forgotten self, forgotten bird
And on the riverbank forgotten the river's name.

The advent of this impersonal universal love that is mirrored clear of self in love's deep river, and that Kevin prays for, is a prayer prayed not by Kevin's will, but by his body. So just as the eggshell is the physical membrane that protects the incubating life inside, so the poem is a form of incubation, a way of keeping safe the fragility of our bodily and spiritual experiences by embodying them in language. It's as if Heaney imagined the eggs in the saint's hand, not only as an instance of the marvelous but also as a marvel of physical and spiritual endurance that depends on Kevin keeping his arm outstretched for as long as it takes for the life inside to hatch and fly away. Just such tenderness and hardheaded endurance inform Heaney's devotion to poetry as a form of linguistic care in which the continual unfolding of little acts of attention and observation will cumulatively create the conditions for life to flourish. At least that is the ideal—and Kevin, having forgotten self, the bird, and even the river's name, becomes the physical embodiment of his prayer to labor and not to seek reward.

Kevin's self-abnegating fulfillment becomes an emblem of what it would mean to be quickened into pure verb. And because this verb becomes the embodiment of an alternate reality to the gravitational pull of the actual, Heaney's use of descriptive language goes beyond the picturesque, or mere notation. The color of the eggs, their heft and texture, are coincident with their fragility in bearing new life into the world—a life that is also, as Heaney says, "a glimpsed alternative, a revelation of potential that is denied or constantly threatened by circumstances." By contrast, the stakes in contemporary poetry can sometimes feel lightweight, a little wispy around the edges, an unconscious capitulation to the *post factum* jabberers and their drive for disembodiment. Careless rather than careful—as if the exploration of sensibility needed no verification from the life of the senses or the surfaces of the world. In the hands of such a poet, the color of the eggs, their heft and texture, aren't so much cared for, as used as an opportunity for mere verbal display.

What I hope Heaney's example can show us is how to go beyond the notion of style as a set of more or less quirky rhetorical maneuvers. Heaney's vision of style as a way to register his care for the surfaces of the world is devoted to transforming the naturalistic into the emblematic, but grounded in bodily sensation. Hence Kevin focuses not on his own beatitude, but on the physical pain that he must endure for the sake of the life inside the eggs. The ordinary circumstance of an egg hatching takes on quietly heroic proportions as the superhuman Saint Kevin is reembodied in Heaney's imagination as just plain old, pain-racked Kevin enduring what he must.

3

I feel something of that quiet heroism about Seamus's relationship to writing, which was at once matter-of-fact, utterly workmanlike, but at the deepest level of inspiration, a marvel of endurance. He tapped into this inspiration not so much at his comfortable digs outside Dublin on the Strand Road, but at his cottage in Glanmore—in comparison, the cottage was very basic, very cold, slate roof, clinking latch. But even though you had to wear your coat all day to keep from shivering, when he invited me to visit him there almost thirty years ago, I loved the "stony, up-againstness" of the place that seemed to say, *Well, look—you may not be exactly comfortable, but go ahead anyway—make yourself at home.*

One warmish afternoon we sat outside the cottage discussing a draft of a translation of Aeneas's descent into the underworld that Seamus was working on—he knocked it out ten to fifteen lines at a time, nothing fussy or angsty in his process, just a severe and un-deluded sense of what was up to the mark and what hadn't yet ar-rived. I came across that draft not long ago tucked into a dog-eared copy of *Field Work* that has worked loose from the binding and bears a faint water stain across the front and back covers' bottom edges. Seamus had inscribed it for me in black ink that has faded to brown, in his serviceable hand that combined cursive and block print, clear loops and vine-like junctures. The date, February 1986, seems both close and far away: "Three scarcities that are better than plentifulnesses: a scarcity of fancy talk, a scarcity of cows in a small pasture, a scarcity of friends around the drink."

As we looked at the translation's typescript with his corrections in black ballpoint, he handed it to me and said, "Now, Sleigh, hit it!" So I tweaked a few words to make them more colloquial, and added a couple of contractions so that the Sybil's speech sounded a shade more casual. Seamus took in the changes as I made them, and when I handed him back the paper, he nodded approvingly, and said, "Good on you, Sleigh." Of course I was glad that he thought my suggestions were of use, but his kindness was such that even if he'd thought they were silly, he'd never have said so. And once, when he asked me to go over a new edition of his selected poems, and I asked if there were any principles guiding him in his selections, he shrugged, laughed, and said with perfect one-downmanship, as op-posed to one-upmanship, "Oh, just the ones I like."

More than anyone I've ever known, Seamus was ready to offer younger writers immediate terms of equality. He never played the éminence grise, the laureate, the literary lion. That was just another example of his generous heart, and the care he took for other people's feelings. Let me give an instance: during that week, we hit on a

routine—him upstairs in his study working away, me downstairs trying to scribble what I could. One evening after dinner, Seamus asked
me if I had any plans to put together a book of essays, since he knew
I'd written a good deal of prose. I shrugged something like, *Well,
that would be nice, but I suppose I needed a theme.* Seamus smiled and
shrugged back, "Oh for God's sake, Sleigh, stop putting on airs: you
don't need a theme, you just need a title!" And after all these years, I
can see what he meant: *theme* is way too cold-blooded a word for the
fragile, warm-blooded subjects who make a theme or an idea mem-
orable. Now that Seamus, too, has joined that "lambent troop" always maneuvering on the edge of vision, I like to think it was this
moment of one-downmanship that planted the seeds for this book.

As a kind of corollary to his generosity, he always played down
his worldly success with a self-skeptical, self-mocking eye. For example, he loved collecting postcards, and he and his friend David
Hammond, the singer, filmmaker, and broadcaster, would mail them
back and forth as a form of friendly banter. Seamus once showed
me a postcard David had sent him of a mountain peak—Everest, I
think it was. David had drawn an X on the highest peak, half-hidden
by a swirl of clouds, and had written in block capitals in heavy black
ink, DEAR MR HEANEY: WILL THIS LOCATION SUIT FOR
THE READING? At any rate, Seamus took friendship very seriously, and once he was your friend, he stuck with you for life.

Once we'd finished with Aeneas, weighting the ink-smudged
drafts under a stone in a rusty wheelbarrow that we used all that
week as a kind of improvised worktable, we sat there in the cool-
ing sunshine, watching a small brown bird busily building a nest
up under the eaves. Our talk rambled along through books and
friends, about what we admired in poet X, or had reservations about
in poet Y, the bird coming and going all the while, grass and little twigs
in its beak. After a few minutes, Seamus got up, walked over to the
eaves, and peered intently at the bird as it wove the grass and twigs together. He craned his neck back, and stood that way for what seemed
like a long time, before coming back and taking his seat. "There's a
little house sparrow up there," he said. "How's the nest coming?" I

asked. "Oh, it's well along—it'll all be built by this time tomorrow." Then I got up and went to take a look, when the sparrow suddenly poked out its head, and looked at me with a sidelong stare before flying off toward the hedgerows. I asked Seamus what I thought later was something of a dopey question: "What do you think the bird sees when he sees us?" But maybe the question isn't so gormless as it sounds: in light of an ethos of care, what did that bird make of the two humans staring up at its nest? Intruders? Destroyers? Fellow creatures under the sun? Maybe the notion that the world of creation looks at us, and that we should be mindful of how we look to it, is a more day-to-day version of the selflessness that Kevin finally arrives at when his saintliness falls away and he becomes just another note in what Seamus once called "the music of what happens." But however that may be, all Seamus did was give a genial shrug and say, "I don't know, lad. Maybe two chaps who need a drink?" And so we went inside the cottage, lit the gas stove, boiled some potatoes, fried up some fish, and nursed several whiskeys before we went to bed.

Acknowledgments

Blackbird: "How to Make a Toilet-Paper-Roll Blowgun" (published in an earlier version)

Los Angeles Review of Books: "Tales of the Marvelous, News of the Strange" and "'Where's the football?'"

Plume: "Momma's Boy" (published under the title "On a 'Sentimental Education'")

Poetry: "To Be Incarnational" and "The Land between Two Rivers" (published under the title "'Six Trees and Two White Dogs . . . Doves?'")

Virginia Quarterly Review: "The Deeds" and "A Violent Prone, Poor People Zone"

The Writer's Chronicle: "Disappearing Act" and "A Man of Care"

All translations but for Anna Akhmatova and Tomas Tranströmer are the author's. My thanks to Judith Hemschemeyer's *Selected Poems of Anna Akhmatova* and to Samuel Charters's version of "Codex," included in *Tomas Tranströmer: Selected Poems, 1954–1986*, ed. Robert Hass. I also owe a debt to Fady Joudah's translation of Mahmoud Darwish's "Murdered and Unknown," upon which my translation is based.

In the interest of transparency, the tales in "Tales of the Marvelous, News of the Strange" are, in the words of a friend, "new ancient tales." That is, I made them up, but like the storytellers before me, I used the conventions and the motifs associated with *The Thousand and One Nights*. However, the story of al-Khansa' appeared in the medieval Arab collection *Tales of the Marvelous and News of the Strange* (trans. Malcolm C. Lyons, Penguin Classics, 2015), from which this essay derives its title. The translation of the poem al-Khansa' wrote for her brother is mine.

I owe a huge debt to the late Andy Needham of Irish Aid and UNHCR for his sense of humor, his intelligence, and street smarts in helping me undertake the most difficult missions.

Deep thanks to Rika Hakozaki of UNHCR, who helped me to open doors that would otherwise have remained closed.

As always my gratitude to Sarah, Alan, Michael, Josh, Chuck, Patrick, and Phil for making these better essays; and to the editors who put their trust in me, Ted Genoways, Don Share and Christian Wiman, Mary Flynn and David Wojahn, Supriya Bhatnagar and David Fenza, Joshua Rivkin and Gabrielle Calvocoressi, and Tom Lutz, Rob Latham, and Tom Zoellner.

And my deepest thanks to Christopher Merrill, who taught me by example: this book wouldn't exist but for you, Chris.

TOM SLEIGH's many books include *One War Everywhere, Station Zed, Army Cats*, winner of the John Updike Award from the American Academy of Arts and Letters, and *Space Walk*, which received the Kingsley Tufts Poetry Award. In addition, *Far Side of the Earth* won an Academy Award from the American Academy of Arts and Letters, *The Dreamhouse* was a finalist for the Los Angeles Times Book Prize, and *The Chain* was a finalist for the Lenore Marshall Poetry Prize. He's also received the Poetry Society of America's Shelley Prize, a fellowship from the Guggenheim Foundation, two National Endowment for the Arts grants, and many other awards. His work appears in the *New Yorker, Poetry*, as well as in *The Best of the Best American Poetry, The Best American Travel Writing*, and *The Pushcart Anthology*. He is a Distinguished Professor at Hunter College and has worked as a journalist in the Middle East and Africa. Sleigh lives in New York.

The text of *The Land between Two Rivers* is set in Adobe Garamond Pro. Book design by Rachel Holscher. Composition by Bookmobile Design & Digital Publisher Services, Minneapolis, Minnesota. Manufactured by Versa Press on acid-free, 30 percent postconsumer wastepaper.